Terror on the Internet

Terror on the Internet

The New Arena, the New Challenges

Gabriel Weimann

UNITED STATES INSTITUTE OF PEACE PRESS
Washington, D.C.

UNITED STATES INSTITUTE OF PEACE
1200 17th Street NW, Suite 200
Washington, DC 20036-3011

© 2006 by the Endowment of the United States Institute of Peace. All rights reserved.

First published 2006

Printed in the United States of America

The paper used in this publication meets the minimum requirements of American National Standards for Information Science—Permanence of Paper for Printed Library Materials, ANSI Z39.48-1984.

Library of Congress Cataloging-in-Publication Data

Weimann, Gabriel, 1950–
    Terror on the internet: the new arena, the new challenges / Gabriel Weimann.
       p.   cm.
    Includes bibliographical references and index.
    ISBN-13: 978-1-929223-71-8 (hardcover: alk. paper)
    ISBN-10: 1-929223-71-4 (hardcover: alk. paper)
    1. Terrorism—Computer network resources. 2. Hate groups—Computer network resources. 3. Internet and communications. 4. Cyberterrorism—Prevention. 5. Terrorism—Prevention. I. Title.
HV6431.W435   2006
363.325—dc22   2005034147

I dedicate this book with admiration and love to my father,
Tibor Weimann, a real hero who survived two world wars in Europe
and six wars in the Middle East and who now celebrates
the hundredth year of an adventurous life.

Contents

Foreword

ONE OF THE ENDURING AXIOMS of terrorism is that it is conceived specifically to attract attention and then, through the publicity it generates, to communicate a message. The terrorist must parlay this illumination (i.e., publicity) into a more effective vehicle of elucidation (i.e., propaganda). The centrality of propaganda to this communications process and its importance to terrorists is as long-standing as it is self-evident. What is different today is that the weapons of terrorism are no longer exclusively guns and bombs; the modern terrorist's arsenal now includes laptop and desktop computers, CD burners and e-mail accounts, and the Internet and the World Wide Web. Indeed, in recent years, the Internet has allowed the art of terrorist communication to evolve to a point where terrorists are able to control the entire communications process: they can determine not only the content and context of their messages but also the means by which their messages are projected into cyberspace and targeted toward specific audiences.

The implications of this development are enormous: the terrorists are challenging the monopoly over mass communication long held by conventional commercial and state-owned television and radio broadcasting outlets and by the state- and privately owned press. But, as Gabriel Weimann alarmingly notes in *Terror on the Internet*, "the story of the presence of terrorist groups in cyberspace has barely begun to be told." Nonetheless, there is no one more qualified or better suited to initiate this process and begin to tell this story than Weimann. The author of such previous, pathbreaking books as *The Theater of Terror: Mass Media and International Terrorism* (1993), *The Influentials: People Who Influence People* (1994), and *Communicating Unreality: Modern Media and the Reconstruction of Reality* (1999), Weimann brings to this subject both fresh insight and well-established scholarly credentials.

Weimann argues that, while considerable concern has arisen in recent years because of the threat of cyberterrorism, comparatively little attention has been paid to the threat posed by terrorist use and exploitation of the Internet. *Terror on the Internet* thus fills a conspicuous gap in the literature. Based on his findings from eight years of monitoring and archiving terrorist Web sites, Weimann sheds important light on terrorist use of the Internet for fund-raising and recruitment, training and instruction, and propaganda and psychological warfare, and for gathering open-source information with which to plan attacks.

One of the book's main arguments is that, despite the multiplicity and diversity of terrorist Web sites, there are nonetheless core, common characteristics that terrorist groups with a presence on the Internet share. As Weimann explains, most terrorist sites are particularly notable for their colorful, well-designed, and visually arresting graphic content, selective presentation of information, and effective message. Other common elements include descriptions of the given terrorist group's history, its aims and objectives, and the depredations inflicted by an enemy state(s) or people(s) upon the constituency that the terrorists purport to represent. The terrorist sites also often contain biographies of the group's leadership, founders, and key personalities; up-to-date news and accompanying feature stories; and speeches, ideological treatises, and, especially, the organization's communiqués and other important statements. Ethnonationalist and separatist movements will also typically post maps of the contested territory they claim to represent or be fighting for. Virtually without exception, all terrorist sites studiously avoid focusing on or drawing any attention to either the violence or the death and destruction that they are responsible for. Instead, issues such as freedom of expression, human rights, and the plight of imprisoned comrades are emphasized. In the case of the more sophisticated organizations, multiple sites are often maintained in different languages.

In addition to providing a thoroughly compelling and trenchant analysis of the content on terrorist sites and terrorist exploitation of the Internet for psychological warfare purposes, Weimann also considers the salience of the cyberterrorist threat itself, outlining the appropriate responses to such a threat and emphasizing the critical importance of striking the proper balance between security and civil liberties. He also discusses how such a balance can best be achieved. His approach to all these issues is characteristically comprehensive, thoughtful, and sober. Weimann's conclusions are firmly rooted in the vast empirical evidence he presents in support of his arguments. Moreover, the policy recommendations he proposes are as practical as they are sensible.

Many books published on terrorism aspire to be described as "cutting edge" or "must read." *Terror on the Internet* unquestionably has earned these accolades. Indeed, it is destined to become the seminal work on this subject.

BRUCE HOFFMAN
WASHINGTON, D.C.

Acknowledgments

THIS BOOK SUMMARIZES MORE THAN eight years of research that was collected mostly in the darkest alleys of cyberspace. This research could not have been conducted without the contributions of many individuals and institutions all over the world. Several grants and foundations contributed directly and indirectly to this project, but the most important hosting and funding organization for this work was the United States Institute of Peace, where I was a Senior Fellow from October 2003 to July 2004. The Institute and its devoted team served as both a home and a family for me during my year in Washington, D.C., and have continued to be a great source of support for me. Many individuals among the Institute's excellent staff deserve my gratitude, but I would first like to single out Joseph Klaits, former director of the Institute's Jennings Randolph Fellowship Program. Without him this book would never have seen the light of day: Joe was a counselor, a friend, a source of advice and guidance, and a spiritual and intellectual mentor. I know that many other scholars and past USIP Fellows owe him a similar debt of gratitude.

Others at the Institute who greatly assisted me include John Crist, my program officer, whose friendship, assistance, and encouragement were so precious; Richard Solomon, the president of the Institute; Sheryl J. Brown, the director of the Institute's Jennings Randolph Fellowship Program; Virginia Bouvier, program officer; Jean Brodeur, the helpful program assistant; Elizabeth Drakulich, program specialist; Kay King, director of the Office of Congressional and Public Affairs; and the librarians and great computer technicians who were often hassled by my inquiries and computer problems.

This research project was also carried out with the help of numerous research assistants. Two of them who worked with me at the Institute deserve my appreciation for their contributions and involvement: Rachel Davis and Alison Foley Talbott. Additionally, several institutions and organizations assisted with data collection and translation of Web sites, including the Pew Internet and American Life Project, the Middle East Media Research Institute, the Northeast Intelligence Network, the SITE Institute, the Project for the Research of Islamist Movements, and the Internet Haganah.

I would also like to thank many of my colleagues and friends for their support, advice, and encouragement, including Bruce Hoffman, Daniel Benjamin, Jerrold Post, Elliott Milstein, Amatzia Baram, Yoram Peri, Edward Luttwak, Reuven Paz, Yariv Tsfati, Boaz Ganor, Joshua Sinai, Yigal Carmon, Lee Rainie, Laura Mansfield, Aaron Weisburd, Deb and Jim Fallows, Josephine and Rami Levi, Gail and Yash Shirazi, Katharina von Knop, and many others I do not name here. I also wish to express my appreciation and gratitude to three anonymous reviewers for their excellent suggestions and comments, and to Nigel Quinney, my editor: I have worked with several editors on my past books and publications, but Nigel is certainly the best. Cory Smith, the legislative counsel for Human Rights First, was more than helpful and offered me not only his important views and insights but also access to vast resources and useful material.

This project, despite its relevance for counterterrorism, was not supported by any security, military, or federal agency. Yet, in my presentations and lectures about my research, I noted the presence of representatives from such agencies and organizations. I hope they learned from my work in this new arena—cyberspace and terrorism—and fully understand the need for democracies to apply limits and boundaries to the war on terrorism in the virtual arena.

Finally, I wish to thank my family, Nava, Oren, and Dana, who provided encouragement and support to me, a husband and parent who was perhaps at times more attentive to his research than to them.

Terror on the Internet

Introduction

I N THE WAKE OF THE SEPTEMBER 11, 2001, TERRORIST ATTACKS, a single question seemed to arise from all quarters: how could U.S. authorities and intelligence agencies have failed so completely to detect the plot? Despite many unknowns, a common thread runs through most of the explanations, the FBI reports, and the numerous analyses: the Internet played a key role in the terrorists' attack—in collecting information, in communications between the various terrorist cells and individuals, and in coordinating and executing the attacks. The hard evidence is overwhelming:

> FBI assistant director Ron Dick, head of the US National Infra-structure Protection Centre told reporters that the hijackers had used the Net, and "used it well." In one instance, two of the hijackers equipped with laptops would not check into a Holly-wood, Florida, hotel unless they had around-the-clock Internet access in their room. When the terrorists learned that such access was not available, they became angry and left. The terrorists also used the Internet to purchase "at least nine of their [airline] tickets for the four doomed September 11 flights." The terror-ists frequently used computers at public libraries to access the

Internet and used the Web to steal social security numbers and obtain fake drivers' licenses.[1]

The events on 9/11 revealed to a shocked world that terrorism had entered a new era and a new arena. This book explores this new arena, examining the ways in which modern terrorist organizations exploit the unique attributes of the Internet and looking at various counter-terrorism measures being applied to the Net. In turning the spotlight on cyberterrorists and exploring the efforts to stop them, we must also take into account the costs of this cyberwar in terms of civil rights. The following research questions have guided this study:

- Who are the terrorists of the Internet?
- How do terrorists use the Internet?
- What rhetorical devices do terrorist Web sites use?
- Who are the target audiences of terrorist sites?
- What counterterrorism measures are in place on the Internet, and how successful are they?
- What are the costs of such measures in terms of privacy and freedom of expression?

The material presented in this book is drawn from an ongoing study, during which the author has witnessed a growing and increasingly sophisticated terrorist presence on the World Wide Web. Terrorism on the Internet is a very dynamic phenomenon: Web sites suddenly emerge, frequently modify their formats, and then swiftly disappear—or, in many cases, *seem* to disappear but actually have only moved by changing their online address, while retaining much of the same content. In exploring this new arena, this study draws on several sources, databases, and methods. The databases used for this project are derived from eight years of monitoring and archiving terrorists' Web sites (1998–2005) and from public opinion surveys (U.S. national samples) conducted by the Pew Internet and American Life Project. The study of counterterrorism measures on the Net and their prices in terms of civil liberties and privacy relies on a survey of various organizations and agencies.[2]

Two earlier studies serve as pilot studies for the current project: Yariv Tsfati and the present author applied a systematic content analysis to a sample of terrorist sites in 1998 and repeated this analysis after three years.[3] These exploratory studies provided the methodological tools as well as the first evidence both of the diffusion of terrorism into the Internet and of the terrorists' growing sophistication. The method used to study Web sites was content analysis, which is defined as "any technique for reaching conclusions by systematic and objective identification of defined properties of messages."[4] To locate the terrorists' sites, we conducted numerous systematic scans of the Internet, feeding an enormous variety of names and terms into search engines, entering chat rooms and forums of supporters and sympathizers, and surveying the links on other organizations' Web sites to create and update our own lists of sites. This is often a Herculean effort, especially since (in the case of al Qaeda's Web sites, for example) locations and contents change almost daily. For the purposes of this book, the Internet was scanned again, in 2003–05. The target population for the current study was defined as "the Internet sites of terrorist movements as they appeared in the period between January 1998 and May 2005." Using the U.S. State Department's list of terrorist organizations (see the appendix),[5] we found more than 4,300 sites serving terrorists and their supporters.

The Structure of This Book

Chapter 1 of this volume, "New Terrorism, New Media," starts with a brief history of the Internet. Ironically, this medium originated from the Cold War and U.S. security services' fears about the vulnerability of strategically vital communications networks to a nuclear attack. Decades later the Internet has become a handy tool of one of Western security's scariest foes: modern-day terrorists. As new communication technologies have emerged, terrorism has kept pace, constantly changing its character and modes of operation, so that today's postmodern terrorism has a new face. It is less centralized, less structured, and less organized, yet far more dangerous than the terrorism of the late twentieth century. In this chapter we will review the attributes of postmodern terrorism and how it depends on modern communication technologies to maintain its decentralized structure, launch global attacks, and control a loosely knit network of operatives and supporters.

We then examine the advantages of using the Net for political activism, and how some political groups and national minorities with Internet access have begun to challenge the state's domination of political discourse and political culture, both of which have traditionally been maintained through the state's control of the media and through its monopoly on the media and education systems. Thus, the Internet's attraction for modern terrorists should come as no surprise: the more severely the interests of a minority group have been ignored, the more attractive the Internet will be for that group. The study distinguishes between various abuses and abusers of the Internet—between, for example, the commonly confused potential and actual damage inflicted by cyberterrorists, and between the relatively benign activities of most hackers and the specter of true cyberterrorism.

Chapter 2, "The War over Minds: The Psychology of Terrorism," gives the theoretical and conceptual framework for this research. Terrorism is a form of psychological warfare, the word itself stemming from "terrorize," meaning "to frighten" or "to scare." Terrorism seeks to threaten a society by spreading fear, distrust, and a sense of helplessness among its citizens. We review the history of psychological warfare and demonstrate how modern terrorism has learned the lessons of state-operated terror campaigns, using the same weapon of psychological warfare with growing sophistication and impact. It is clear that such psychological impact relies on the mass media: the desired panic is produced via a constant broadcasting, by radio and television, videos, and the Internet, of vicious acts, threats, and declarations—all according to the familiar, tried-and-true methods of psychological warfare.

This leads us to an examination of the media's role in modern terrorism, applying the theory of "terrorism as theater." The theater metaphor is used to examine modern terrorism as an attempt to communicate messages through the use of orchestrated violence.[6] As we suggest, the growing use and manipulation of the mass media by terrorist organizations led governments and several media organizations to consider certain steps in response. These included limiting terrorists' access to the conventional mass media, reducing and censoring news coverage of terrorist acts and their perpetrators, and minimizing the terrorists' capacity for manipulating the media. However, new media technologies, especially computer-mediated communication and the Internet, allow terrorist organizations to transmit messages more easily and freely than through other means of communication. Finally, this chapter examines the advantages that the Internet provides to modern terrorism, ranging from easy access and rapid flow of information to multimedia applications. Web sites are only one of the Internet applications used for terrorism; many terrorists are adept at manipulating other services on the Net, including e-mail, chat rooms, e-groups, forums, online magazines, virtual message boards, and online manuals and guidebooks. It is especially this interactive aspect of the Internet that enables terrorists to activate their audiences in a manner and to a degree unachievable by other mass media.

In chapter 3, "Communicative Uses of the Internet for Terrorism," we see how terrorist organizations are increasingly using the Internet for communication purposes from propaganda and dissemination of messages to psychological warfare. Numerous organizations have entered cyberspace and created Internet sites. The search for Internet-based organizations reveals much about the identities and characteristics of those groups and movements that use this new communication channel. In this chapter we present the scope and content of terrorist Web sites, their messages and rhetoric, target audiences, and persuasive appeals. Who do the terrorist Web sites target? Are they appealing to potential supporters, to their enemies (namely, the public who is part of the opposing sociopolitical community in the conflict), or to international public opinion? Judging from the content of many of the sites, we infer that journalists constitute another target audience. Our findings reveal a proliferation of radical Islamic Web sites. This is not a methodological bias but rather a significant trend highlighted in our study. This study explores how the freedom offered by the Internet is vulnerable to abuse from groups that, paradoxically, are themselves hostile to uncensored thought and expression, and how extreme anti-Western and antimodernity forces are using the most sophisticated tools of modern Western culture.

Applying the theory of selective moral disengagement to terrorist Web sites, we reveal their use of all the various disengagement practices, including displacement of responsibility, diffusion of responsibility, dehumanization of targets, euphemistic language, advantageous comparisons, distortion of sequence of events, and attribution of blame. The most popular theme is the displacement of responsibility: violence is presented as a necessity foisted upon the weak as the only means for dealing with an oppressive enemy. The blame is thus attributed to others. Another rhetorical structure used to legitimize violence is the demonizing and delegitimizing of the enemy by shifting the responsibility to the enemy and displaying his brutality, inhumanity, and immorality: "Terrorist rhetoric on the Internet tries to present a mix of images and arguments in which the terrorists appear as victims forced to turn to violence to achieve their just goals in the face of a brutal, merciless enemy devoid of all moral restraint. Demonizing the enemy, playing down the issue of terror victims, shifting blame for the use of violence, and proclaiming peace-loving messages are all strategies used on most terror sites."[7]

As illustrative examples, this chapter presents a more detailed analysis of several groups' presence on the Net. We chose them because they represent a variety of motives, locations, types of action, and aggression levels and because each has an impressive presence on the Net. The use of the Internet for conveying terrorist propaganda is well illustrated by the Web site of the Japanese Aum Shinrikyo (meaning "Supreme Truth"). Another section focuses on the "phoenix of the Internet": al Qaeda and its numerous Web sites. We see how this widespread network of Web sites is used by al Qaeda's leaders to spread information, incitement, and instructions to supporters and sympathizers around the world. Al Qaeda publishes several online magazines, including *Sawt al-Jihad*, or *The Voice of Jihad*, highlighted in this chapter because it serves as al Qaeda's tool of ideological indoctrination. All the attempts to prevent al Qaeda from using the Internet are futile. If one Web site is hacked or removed from the Net, many others will surface, using other service providers, new URLs, and new formats. Our study describes how al Qaeda changes its Web site names and URLs every few days to avoid being hacked, and how it directs followers and supporters to these new sites. Other case studies of Internet-based campaigns of propaganda and indoctrination include FARC (Revolutionary Armed Forces of Colombia), Hamas, Hezbollah, the IRA splinter groups, and the insurgents in Iraq. Finally, this chapter discusses the impact of these campaigns, suggesting several indirect measures to assess the real effectiveness and impact of terrorist uses of the Internet, including testimonies of terrorists and affected individuals.

Along with communicative uses, terrorists also use the Internet for practical purposes: chapter 4, "Instrumental Uses of the Internet for

Terrorism," presents seven different, though sometimes overlapping, means by which contemporary terrorists take advantage of the Internet for such purposes. Some of these parallel the uses to which everyone puts the Internet—information gathering, for instance. Some resemble the uses made of the medium by traditional political organizations—for example, raising funds and coordinating actions. Others, however, are much more unusual and distinctive—for instance, hiding instructions, manuals, and directions in coded messages or encrypted files. The Internet may be viewed as a vast digital library. It offers more than a billion pages of information, much of it free and much of it of interest to terrorist organizations. Terrorists, for instance, can learn from the Internet about the schedules and locations of targets such as transportation facilities, nuclear power plants, public buildings, and air- and seaports, and can even reveal and preempt or avoid counterterrorism measures. This chapter presents evidence of the data mining done by Internet-savvy terrorists and looks at the numerous tools that are available to facilitate such data collection, including search engines, e-mail distribution lists, chat rooms, and discussion groups. While some of this information may also be available in the traditional media, online searching capabilities allow terrorists to capture it anonymously and with very little effort or expense.

Other instrumental uses of the Internet for modern terrorists include the sharing and distribution of information, instructions, manuals, and guidebooks. The World Wide Web is home to dozens of sites that provide information on how to build explosive and chemical weapons, providing maps, photographs, directions, codes, and technical details of how to use explosives. The Internet can serve as a virtual training camp, as illustrated by al Qaeda's *Al Battar Training Camp.* This bimonthly online magazine contains detailed articles on cell organization and management, weapons training, physical fitness, and even wilderness survival training. Some issues focus on how to conduct kidnapping operations, negotiate release of hostages, and collect information on targets. The Internet, as this chapter demonstrates, was used for networking terrorists, coordinating attacks, and planning actions including the attacks of September 11, 2001, as well as those of March 11, 2004, in Madrid and of July 2005 in London. The Internet is used to recruit and mobilize supporters to play a more active role in supporting terrorist activities or causes. In addition to seeking converts by using the full panoply of Web site technologies (audio, digital video, and so on) to enhance the presentation of their message, terrorist organizations capture information about the users who browse their Web sites (culled, for instance, from personal information entered on online questionnaires and order forms). Users who seem most interested in an organization's cause or who are well suited to carrying out its work are then contacted. Here we also explore the sophisticated methods used by terrorists to refine or customize recruiting techniques on the Net.

Like many other political organizations, terrorist groups use the Internet to raise funds. We reveal how the Internet allows terrorists to identify users sympathetic to a particular cause or issue. These individuals are then asked to make donations, typically through e-mails sent by a front group (an organization broadly supportive of the terrorists' aims but operating publicly and legally, and usually having no direct ties to the terrorist organization). Finally, the Internet serves as a battlefield between and within terrorist organizations, which use the Net to conduct ideological debates or even personal disputes and internal power struggles, some of which are discussed in this chapter.

Chapter 5, "Cyberterrorism: How Real Is the Threat?," is devoted to the scariest scenario: using the Internet as a weapon of terrorism. The growing reliance of modern society on information technology has created a new form of vulnerability, giving terrorists the chance to approach targets that would otherwise be utterly unassailable, such as national defense systems, nuclear plants, and transportation control systems. The threat posed by cyberterrorism has grabbed headlines and the attention of politicians, security experts, and the public. But just how real is the threat? Could terrorists cripple critical military, financial, and service computer systems? This chapter charts the rise of cyberangst and examines the evidence cited by those who predict imminent catastrophe. Many of these fears, the chapter contends, are exaggerated: not a single case of cyberterrorism has yet been recorded, hackers are regularly mistaken for terrorists, and cyberdefenses are more robust than is commonly supposed. Even so, the potential threat is undeniable and seems likely to increase, making it all the more important to address the danger without inflating or manipulating it.

This chapter examines the reality of the cyberterrorism threat, present and future. It begins by outlining why cyberterrorism angst has gripped so many people, defines what qualifies as "cyberterrorism" and what does not, and charts cyberterrorism's appeal for terrorists. The text then looks at the evidence both for and against Western society's vulnerability to cyberattacks, drawing on a variety of recent studies and publications to illustrate the kinds of fears that have been expressed and to assess whether we need to be so concerned. The conclusion looks to the future and argues that we must remain alert to real dangers while not becoming victims of overblown fears.

In chapter 6, "Fighting Back: Responses to Terrorism on the Internet, and Their Cost," we examine the war on terrorism as it is being waged on the Net. Up to now, most of the counterterrorism effort has been devoted to tracking down the terrorist networks, the perpetrators of terrorist attacks, and the transfer of money and funds. This chapter describes the post-9/11 counterterrorism measures on the Net, including the USA PATRIOT Act and the Domestic Security Enhancement Act of 2003, or "PATRIOT II," as it has been labeled informally, which expand surveillance power, increase government access to private data, and broaden the definition of "terrorist activities." We describe the United States' Internet-wide monitoring center, which "detects and responds to attacks on vital information systems and key e-commerce sites."[8] According to the *Washington Post*'s Brian Krebs, this center "is a key piece of the White House's national cybersecurity strategy and represents a major leap in the federal government's effort to achieve real-time tracking of the Internet."[9]

As we study Internet security and the legal measures to protect it, Asian countries may provide a useful and perhaps alarming example. Governments in Asia have become increasingly interested in cybersurveillance, both to monitor and to intimidate Internet users. The Singapore government's system of Internet control has been a model for authoritarian states in Asia, and so we discuss the Singaporean model in particular. Then we explore the routine U.S. monitoring of e-mail traffic, presenting and explaining various monitoring procedures and techniques such as "sniffers," Carnivore (DCS1000), Magic Lantern, Echelon, and others. We also discuss the criticism of these measures as abusing privacy or civil liberties. Another counterterrorism measure applied to the Net is the removal of specific Web sites (entirely or partially) from the Internet. Is this removal of information from Web sites an efficient step in combating terrorism? As this chapter reveals, not really. Finally we examine cyberattacks against terrorist Web sites, and the banning of them, as relatively futile attempts to restrict terrorists' access and exposure.

The most important challenge presented to modern democracies by terrorism is addressed in chapter 7, "Balancing Security and Civil Liberties." Since September 11, 2001, many governments have sought ways to limit or minimize terrorists' use of the Internet. These measures have inspired fears among civil libertarian activists. It has been said that the first casualty of war is truth. In the digital war on terrorism, however, the first victim may be our civil liberties. In this chapter we review the counterweight of counterterrorism: while some argue that we must surrender some freedoms in order to enjoy the ones we cherish most, others emphasize the price in freedom that we pay for this war. Many in the Western world and especially in the United States worry about the abuse of civil liberties in the name of fighting terrorism. We review some of these voices of concern and their calls for some important modifications to the surveillance system of the Net.

We also discuss the missed opportunities: demonizing the Internet as a terrorist tool diverts our attention from its potential for nonviolent management of conflicts and for virtual diplomacy. The Internet furnishes advocacy groups and individuals with a free, easy-to-access mass medium where they can publish information to further policy objectives and present political grievances in nonviolent forms. The Zapatistas in Mexico represent one of the most successful examples of the positive use of computer communications by grassroots social movements. When activists turn to the Internet and use it efficiently to disseminate information, attract support and sympathy, and transform their conduct of the conflict, a traditional guerrilla insurgency is changed into a nonviolent political campaign.

Another missed opportunity presented in this chapter is virtual diplomacy. Computer-mediated communication can serve as an ideal channel for supporting good governance or managing international conflicts and crises effectively and expediently. A good example, though sadly one of very few, is the United States Institute of Peace's initiative on peace in Liberia; another virtual approach to training for peace is the use of computer simulation to create peace support operations. The potential for virtual diplomacy, however, has yet to be fully employed.

The book concludes with policy recommendations. We should recognize that terrorism has been around for thousands of years and is not likely to go away soon. Modern societies, it appears, will have to learn to live with some terrorism, which leads to the issue of trade-offs between securing our safety and securing our liberties. Thus, a more realistic way to protect the Internet, prevent its abuse by terrorism, and at the same time protect civil liberties is to look for the "golden path," or best compromise. This means that we will have to accept both some vulnerabilities of the Internet to terrorism and some constraints on civil liberties; the underlying guidelines, determined by examining the trade-offs between securing our safety and securing our liberties, should minimize the threats to both. Among the recommendations presented here for following that golden path to a balanced "middle ground" are modifying the USA PATRIOT Act, encouraging self-policing of the Internet, applying the social responsibility model, developing international collaboration, building a proactive presence on the Internet, and promoting peaceful uses of the Internet.

1

New Terrorism, New Media

THE STORY OF TERRORIST GROUPS OPERATING IN CYBERSPACE has only just begun to be told. In 1998, fewer than half of the thirty organizations designated as foreign terrorist organizations by the U.S. Department of State maintained Web sites;[1] by the end of 1999, nearly all thirty terrorist groups had established their presence on the Net. Today there are more than forty active terrorist groups, each with an established presence on the Internet. A thorough and extensive scan of the Internet in 2003–05 revealed more than 4,300 Web sites serving terrorists and their supporters.[2] That these Web sites, regardless of whatever other language versions they might be available in, are almost invariably available in English raises complex and hitherto unexplored questions about the constituencies that find cyberspace hospitable for the fulfillment of their political goals. This chapter explores how modern terrorism and the Internet met: we review the history of the Internet, the new faces of postmodern terrorism, and the compatibility of the two.

A Brief History of the Internet

Paradoxically, the conspicuously decentralized network of computer-mediated communication that U.S. security services created out of concern over the Soviet Union now serves the interests of the greatest foe of the world's security services since the end of the Cold War: international terror. The nature of the network—its international character and chaotic structure, its global reach, its simple access, and the anonymity it offers—furnishes terrorist organizations with an ideal arena for action. The same advantages that advanced computer-mediated communication brings to the public and to "innocents" are enjoyed by modern terrorist groups.

How did the Internet emerge? Much of the following description of the history of the Internet relies on the essay "Brief History of the Internet," written by the very people who created the medium, namely, Barry M. Leiner, Vinton G. Cerf, David D. Clark, Robert E. Kahn, Leonard Kleinrock, Larry G. Roberts, and others.[3] The network that was to become the Internet, or Net, started in earnest during the Cold War, when the U.S. Department of Defense was concerned about the vulnerability of its computer network to nuclear attack. The basic idea was to decentralize the whole system by creating an interconnected web of computer networks. The Net was designed so that every computer could "talk" to every other computer. Information was bundled in a packet, called an Internet protocol packet (IPP), which contained the destination address of the target computer. In the early 1970s, the U.S. Defense Advanced Research Projects Agency (DARPA) commissioned a research project to investigate techniques and technologies for connecting various packet networks. This project, named "the Internetting project," resulted in a system of networks that became known as the Internet.

In 1965, a computer in Massachusetts was linked to a computer in California using a low-speed dial-up telephone line, creating the first (however small, slow, and expensive) computer network ever built. The result of this experiment was the realization that by using the network the computers could work together, although the telephone system was woefully inadequate for the job. In late 1966 Larry G. Roberts, working for DARPA, introduced his concept of a computer network for the Advanced Research Projects Agency Network (ARPANET). The Network Measurement Center at the University of California–Los Angeles was the first node on the ARPANET, and Stanford Research Institute (SRI) was the second. The University of California–Santa Barbara and the University of Utah became the next two nodes, so that by the end of 1969, four host computers were interconnected to form the ARPANET. The embryonic Internet was up and running. As other computers were added, the network grew, and soon there were comprehensive host-to-host protocols, network software, and various applications. One of the most important applications was the e-mail, introduced in the early 1970s:

> In October 1972 Kahn organized a large, very successful demonstration of the ARPANET at the International Computer Communication Conference (ICCC). This was the first public demonstration of this new network technology to the public. It was also in 1972 that the initial "hot" application, electronic mail, was introduced. In March Ray Tomlinson at BBN wrote the basic email message send and read software, motivated by the need of the ARPANET developers for an easy coordination mechanism. In July, Roberts expanded its utility by writing the first email utility program to list, selectively read, file, forward, and respond to messages. From there email took off as the largest network application for over a decade. This was a harbinger of the kind of activity we see on the World Wide Web today, namely, the enormous growth of all kinds of "people-to-people" traffic.[4]

The new network's potential for communication quickly became clear and led to further developments that changed ARPANET to the Internet. The word "Internet" is composed of two words "inter," which is Latin and means "between," and "net," the short form of "networking." Thus, the term "Internet" means a network of computer networks:

> The Internet was based on the idea that there would be multiple independent networks of rather arbitrary design, beginning with the ARPANET as the pioneering packet switching network, but soon to include packet satellite networks, ground-based packet radio networks and other networks. The Internet as we now know it embodies a key underlying technical idea, namely that of open architecture networking. . . . In an open-architecture network, the individual networks may be separately designed

and developed and each may have its own unique interface which it may offer to users and/or other providers.[5]

The users of this early network were primarily scientists, scholars, and computer specialists. Widespread development of personal computers and workstations in the 1980s helped the burgeoning Internet to grow until, by the late 1980s, other communities were beginning to adopt Internet technology for day-to-day computer communications.

> Electronic mail was being used broadly across several communities, often with different systems, but interconnection between different mail systems was demonstrating the utility of broad-based electronic communications between people. At the same time that the Internet technology was being experimentally validated and widely used amongst a subset of computer science researchers, other networks and networking technologies were being pursued. . . . With the exception of BITNET and USENET, these early networks (including ARPANET) were purpose-built—i.e., they were intended for, and largely restricted to, closed communities of scholars; there was hence little pressure for the individual networks to be compatible and, indeed, they largely were not.[6]

And so the need arose for a wide networking infrastructure to serve the growing community of users. The next step was the commercialization of the Net:

> Starting in the early 1980's and continuing to this day, the Internet grew beyond its primarily research roots to include both a broad user community and increased commercial activity. Increased attention was paid to making the process open and fair. This coupled with a recognized need for community support of the Internet eventually led to the formation of the Internet Society in 1991. The recent development and widespread deployment of the World Wide Web has brought with it a new community, as many of the people working on the WWW have not thought of themselves as primarily network researchers and developers. A new coordination organization was formed, the World Wide Web Consortium. . . . Commercialization of the Internet involved not only the development of competitive, private network services, but also the development of commercial products implementing the Internet technology.[7]

During the late 1980s and even more so in the 1990s, the Internet network expanded worldwide, adding the private networking facilities of businesses, educational and research institutions, and government organizations and agencies. The global "penetration rate" of the Internet now averages 12.7 percent, meaning that about thirteen out of every hundred persons in the world use the Internet.[8] Today the Internet provides access to communication services and information resources for almost a billion users worldwide. These users depend on the Net for direct communication (e-mail and chat rooms), online conferencing (e-mail discussion lists and Usenet News), distributed information resources (the World Wide Web), remote log-in and file transfer (ftp and telnet), and a host of other resources, many of which have become virtually indispensable.

Students, scientists, government officials, and in fact anyone else can have access to the information superhighway, to worldwide databases, and to the entire cyberspace network; thus, the number of users, the amount of information exchanged, and the time spent surfing in cyberspace have increased tremendously. In the mid-1990s the Internet connected more than 18,000 computer networks, with those numbers increasing daily. Hooked into these networks were about 3.2 million host computers, and experts estimate that some 1,000 host computers are added daily. From 2000 to 2005 the global Internet community grew by 126.4 percent, reaching 817,447,147 users in February 2005. While worldwide penetration rates average 12.7 percent, certain regions of the globe have rates that are far higher (for example, 66.5 percent in North America).[9]

As it burgeoned, the Internet was hailed as an integrator of cultures and a medium for businesses, consumers, and governments to communicate both internally and to one another. It appeared to offer unparalleled opportunities for the creation of a forum in which the "global village" could meet and exchange ideas, stimulating and sustaining democracy throughout the world.[10] However, with the enormous growth in the size and use of the network, utopian visions of the promise of the Internet were challenged by the proliferation of pornographic and violent content on the Web and by the use of the Internet by extremist organizations of various kinds. Groups with very different political goals but with the same readiness to employ terrorist tactics started using the network to distribute their propaganda, communicate with their supporters, foster public awareness of and sympathy for their causes, and even execute operations.

The Nature of Modern Terrorism

In order to study terrorism, whether on the Internet or elsewhere, it is first necessary to define just what constitutes a terrorist organization. Although most people know terrorism when they see it, academics and scholars are unable to agree on a precise definition. As Wayman Mullins argues, "Terrorism is an extremely difficult concept to define. Terrorism is an ethereal philosophy, and terrorist actors engage in terrorism for a variety of purposes, motivations, and ideologies."[11] One of the problems with defining terrorism (and with the entire "war on terrorism") is that terrorism is a tactic, not a palpable foe or group, not even a political or ideological category (such as Islam or communism or capitalism). More than a hundred different definitions are offered by scholars.[12] Some definitions are based on the nature of the act; some focus on the victims of the act; some highlight the objective of the terrorists; others focus on the characteristics of the perpetrators. Joseba Zulaika and William A. Douglass argue: "It is not simply that, like 'Communist' or 'fascist,' the word 'terrorist' is being abused; rather the word itself is an abuse, a banality that disguises reality while impoverishing language and thought by obliterating distinction."[13]

Thus, rather than trying to define terrorism, we should try to identify its hallmarks—that is, characterize it. Mullins provides a starting point by highlighting "the terror of terrorism," that is, the argument or precondition that "without the terror induced by the terrorist, there can be no terrorism."[14] Fear, therefore, is a key element in terrorism, and it is "the fear evoked by the individuals or the small groups of individuals whose capacity to constrain the behavior of others resides not in reason, in numerical preponderance, or in any legitimate exercise of authority, but only in their perception that they are able and willing to use violence unless their demands are satisfied."[15] The U.S. State Department characterizes terrorism as "premeditated, politically motivated violence perpetrated against noncombatant targets by subnational groups or clandestine agents, usually intended to influence an audience."[16] Paul Pillar, a former deputy chief of the CIA's Counterterrorist Center, offers a similar characterization of terrorism:[17]

- It is premeditated—planned and prepared in advance, rather than an impulsive outburst of rage.
- It is political—designed to change the existing political order—and not criminal.
- It is directed at civilians—not at troops or other military targets.
- It is perpetrated by subnational groups rather than by the army of a state.

Boaz Ganor, in his article "Defining Terrorism," cites the book *Political Terrorism* by Alex P. Schmid and Albert J. Jongman, in which the authors present the results of a survey of leading academics in the field, each of whom was asked to define terrorism.[18] "From these definitions, the authors isolated the following recurring elements, in order of their statistical appearance in the definitions: Violence, force (appeared in 83.5% of the definitions); political (65%); fear, emphasis on terror (51%); threats (47%); psychological effects and anticipated reactions (41.5%); discrepancy between the targets and the victims (37.5%); intentional, planned, systematic, organized action (32%); methods of combat, strategy, tactics (30.5%)."[19] From this survey, they determined that acts of terrorism are characterized by the following key elements:

- the use of violence
- a symbolic choice of victims
- performance by an organization
- operational seriality
- advance planning
- an absence of moral restraint
- political motivation
- the use of fear and anxiety

But terrorism is changing—now it has a new face. It is less centralized, less structured, less organized, and less local, yet it is much more danger-ous than the terrorism of the pre-2000 era. Xavier Raufer states that this new model of terrorist organization, such as al Qaeda, is marked by

- deterritorialization, or an interstate nature
- an absence of state sponsorship (generally speaking), which makes it more unpredictable and uncontrollable
- a hybrid political and religious-fanatic character
- an ability to mutate rapidly according to circumstances
- a pragmatic approach
- enormous killing power, compared with Cold War terrorism, which was usually little more than symbolic[20]

Using a somewhat oversimplified dichotomy of "old" and "new" terrorism, Shabtai Shavit points to several differences between the two types.[21] Shavit argues that while old terrorism was usually local, new terrorism is more global and intended to "export" conflict and widen the threat in order to challenge the world order. While old terrorism was secular, new terrorism is mostly fundamentalist. While old terrorism was nationalist and state related, new terrorism is more transnational and global. While old terrorism was international in the sense of collaboration and solidarity among various groups and organizations, new terrorism is international in terms of scope of the "targets" (e.g., the West and Christians). While old terrorism directed its messages to specific target populations defined by location, state, or territory, new terrorism is addressing global communities. Finally, while old terrorism was based on structured organizations, new terrorism is based on loosely knit networks that lack hierarchical structures.

The emerging nature of modern terrorists is very relevant to their growing reliance on modern communication technologies. As Michele Zanini and Sean Edwards note:

> Several of the most dangerous terrorist organizations are using information technology (IT)—such as computers, software, telecommunication devices, and the Internet—to better organize and coordinate dispersed activities. Like the large numbers of private corporations that have embraced IT to operate more efficiently and with greater flexibility, terrorists are harnessing the power of IT to enable new operational doctrines and forms of organization. And just as companies in the private sector are forming alliance networks to provide complex services to customers, so too are terrorist groups "disaggregating" from

hierarchical bureaucracies and moving to flatter, more decentralized, and often changing webs of groups united by a common goal.[22]

Cyberpolitics: Political Activism and the Net

The Internet is most likely the ideal channel of communication for political activists, especially those deprived of media attention. Discussing the nature of cyberpolitics, the CLC Media Policy Program argues:

> Perhaps one of the most promising features of the Internet is that it gives voice to many who have been unable to buy or generate media attention. Minor parties are using the Internet to spread their messages and recruit members. Interest groups are likewise drumming up support on the Net. Moreover, the low cost of the Internet means that poorly financed challengers can compete at some level with incumbents. For some, the Internet may be their only chance to address a large audience. . . . In addition to providing information, the Internet can facilitate communications that might not otherwise be possible. Ubiquitous chat rooms provide users with a chance to exchange ideas with one another. . . . Websites also act as de facto grassroots organizers; many candidates use their sites to recruit volunteers for their campaigns. Finally, because many sites permit users to e-mail candidates directly, there is a type of interaction that is not possible through more traditional campaign communications.[23]

Using the Net's capabilities, individuals and groups are now able to connect virtually with millions of people who share their attitudes, values, and ideas. Unlike the conventional mass media, argues Rob Kitchin, "cyberspace is not a broadcast medium with a few producers and many consumers, but rather a decentralized communication system where individuals are both the consumers and the producers . . . cyberspace is interactive; users can choose what information they receive and send."[24] This new medium may change the nature of political activism, as argued by Robert A. Saunders: "The ramifications of selective consumption and community-building for national minorities, previously at the mercy of elite-dominated media platforms, are substantial. The Internet has eliminated the barriers of distance and time between widely dispersed ethnic groups creating conceptual contiguity among members of these groups."[25]

The main advantage of the Internet for political activism when compared to "conventional" mass media is its interactive nature. Because many sites offer online response, cyberpolitics is more interactive than most traditional communications: "As attendance at town meetings or campaign rallies diminishes, the Internet may be a chance to create such events on line, and, at the same time, inspire people to leave their computers long enough to become involved in their communities."[26] Moreover, cyberspace also offers great promise for the creation and preservation of political identity and national culture. Political activism on the Net may take many forms, "from sites proclaiming the virtues of one party or candidate over another to scrupulously nonpartisan suppliers of political information."[27] Using the Internet, communities and groups "have the ability to maintain and reinforce their identity in new and compelling ways. Anthems, legends, genealogies, histories, photographs, manuscripts, and other tangible assets of political or national culture are being protected, distributed, and accessed in cyberspace."[28] The environment this created has been termed the "postinternational world," a concept defined and examined in Yale Ferguson and Richard Mansbach's book *Remapping Global Politics: History's Revenge and Future Shock.*[29] Postinternationalists see a world in which the primary actors are no longer representatives of the nation-state, and where power and authority have been transferred to countless spheres of authority or polities.

As Saunders argues, "The emergence of a postinternational world is closely tied to the communication and transportation revolutions of the past 50 years. The Internet is arguably the most important manifestation of this new milieu."[30] In effect, the emergence of cyberspace combined with the communicative powers of the Internet has prompted a paradigm shift in the power structures of modern society. Ronald J. Deibert identifies this large-scale shift in the modes of communication as a "distributional change" that is leading to a "world order transformation" on a par with the shift from parchment to printing in the waning days of the medieval period.[31] Such changes have enormous potential for altering political authority. Saunders claims that political and national minorities are especially well served in cyberspace:

> Historically, national minorities have been marginalized by their
> states of residence and cut off from contact with their co-
> nationals residing in other states. The dynamics of communica-
> tion and consumption on the Internet has broken the state's
> monopoly on information distribution and disrupted the politi-
> cal, cultural and economic elite's—that is, those representing the
> core nationality—ability to dominate thought, common sense
> and everyday assumptions within societies. Cultural, national
> and state identity is no longer exclusively in the hands of few
> authors—instead the power has shifted to multiple nuclei resem-
> bling a galactic configuration rather than a solar system.[32]

Among the political groups joining the Internet are extremist and
violent movements and organizations. In the late 1990s terrorist movements made their first appearance on the Net.[33] This should come as no
surprise: the more severely the interests of an extremist group have been
ignored, the more attractive the Internet will be for them. In a 1994
study on terrorism and the media, the present author and Conrad Winn
used the metaphor of the "theater of terror" to describe and analyze the
terrorists' use of violence as motivated by their need to stage events that
would attract the mass media.[34] In line with this argument, marginal
groups may be expected to seek to advance their interests in cyberspace
since their causes have been largely ignored by the conventional media.

Terrorism and the Internet have been associated in two ways. First,
the Internet has become a useful channel of communication, linking terrorists and their followers, spreading propaganda and instructions,
launching psychological scare campaigns, and networking terrorist
groups and organizations. Second, instead of using the Net, terrorists
may try to attack it, in what has come to be called cyberterrorism. At
present, terrorists are using and abusing the Internet and benefiting from
it more than they are attacking it.

The Advantages of the Internet for Modern Terrorism

The network of computer-mediated communication (CMC) is ideal for
terrorists-as-communicators: it is decentralized, it cannot be subjected
to control or restriction, it is not censored, and it allows access to anyone
who wants it. Moreover, the structure of modern terrorist organizations
in many ways is compatible with the structure of the Internet. The

loosely knit network of cells and subgroups typical of modern terrorist groups takes full advantage of the Internet for intergroup and intragroup networking. Al Qaeda, for example, has shown itself to be a remarkably nimble and adaptive entity, mainly due to its decentralized structure.[35]

The emergence of terrorist networks is a process noted by John Arquilla and David F. Ronfeldt as a shift toward "netwar":

> Netwar refers to an emerging mode of conflict and crime at societal levels, involving measures short of traditional war in which the protagonists are likely to consist of dispersed, small groups who communicate, coordinate, and conduct their campaigns in an internetted manner, without a precise central command. Netwar differs from modes of conflict in which the actors prefer formal, stand-alone, hierarchical organizations, doctrines, and strategies, as in past efforts, for example, to build centralized revolutionary movements along Marxist lines.[36]

The use of the Internet by modern terrorists is also a key ingredient in the concept of terrorism as psychological warfare. Timothy Thomas argues:

> Cyber-fear is generated by the fact that what a computer attack *could* do (i.e., bring down airliners, ruin critical infrastructure, destroy the stock market, reveal state secrets, etc.) is too often associated with what *will* happen. . . . It is clear that the Internet empowers small groups and makes them appear much more capable than they might actually be, even turning bluster into a type of virtual fear. The net allows terrorists to amplify the consequences of their activities with follow-on messages and threats directly to the population at large, even though the terrorist group may be totally impotent. In effect, the Internet allows a person or group to appear to be larger or more important or threatening than they really are.[37]

A terrifying example of this is the way that Pakistani captors used the Net to entrap the Jewish-American reporter Daniel Pearl through false e-mail communications. After kidnapping and murdering him, they posted the gruesome video of his death on the Internet.[38] This pattern was later repeated by Abu Musab al-Zarqawi and the insurgents in Iraq, who beheaded numerous hostages and posted the videotaped executions online.

Terrorist Web sites are often used to launch scare campaigns: for example, in early 2003, a number of sites announced that al Qaeda was preparing "a large attack" on American targets that would coincide with the start of the U.S.-led war on Iraq.

> This announcement was also published on several Islamic Internet web sites that support the global Jihad and al-Qaida. These announcements followed a whole string of previous declarations which have festooned websites and media reports since later January 2003. The end result of all these declarations and warnings of imminent attack has been to build up a sense of dread in expectation of "the big one"; we are told that a "mega attack" is in the works and that "it is only a matter of time." All of this may be grounded in fact, but it is equally true that the media hype has played into al-Qaida's strategy of psychological warfare.[39]

The desired impact of increasing public anxiety can be achieved even without any supporting evidence, detailed information, or materialization of the threats. For example, the Global Islamic Media published a communiqué in November 2003 at a Yahoo! Groups Web site, warning Muslims that they should leave three major U.S. cities.[40] According to the Middle East Media Research Institute (MEMRI), "The same website has published in recent months many communiqués by jihad groups around the world, as well as Islamic ideological material."[41] The announcement was signed "Ramadan" and bore the title "A Warning to the Muslims in America." Its opening statement read: "You did not think that they would go forth and they thought that their fortresses would protect them against Allah. But Allah came upon them whence they did not expect and cast terror into their hearts, so that they destroyed their homes with their own hands and the hands of the believers."[42] The communiqué continued: "Our Muslim brothers in America, we ask you to leave the following cities: Washington, D.C., New York, and Los Angeles. We are serious in our warning. The next few days will prove to you the truth of this warning. . . . To the oppressive rulers of America we say: Expect our terms following the first rule of Allah's believing soldiers (Koran, Chapter 59, Verse 2–3)." The message ends with another Koranic verse: "Fight them: Allah will punish them at your hands, and will humiliate them, and will help you to overcome them, and will relieve the minds of the believers (Koran, Chapter 9, Verse 14)." As one counter-terrorism expert concluded in his report on these virtual cyberthreats, "By creating the expectation of terrorism after each broadcast of a bin Laden video or audiotape, al Qaeda has built a pattern of stimulus and response. The public is conditioned to believe that these announcements will be followed by another terror attack in the near future. A conditioned reflex is thus established between the terrorists and the public, whereby a state of anxiety is fostered among the general populace in expectation of future attacks."[43]

It is relatively easy for terrorists to set up a Web site. Take, for example, alneda.com, al Qaeda's long-lasting former Web site (*alneda* means "the call" or "the calling"). This site was created by a fictitious organization, "The Center for Islamic Studies and Research," with a fake street address in Venezuela and a free Hotmail e-mail account (using a Web-hosting company in Malaysia). Al Qaeda then deposited eighty-seven dollars by wire in a Malaysian bank to cover the cost of the Web site for a year. Just before alneda.com was shut down, it posted warnings to its "customers" that the FBI, CIA, and U.S. Customs Service were probably monitoring the site. It informed them that they could find the new site's address in chat rooms on other terror sites, such as Hamas's qassam.net, and it even promised to e-mail them the new address. A statement on azzam.com, a Web site used by jihadists and al Qaeda, reads: "We strongly urge Muslim Internet professionals to spread and disseminate news and information about the jihad through e-mail lists, discussion groups and their own Web sites. The more Web sites, the better it is for us. We must make the Internet our tool."[44]

Web sites are only one of the Internet's services used by modern terrorists; many other facilities on the Net—e-mail, chat rooms, e-groups, forums, online magazines, and virtual message boards—are used more and more by terrorists. For example, according to Rita Katz and Josh Devon,

> Yahoo! has become one of al Qaeda's most significant ideological bases of operation. Utilizing several facets of Yahoo!'s service, including chat functions, e-mail, and most importantly, Yahoo! Groups, al Qaeda and its supporters have inserted themselves like a cancer into a company that screams, "American pop culture," and made it as much their own as a training camp in

> Khost. . . . Creating a Yahoo! Group is free, quick, and extremely
> easy, and al Qaeda and its supporters have wasted no time in
> starting up several Yahoo! Groups with topics related to the ter-
> rorist group and the downfall of Western civilization. Very often,
> the groups contain the latest links to jihadist websites, serving as
> a jihadist directory, and are sometimes the first to post al Qaeda
> communiqués to the public.[45]

Thus, by using Yahoo! Groups, "al Qaeda supporters chronicle the
terrorist group's victories, disseminate hatred of non-Muslims, and provide multimedia jihad frenzy for sympathetic viewers and other al Qaeda
members."[46] Moreover, "through these Yahoo! Groups, one can view
sickening media presentations posted by al Qaeda zealots. Videos
of Russian soldiers being tortured by Chechen mujahideen, vehicle-
bombing operations, sermons by jihadist sheikhs, homages to bin Laden,
and glorified, mutilated bodies of mujahideen fill these Yahoo! Groups."[47]
One of these sites, the Jundallah Web site, is hosted on Geocities, which
is owned by Yahoo! and provides free access and free Web pages to anyone interested. Katz and Devon report that "investigations into the
activities of captured members of an Al-Jihad splinter group in Egypt
called Jundallah (Soldiers of God) indicated that they utilized the Internet to recruit new members and to aid operatives."[48] Finding these Web
sites is not hard, but stopping them is an almost impossible task because
of the huge volume of traffic in Yahoo!'s free services. Moreover, if one
Web site is removed or blocked, others will emerge as substitutes, using
the unrestricted access provided by Yahoo! and similar companies.

The great virtues of the Internet have been converted to the advantage of groups committed to terrorizing societies in order to achieve
their goals. The anonymity offered by the Internet is especially attractive
to modern terrorists.[49] Due to their extremist beliefs and values, terrorists require anonymity to exist and to operate in social environments
that may not agree with their particular ideology or activities. The Internet provides this anonymity as well as easy access from virtually anywhere, with the ability to post messages, to send and receive e-mail, to
upload and download information, and to then disappear into the dark.
By its very nature, the Internet is in many ways an ideal arena for the
activities of terrorist organizations. Most notably, it offers:

- easy access
- little or no regulation, censorship, or other forms of government control
- potentially huge audiences spread throughout the world
- anonymity of communication
- fast flow of information
- interactivity
- inexpensive development and maintenance of a Web presence
- a multimedia environment (the ability to combine text, graphics, audio, and video and to allow users to download films, songs, books, posters, and so forth)
- the ability to shape coverage in the traditional mass media, which increasingly use the Internet as a source for stories

* * * * *

In July 2004, the independent National Commission on Terrorist Attacks upon the United States (the 9/11 Commission) released its findings in a 570-page report. This bipartisan commission was established by the U.S. Congress to investigate events before, during, and immediately after the attacks on New York and Washington that killed nearly three thousand people. The commission "reviewed more than 2.5 million pages of documents and interviewed more than 1,200 individuals in ten countries, held 19 days of hearings, and took public testimony from 160 witnesses."[50] The report starts with this short conclusion: "We learned about an enemy who is sophisticated, patient, disciplined, and lethal. The enemy rallies broad support in the Arab and Muslim world by demanding redress of political grievances, but its hostility toward us and our values is limitless."[51] The report points to the use of modern communication technologies in the planning and execution of the 9/11 attacks: "Terrorists . . . have benefited from this same rapid development of communication technologies."[52] The importance of the Internet, and its uses by al Qaeda for the attacks, was noted, too:

> The emergence of the World Wide Web has given terrorists a much easier means of acquiring information and exercising command and control over their operations. The operational leader

of the 9/11 conspiracy, Mohamed Atta, went online from Hamburg, Germany, to research U.S. flight schools. Targets of intelligence collection have become more sophisticated. These changes have made surveillance and threat warning more difficult.[53]

The report notes the uses of the Internet by the al Qaeda operatives, including searching the Web for information on U.S. flight schools (p. 157), using Internet communications (p. 157), equipping the hijackers with e-mail accounts (p. 529, note 140), coordinating the attackers' actions using e-mail (p. 530, note 152), downloading anti-American Web pages (p. 221), and gathering flight information from the Internet (p. 222). Given this compatible relationship between the Internet and modern terrorism, the use and abuse of these new electronic communications and capabilities by terrorists is inevitable, as we will see in chapters 3 and 4, which highlight the communicative and instrumental uses of the Internet by terrorists. First, however, we will examine the psychology of terrorism.

2

The War over Minds

The Psychology of Terrorism

The only thing we have to fear is fear itself.
—Franklin Delano Roosevelt, first inaugural address,
March 4, 1933

Psychology and Terrorism

Terrorism has always had a major psychological dimension: the word "terror" comes from the Latin "terrere," meaning "to frighten" or "to scare." The first use of large-scale terrorism occurred during the "popular" phase of the French Revolution: in September 1793, the Reign of Terror was launched, and over its course seventeen thousand people were executed. These executions were conducted before large audiences and were accompanied by sensational publicity, thus spreading the intended fear.

As a result of technological advances in communications and transportation, modern-day terrorists have new opportunities for exerting mass psychological impacts. According to the American Psychological Association's report "Coping with Terrorism,"

> Terrorism threatens a society by instilling fear and helplessness in its citizens. It seeks to hold a society or government hostage by fear of destruction and harm. When terrorist acts occur, people generally look for ways to cope with the acute stress and

trauma. Terrorism evokes a fundamental fear of helplessness. The violent actions are random, unprovoked, and intentional, and often are targeted at defenseless citizens. Trying to cope with the irrational information that is beyond normal comprehension can set off a chain of psychological events culminating in feelings of fear, helplessness, vulnerability, and grief.[1]

The psychologist Clark McCauley argues that terrorist acts can be perceived as acts of aggression against society: "Psychologists recognize two kinds of aggression: emotional and instrumental. Emotional aggression is associated with anger and does not calculate long-term consequences."[2] Emotional aggression rewards the aggressor by hurting someone who has hurt him or her, while instrumental aggression is the use of aggression as a means to other ends. "Terrorist aggression may involve emotional aggression," asserts McCauley, "especially for those who do the killing, but those who plan terrorist acts are usually thinking about what they want to accomplish. They aim to inflict long-term costs on their enemy and to gain long-term advantage for themselves. Terrorism inflicts immediate damage in destroying lives and material, but terrorists hope that the long-term costs will be much greater. They want to create fear and uncertainty far beyond the victims and those close to them. They want the enemy to spend time and money on security."

Terrorists want to attract attention to their cause and create fear, doubt, and uncertainty far beyond the first circle of immediate victims. As terrorism expert Boaz Ganor argues: "Modern terrorism, in defiance of the norms and laws of combat, focuses its attacks on civilians, thus turning the home front into the frontline. . . . The message is: anyone, anywhere, at any time, may be the target of the next attack. This threat undermines the ability of the civilian population to live a normal life. When every action must involve planning for how to survive a potential terror attack at a random time and place, the daily routine becomes fraught with anxiety."[3]

Terrorists seek to promote an overreaction: "The terrorists hope that a clumsy and over-generalized strike against them will hit some of their own side who are not yet radicalized and mobilized, will enlarge their base of sympathy, will turn the sympathetic but immobilized to action and sacrifice."[4] Terrorists also try to provoke expressions of prejudice, turning them into propaganda themes; they portray themselves as representing not just themselves but the entire population that is the subject of prejudice. For example, ETA in northern Spain claims to be fighting Spanish authority and governance on behalf of the entire Basque region. But ETA's opposition often comes from the Basque people themselves, especially the moderates who seek alternatives to violence. If ETA is able to instigate a closing of ranks among all those who sympathize with the cause the organization espouses, then the moderates are undermined and even silenced.

Finally, there is the personal dimension, or the psychopathology of terrorism.[5] McCauley points to a common notion that "there must be something wrong with terrorists. Terrorists must be crazy, suicidal or psychopaths without moral feelings or feelings for others."[6] For many years this idea was taken very seriously, but numerous studies have found no differences in terms of psychopathology and personality disorder between terrorists and nonterrorists. Such comparisons of terrorists with nonterrorists found similar psychopathology rates for both groups. Not only are terrorists not crazy, mentally sick, or psychologically damaged, but also they do not share a personality type: Martha Crenshaw argues that "no comparative work on terrorist psychology has ever succeeded in revealing a particular psychological type or uniform terrorist mindset."[7]

We should not, however, underestimate the allure of joining a terrorist group. Many groups offer persuasive incentives to would-be suicide terrorists, including detailed descriptions of the afterlife and its benefits. Palestinian suicide bombers, for example, are often seen as heroes and promised eternal glory as well as various other benefits in the next world. On earth their pictures, names, and descriptions are plastered on walls and Web sites. Their families are praised and usually receive some economic reward.

If psychology can be a useful tool in understanding modern terrorists, it is much more useful in decoding their motives, strategies, tactics, and impact than in profiling them according to psychological models.

Terror as Psychological Warfare

The term "psychological warfare" was coined in 1941 by the Nazi regime, with the German word *Weltanschauungskrieg* ("worldview warfare"). This strategy called for the psychological application of propaganda, pressure, and terrorism to secure both obedience and ideological victory over enemies of the Reich. Psychological warfare and propaganda were widely used during World War II and thoroughly studied after the war. William Donovan, director of the Office of Strategic Services (OSS) during the war, "viewed Nazi psychological tactics as a vital source of ideas to be used by American agencies. Donovan sought to use psychological warfare as a major military tool."[8] A personal friend of President Franklin D. Roosevelt, he convinced the president to launch the Office of the Coordinator of Information in 1941. With Donovan in charge, this agency was meant to conduct propaganda campaigns and secret operations both at home and abroad. It was soon reconfigured by a division that assigned the "white," official propaganda operations to the Office of War Information (OWI), while the "black," clandestine functions were delegated to the OSS. During World War II, the Psychological Warfare Division of U.S. forces in Europe grew to 460 employees. After the war, almost all the scientists in the field of communication studies emerged from wartime operations; wartime techniques were subsequently documented, studied, and developed and are now applied to a whole gamut of endeavors ranging from commercial marketing to political campaigning. The United States engaged in significant psychological warfare during the first Gulf War in Iraq.[9] More recently, in 1998, the United States Army activated the fourth Special Operations Regiment, the Psychological Operations Regiment, known as PsyOp and bearing the motto "Persuade, change, and influence."

Today it appears that modern terrorism has learned the lessons of state-operated campaigns and now uses the weapon of psychological warfare with growing sophistication and impact. According to Jerrold Post, professor of psychiatry, political psychology, and international affairs at George Washington University, "Terrorism at heart is a vicious species of psychological warfare; it is violence as communication. Smart bombs and missiles will not win this war. The only way to counter psychological warfare is with psychological warfare."[10] Hezbollah, the militant Shiite organization in Lebanon, has made clear its desire to employ psychological warfare: al-Manar, a TV station operated by Hezbollah, declared on its Web site (web.manartv.org), "Al-Manar is the first Arab establishment to stage an effective psychological warfare against the Zionist enemy." The psychologically astute terrorists study the target population to learn about weaknesses and sensitivities. According to Ganor,

> Dissenting views in the society are carefully collected and used to undermine the population's beliefs in the rightness of its own ways. The terror organization knows from the outset that it will not achieve its goals purely by means of terror attacks. It must enlist the help of its victims themselves in gaining its objectives. A victory that would be impossible by military means is thus brought within reach through a protracted, gnawing campaign of psychological warfare—a war of attrition that gradually erodes the target population's will to fight and turns the tables against the stronger power.[11]

The psychological impact of modern terrorism is designed to reach beyond the immediate victims to others who were not victimized directly by the attack. Statistically, one is far less likely to be the victim of a terrorist attack than to be the victim of a traffic accident or even a workplace accident. Nonetheless, by using psychological manipulation, argues Ganor, the terrorists produce a level of anxiety that is disproportionate to the actual danger:

> Terrorism is psychological warfare pure and simple. It aims to isolate the individual from the group, to break up a society into so many frightened individuals, hiding in their homes and unable to go about their daily lives as citizens, employees, and family members. Further the terrorist aims to undermine the individual's belief in the collective values of his society, by amplifying the potential threat to the extent that security appears to outweigh all other political concerns. Terrorism uses the victim's own imagination against him.[12]

Thus modern terrorists are not necessarily interested in the death or injury of their direct victims as much as in the impact of this psychological victimization on a wider public. In fact, Alex Schmid distinguishes between the target of violence and the target(s) of attention, of which he notes three: the target of terror, the target of coercion, and the target of influence.[13] It is clear that such psychological impact relies on the mass media: the desired panic is produced by the continuous broadcast of the horrible acts of violence and the terrorists' threats and declara-

tions—via radio and television, videos, and the Internet—all according
to the very familiar methods of psychological warfare.

The Theater of Terror

> *When one says "terrorism" in a democratic society, one also says*
> *"media." For terrorism by its very nature is a psychological weapon*
> *which depends upon communicating a threat to a wider society.*
> *This, in essence, is why terrorism and the media enjoy a symbiotic*
> *relationship.*
>
> —Paul Wilkinson, *Terrorism versus Democracy*

A terrorist campaign usually has four target audiences for its messages:
supporters of the terrorist organization; the population that the organization purports to serve; the enemy, or those attacked by the organization;
and international public opinion. The messages vary from one target
audience to another. To the terrorist organization's supporters, purported
community, and potential recruits, the message is of pride, success, commitment, and vision. To the enemy population, the terrorists' message is
of threat and fear, with the intention that this fear translate into moral
breakdown, collapse of confidence in the government, and pressure on
decision makers to accept the terrorists' demands. The success of this
strategy depends on the degree to which fear or panic can be blown out
of all proportion to the actual threat. Finally, to the rest of the world, the
terrorists' message is usually based on the determination to achieve noble
political goals such as freedom, equal rights, self-expression, a free state,
liberation of prisoners, and so on. The use of violence is justified as the
only way to get world attention. One of the terrorists who orchestrated
the attack on the Israeli athletes during the 1972 Munich Olympic
Games testified:

> We recognized that sport is the modern religion of the Western
> world. We knew that the people in England and America would
> switch their television sets from any program about the plight of
> the Palestinians if there was a sporting event on another chan-
> nel. So we decided to use their Olympics, the most sacred cere-
> mony of this religion, to make the world pay attention to us. We
> offered up human sacrifices to your gods of sport and television.

And they answered our prayers. From Munich onwards, nobody could ignore the Palestinians or their cause.[14]

The emergence of media-oriented terrorism led several communication and terrorism scholars to reconceptualize modern terrorism within the framework of symbolic communication theory.[15] Philip Karber has argued that "the terrorist's message of violence necessitates a victim, whether personal or institutional, but the target or intended recipient of the communication may not be the victim."[16] Ralph Dowling applied the concept of "rhetoric genre" to modern terrorism, arguing that "terrorists engage in recurrent rhetorical forms that force the media to provide the access without which terrorism could not fulfill its objectives."[17] The present author and Conrad Winn adopted the "theater of terror" metaphor to examine modern terrorism as an attempt to communicate messages through the use of orchestrated violence.[18] This metaphor materialized in dramatic form in October 2002, when forty-one Chechen terrorists took more than eight hundred people hostage in a Moscow theater, demanding an end to Russia's war against the Chechen homeland. Playing at the Moscow Theater that evening was a Russian musical about the Red Army during World War II. When heavily armed masked gunmen appeared onstage, the audience thought that it was a part of the production. A member of the audience in the Moscow Theater recalled thinking to herself, "Great acting!" However, it was acting in a very different sense, and the Moscow Theater was about to become the world's stage for yet another monstrous terrorist drama. When the terrorists exposed their explosive belts and declared that if the Russian army did not leave Chechnya they would blow up the entire theater, the hostages realized that they had just become actors in a horrifying and very realistic drama. Videotapes of the event as well as dramatic first-person interviews with the hijackers, the hostages, and the survivors give a vivid illustration of the "theater of terror" being actualized.

The most powerful and violent performance of modern terrorism to date, however, was the September 11, 2001, attack on U.S. targets. "The greatest irony," argues Brigitte Nacos, professor of political science at Columbia University, "was that the very terrorists who loathed America's pop culture as decadent and poisonous to their own beliefs and ways of life turned Hollywood-like horror fantasies into real life hell."[19] In

November 2001, shortly after the 9/11 attacks, Osama bin Laden discussed the attacks, describing the suicide terrorists as "vanguards of
Islam" and arguing that "those young men said in deeds, in New York
and Washington, speeches that overshadowed other speeches made
everywhere else in the world. The speeches are understood by both Arabs
and non-Arabs, even Chinese."[20] With these remarks, argues Nacos, "bin
Laden revealed that he considered terrorism first and foremost as a vehicle to dispatch messages—'speeches,' in his words—and regarding the
events of 9/11, he concluded that Americans in particular had heard and
reacted to the intended communication."[21] From the "theater of terror"
perspective, the September 11 attack on the United States introduced a
new level of mass-mediated terrorism, a perfectly choreographed production aimed at international, Muslim, and U.S. audiences.

In her study "The Terrorist Calculus behind 9-11," Nacos notes that
the terrorists could have struck at night, sparing many lives, and still
gained enormous publicity, "but the bright daylight guaranteed the most
'spectacular' visuals and the loss of life for which they undoubtedly
aimed. In all these respects no previous act of terrorism came even close
to the events of 9-11."[22] With the first World Trade Center bombing in
1993 and the Oklahoma City bombing in 1995, Americans were introduced to a new age of terrorism, and this new form of terrorism is a
more powerfully media-oriented production than ever before. The targets chosen for September 11, for example, were symbols of American
wealth, power, and national heritage. A detailed manual of the Afghan
jihad, taken from al Qaeda's training camps, advised the would-be terrorists to target "sentimental landmarks" such as the Statue of Liberty in
New York, Big Ben in London, and the Eiffel Tower in Paris because
their demolition would "generate intense publicity."[23]

In the attacks on New York and Washington, argues Nacos, "the archi-
tects of terror were successful in realizing some of their objectives. . . .
With their deadly assault Bin Laden and his followers managed to set
America's public agenda for many months, perhaps even years."[24] Nacos
cites several opinion polls revealing that literally all Americans followed
the news of the terrorist attacks by television, radio, and the Internet. All
over the world there was a wave of shock and fear and a general tuning
in to the mass media. The terrorists were spectacularly successful in the
agenda-setting goal for which all terrorists strive. During the 1972

Olympic Games at Munich, the Black September terrorists' attack was watched live by an estimated audience of 800 million viewers all over the world. The advances in communication technology in the ensuing three decades and the staggering visual images of the events on September 11 combined to make the al Qaeda attacks on the United States the most-watched terrorist spectacle ever.

Another objective of media-oriented terrorism is to spread fear and anxiety and to intimidate the target audience through exposure to terrorism via the mass media. Nacos notes that

> opinion polls revealed that the terror attacks on New York and Washington heightened Americans' fear of more terrorism to come and of the likelihood that they themselves or a member of their family might become victims. This effect on the targeted population was not lost on bin Laden and his associates. In commenting on the impact of the terror attack on the American enemy, the Al Qaeda leader remarked with obvious satisfaction, "There is America, full of fear from north to south, from west to east. Thank God for that."[25]

Moreover, by striking hard at the United States, argues Nacos, the terrorists led the world media to present and discuss their claims and grievances in ways that far transcended the amount and prominence of the coverage before the attacks. Media coverage of Islam-related issues changed in a dramatic fashion after al Qaeda's attacks on September 11. Much of the coverage focused on attempts to answer President Bush's question: "Why do they hate us?" Such coverage served the terrorists by publicizing their causes, grievances, and demands. The intensive coverage of these topics in the mass media increased the U.S. public's comprehension of Muslims and Islam:

> According to a CBS News survey, 55% of Americans said at the end of February 2002 that they knew more now about Islam than they did before September 2001. The same survey showed that 30% of the public had a positive, 33% a negative view of this religion. But this was actually a net gain in favor of Americans' positive attitudes toward Islam compared to a 1993 survey conducted by the *Los Angeles Times*, when 14% revealed positive and 22% negative feelings toward Islam.[26]

But bin Laden's most important target audience was not the American public but rather the populations of Muslim countries. In the eyes of many Muslims, Osama bin Laden was the biggest hero: the Arab media and especially the Arab news network al Jazeera presented him as a world leader, a rising icon, and America's public enemy number one, thus promoting his status, popularity, and legitimacy among millions of Muslims. In the international media, from CNN to *Time* magazine and from al Jazeera to al Arabiya, bin Laden appeared frequently and prominently, sometimes even more frequently and prominently than the leaders of the world's most powerful states. The "status conferral" function of the mass media elevated him to the level of a leading global figure. Thus, Nacos concludes,

> There is no doubt, then, that the architects of 9/11 had a perfect score with respect to the three media-centered objectives of the calculus of terror: they raked unprecedented media attention, publicized their causes and motives and in the process the grievances of many Muslims, and gained global prominence and notoriety otherwise only accorded to nation-states and their leaders.[27]

An impressive and frightening potential of psychological warfare launched by media-wise terrorists was the use of the anthrax envelopes, sent in 2001–02 to post offices and then to the mail rooms of two U.S. media companies. "If the idea was to increase the jitters in a grieving, nervous population, the people who dispatched the anthrax-carrying mail and those who sent the frightening copycat letters containing what appeared to be harmless white powder also succeeded. Just as one group of terrorists brought mass killings to American soil, turning local reporters into war correspondents, that group or other groups or individuals turned the news offices into battlefields . . . of psychological warfare."[28] "It's brilliant," said Jessica Stern, a lecturer on terrorism at the Kennedy School of Government at Harvard University. "What better way to guarantee that you're going to get attention than to attack the media directly?"[29] This attack could have been produced by bin Laden, by Islamic fundamentalist groups, or by right-wing groups in the United States. The perpetrators have yet to be determined.

The emergence of media-oriented terrorism and its growing sophistication in manipulating the media have led governments and media organizations to react by limiting terrorists' access to the conventional mass media, reducing and censoring news coverage of terrorist acts and their perpetrators and minimizing the terrorists' capacity for manipulating the media.[30] However, the new media technologies, and especially computer-mediated communication and the Internet, allow terrorist organizations to send messages more freely and easily than through other means of communication.

Al Qaeda, for example, is using multimedia propaganda and advanced communication technologies in a most sophisticated way. In his assessment of al Qaeda, RAND specialist Bruce Hoffman notes this "long-established sophistication of bin Laden and al Qaeda's propaganda efforts—employing multimedia vehicles, including prerecorded video and audiotapes, CD-ROMs, DVDs, and the Internet; dramatically choreographed and staged dissemination opportunities; and other mass outreach techniques (e.g., via al Qaeda's phantom Alneda website and those of sympathetic, above-ground radical Islamic sites and organizations)."[31] Despite the massive attacks on al Qaeda in recent years, the heavy losses of operatives, and the dismantling of its operational bases and training camps in Afghanistan, al Qaeda quickly reacted with an impressive campaign. A professionally produced seven-minute videotape appeared, intended to serve both recruitment and propaganda uses. It was circulated in various Muslim countries and communities all over the world. This video, seized by U.S. authorities in the spring of 2002, openly prescribed martyrdom and suicide attacks and solicited new recruits to bin Laden's camp. The tape presented martyrs in training camps and in combat and then showed images of twenty-seven martyrs in rapid succession, including their names, where they came from, and where they died. The voiceover in the concluding segment recited a Koranic verse: "They rejoice in the bounty provided by Allah: And with regard to those left behind, who have not yet joined them (in their bliss), the (Martyrs) glory in the fact that on them is no fear, nor have they (cause to) grieve." The persistent reappearance of al Qaeda's Web sites (see "The Phoenix of the Internet" in chapter 3) is another example of the organization's determination to use modern media technologies. The sites, published in Arabic only, continue to disseminate anti-American, anti-Western, and anti-Israeli messages.

In February 2004, the first online issue of the al Qaeda biweekly magazine *Sawt al-Jihad (Voice of Jihad)* was released.[32] This first issue was devoted entirely to propaganda, especially Internet propaganda. One of the articles presents the achievements of the mujahedeen (Muslim guerrilla warriors engaged in a jihad), arguing that their most prominent victory was to "prove the truth of their belief." The online magazine sheds some light on al Qaeda's view of its main objectives. Orchestrating attacks against Western targets is important, but the main objective remains that of mobilizing public support and gaining grassroots legitimacy among Muslims. Another article in the same issue of *Sawt al-Jihad* refers to the video *Badr al-Riyadh,* produced, posted, and distributed by al Qaeda. According to the article, 300,000–400,000 people downloaded the movie in less than five days, segments of it were broadcast on various TV news channels, and the video was also duplicated and distributed on videocassettes. The article argues, "This video had a great impact on the tyrants of the Peninsula, it baffled them, it destroyed everything they had done. . . . Months, and even years of organized deceit went to waste in a mere 90 minutes."[33]

Al Qaeda's propaganda, argues Hoffman, has three basic themes: the West is implacably hostile to Islam; the only way to address the West is in the language of violence; and jihad is the only way for true believers.[34] The Islamic theory of jihad, or holy war, is presented as a commitment to spread the faith by the sword. Al Qaeda's Web sites, videos, and audiotapes carry updated news summaries, reporting the struggle of Islam against the West, along with ideological material that includes recommended readings, books, and articles by selected authors. In many messages, al Qaeda claims responsibility for the 9/11 attacks, praises the operation, and cites Islamic arguments to justify the killing of the "enemies." As do many terrorist sites, al Qaeda's uses impressive graphics, recorded television footage (mostly of bin Laden), and even poetry to glorify the sacrifices of the martyrs and the merciless struggle against Islam's enemies. According to Paul Eedle, "The site works to maintain the morale of al Qaeda supporters in the face of obvious reverses since 11 September."[35] Interestingly, a consistent theme is the symbolic link made between the destruction of the World Trade Center and damage to the U.S. economy: the September 11 attacks are depicted as an assault on the trademarks of the U.S. economy, and the site offers as evidence the weakening of the U.S. dollar, the decline of the U.S. stock exchange, and the loss of confidence, both at home and abroad, in the U.S. economy. Again, in a very typical style of rhetoric found in terrorist propaganda, a comparison is made with the decline and collapse of the Soviet Union. In one of bin Laden's numerous publications, he stated that "America is in retreat by the Grace of Almighty and economic attrition is continuing up to today. But it needs further blows. The young men need to seek out the nodes of the American economy and strike the enemy's nodes."[36] In addition, the thirteen-volume *Encyclopedia of Jihad* and the single-volume *Jihad Manual* were posted on the Net, transferred onto discs and CD-ROMs, and e-mailed to supporters, jihadists, and would-be jihadists all around the world.

A dramatic example of the multimedia propaganda of al Qaeda were the wills of the May 12, 2003, suicide bombers in Riyadh, which were videotaped, broadcast, and posted on the Internet. In October 2003, al Qaeda released a videotape that included an audio recording of the actual attack, excerpts from speeches of Osama bin Laden, and the wills of the attackers, which were reportedly recorded two weeks before the attacks.[37] The video was produced by the Sahhab Institute, which had previously produced other al Qaeda videos and films, including the videotaped wills of two 9/11 hijackers. The October 2003 video shows two attackers (Hazem al-Kashmiri, also known as Abu Umar al-Ta'ifi, and Muhammad bin Abd al-Wahhab al-Maqit) reading their wills and addressing a message in English to "the American soldiers" and to "the West." Al-Kashmiri introduces himself as the son of General Muhammad Said Abdallah al-Kashmiri, a retired high-ranking officer in the Saudi domestic intelligence apparatus. The following are excerpts from statements of the two suicide bombers:

> HAZEM AL-KASHMIRI: For the American soldiers, we say you have to know that your government has become a big evil killing innocent people, destroying homes, stealing our money and holding our sons in jail. We promise that we will not let you live safely and you will not see from us anything else—just bombs, fire, destroying homes, cutting your heads. Our Mujahedeen is coming to you very soon to let you see what you didn't see before.

MUHAMMAD BIN ABD AL-WAHHAB AL-MAQIT: I invite you to accept Islam by saying "Ashhadu Anna La Ilaha Illa Allah Wa-Muhammad Rasul-ul-Allah"—"I bear witness that there is no God but Allah and Muhammad is his messenger" . . . and you will be my brother in Islam. And it doesn't matter what your nationality or your color is until you accept Islam—if any enemy attacked you, I will do what I can even if it cost my life to save you. We want from all Christians and Jews to go out from our Islamic countries and release our brothers from jails and stop killing Muslims or we will kill you as you are killing Muslims. We will continue in our fighting until we get what we want. The real Muslims they mean what they say. Very soon all the world will see what we will do. You will not enjoy in your life forever Allah Akbar and glory to Allah.[38]

Bin Laden's mass-mediated propaganda also relies on the popular al Jazeera satellite television. In numerous videotapes, released to al Jazeera or on the Internet, bin Laden attempts to justify in a rational and moral framework the mass murder perpetrated by his followers. Yoram Schweitzer, a terrorism expert, studied al Qaeda's propaganda and found that "Bin Laden, like some of his psychopathic predecessors in history, justified his responsibility for cold-blooded murder. The slaughter of men, women, and children in Kenya, Tanzania, and the United States, along with the atrocities committed by his associates in Egypt, Algeria, Pakistan, and India were merely acts of retaliation for the actions of the U.S.A. and its proxy, Israel. . . . Bin Laden typically selects a few historical incidents, takes them out of their context and twists their significance, and uses them as a rational and moral pretext for his terrorist crimes."[39] Bin Laden's propaganda is based on his perception of a struggle between good and evil. He describes the attacks on the United States as part of an inevitable clash between two parts of mankind: "the part of belief without hypocrisy versus the part of the heresy."[40] In his Internet and television campaign, bin Laden explains the motives for the 9/11 attacks on the United States: they were meant to trigger a universal war between "Islam of the true believers" and "the camp of the heretics." According to Schweitzer, "Bin Laden hopes to force all Muslims in every corner of the world to choose sides; he believes that most Muslims will ultimately come to support his struggle."[41]

These messages target various audiences through multimedia channels of communication. As Hoffman concludes, "[A]l-Qaeda's abiding faith in the power of communication, whether through propaganda or instructional treatises, has ensured a steady flow of information to its far-flung sympathizers and supporters. . . . The main challenge for al Qaeda, however, will be to promote and ensure its durability as an ideology and concept. It can only do this by staying in the news."[42]

Terrorism functions by instilling fear in its enemies. Whether through the public arenas of France's Reign of Terror or the global coverage of the 9/11 attacks, terrorists have been dependent on whatever means were available to let their actions and threats be known. With the advent of the Internet, the means of communication have become internalized and controlled by the terrorists themselves.

3

Communicative Uses of the Internet for Terrorism

ONE OF THE OBJECTIVES OF MODERN TERRORISM is to generate publicity and draw attention to the terrorists and their cause. How do terrorist groups use the Internet to advance their organizations' political, religious, and ideological agendas? We know that terrorists "are increasingly resorting to the internet to disseminate their views to a wider public, and that they have come to the realization that establishing their presence in cyberspace is nearly just as critical to their long-term success as any military triumph or act of sabotage."[1] Terrorist groups can maintain Web pages to present their case, disseminate propaganda, and recruit followers and supporters. Through the Internet they can easily reach a vast audience in a direct and uncensored way and place themselves on the international stage. In the conventional media, if some message should seem dangerous to a government or the public, it can be censored or filtered. However, the Internet does not allow for the same degree of control. According to Timothy Thomas in his article on cyberplanning, "The web allows an uncensored and unfiltered version of events to be broadcast worldwide. Chat rooms, websites, and bulletin boards are largely uncontrolled, with few filters in place. This climate is perfect for an underfunded group to explain its actions or to offset both internal and international condemnation, especially when using specific servers. The Internet can target fence-sitters as well as true believers with different messages, oriented to the target audience."[2]

In this chapter we will review the ways in which terrorists use the Internet to communicate their messages to various target groups. We present the scope and content of terrorist Web sites, their target audiences, and their persuasive appeals, including the rhetoric of moral disengagement. As illustrative examples, this chapter presents a detailed analysis of several groups' use of the Internet. We chose these groups because they represent a variety of motives, locations, types of action, and aggression levels and because they all share an impressive presence on the Net. They include the Web sites of the Japanese Aum Shinrikyo, or "Supreme Truth"; al Qaeda, the "phoenix of the Internet"; FARC, the Revolutionary Armed Forces of Colombia; Hamas; Hezbollah; the IRA splinter groups; and the insurgents in post-Saddam Iraq. We conclude this chapter with an examination of the impact of these campaigns, suggesting several indirect measures to assess the real effectiveness and impact of terrorist uses of the Internet, including testimonies both from terrorists and from affected individuals.

An Overview of Terrorist Web Sites: Scope and Contents

Terrorists use the Internet for its commonly accepted benefits: communication, propaganda, marketing, and fund-raising. And yet, despite this growing terrorist presence, when policymakers, journalists, and academics discuss the combination of terrorism and the Internet, they focus on the overrated threat posed by cyberterrorism or cyberwarfare (i.e., attacks on computer networks, including those on the Internet) and largely ignore the numerous uses that terrorists make of the Internet every day.

Who are the terrorist organizations on the Web? As the following illustrative list shows, these organizations and groups come from all corners of the globe. (This geographical categorization, it should be noted, reveals the geographical diversity of terrorist groups but obscures the fact that many of them are truly transnational, and even transregional, in character.)

- From the Middle East: Hamas (the Islamic Resistance Movement), the Lebanese Hezbollah (Party of God), the al-Aqsa Martyrs Brigades, Fatah Tanzim, the Popular Front for the Liberation of Palestine (PFLP), the Palestinian Islamic Jihad, the Kahane Lives movement, the People's Mujahedin of Iran (PMOI, Mujahedin-e Khalq), the Kurdish Workers' Party (PKK), the Turkish-based Popular Democratic Liberation Front Party in Turkey (DHKP/C), and the Great East Islamic Raiders Front (IBDA-C), also based in Turkey
- From Europe: the Basque ETA movement, Armata Corsa (the Corsican Army), and the Real Irish Republican Army (RIRA)
- From Latin America: Peru's Tupac-Amaru (MRTA) and Shining Path (Sendero Luminoso), the Colombian National Liberation Army (ELN-Colombia) and the Armed Revolutionary Forces of Colombia (FARC), and Mexico's Zapatista National Liberation Army (EZLN)[3]
- From Asia: al Qaeda, the Japanese Supreme Truth (Aum Shinrikyo), Ansar al Islam (Supporters of Islam) in Iraq, the Japanese Red Army (JRA), Hizb-ul Mujehideen in Kashmir, Sri Lanka's Liberation Tigers of Tamil Eelam (LTTE), the Islamic Movement of Uzbekistan (IMU), the Moro Islamic Liberation Front (MILF) in the Philippines, the Pakistan-based Lashkar e-Tayba (LeT), and the rebel movement in Chechnya

Many of the terrorists on the Net belong to radical Islamist groups and organizations. Paradoxically, it is those who criticize and attack Western modernity, technology, and media who are using the West's most advanced modern medium, the Internet.[4] This should come as no surprise after the publication of several studies, especially Gary Bunt's books *Virtually Islamic* and *Islam in the Digital Age*,[5] that describe the diverse manifestations of the Islamic presence online. Bunt suggests that there has been a significant redirection of resources into the Net by Islamic organizations that have adapted to the digital age, preferring the Net over traditional channels of communication. This trend is reflected in the volume of militant Islamic materials online and in the growing sophistication of Islamic Web sites. For example, the presentation of video clips and audio broadcasts on Islamic sites applies some of the most recent developments in computer technology.

According to Bunt, "The Islamic Internet landscape changes frequently, with new sites emerging on a daily basis. Some very proactive players change their content and format regularly, attempting to draw readers to their message(s) in order to establish links or a sense of community."[6] Chat rooms are often unregulated and unmonitored by scholars and clerics, can provide a virtual hangout for teenage and young adult Muslims, and are sometimes rife with anti-*kuffar* (-nonbeliever) sentiment. Bunt adds, "The Internet is clearly important in disseminating a broad range of Islamic political-religious opinions and concerns to a global audience. Thus, many extremist Islamist activists and terrorists now see the Internet as a vital tool."[7]

Given that terrorists are present on the Internet, what does this presence look like? What are the contents of terrorist sites? A typical Web site usually includes information about the history of the group or organization; biographies of its leaders, founders, heroes, and commanders; information on the political, religious, or ideological aims of the organization; and news bulletins and updates. Most of the sites present a review of the group's social and political background including its notable activities in the past and its current and future plans. The sites of national organizations generally display maps of the areas in dispute: the Hamas site shows a map of Palestine; the ETA sites present maps of Spain and the Basque land; the FARC site shows a map of Colombia; the Tamil site presents a map of Sri Lanka.

A good example of an informative campaign is found on one of the Web sites of ETA. This site *(Euskal Herria Journal)* is in English, with some documents in Basque, French, and Spanish.[8] The Web site presents itself as a factual and professional journal espousing Basque culture, history, and independence. It argues that Navarre is the seat of the Basque country and maintains that the Spanish and French Basque regions are an occupied sovereign Basque state and should be independent. In the "history" segment, the objective is clearly to show Spanish and French transgressions, stressing the long history of the Basque people and their existence in the area before other European cultures. In the review of Basque nationalism, the writing takes on a biting tone, accusing the "founding fathers" of the movement and later the Basque Nationalist Party of selling out, aligning with the Spanish government, and giving up on the French provinces in order to "get at least an inch of hegemony in their little fiefdom." The segment on repression details actions taken by the Spanish and French governments against the Basque people and

ETA, such as the outlawing of the Basque language and the targeting of ETA members by Spain's Antiterrorist Liberation Groups (which the journal calls "death squads"), and describes "Spain's Dirty War" (which was a paramilitary campaign against ETA sanctioned by the Spanish government). Although the text mentions some acts of violence committed by ETA (which is rare for a terrorist group—see below), it largely focuses on tactics by the Spanish government. The site also has a news section, which is divided into segments on the conflict and its politics, the "econo-myth"—arguing against foreign companies and the European Union—the environment, society, and women. This Web site contains Basque language lessons and talks about human rights and free speech. Despite its cultural, ideological, and informative nature, this site supports ETA, its goals, and its activities, including violent actions. As Yariv Tsfati and the present author noted in our 2002 report,

> Almost all the terror sites detail their goals in one way or another. Sometimes this is done explicitly, sometimes indirectly. Sometimes it is a separate section, and sometimes intermixed with other content. The most common presentation of aims is through a direct criticism of their enemies or rivals. For example, the Hamas site presents a historical account of "the birth of the Zionist entity in Palestine"; the Shining Path site has information about "the crimes of the Fujimori regime" (supported by the United States); a considerable part of the Hezbollah site focuses on Israeli activity ("Israeli terrorism" from the Hezbollah standpoint); the Tamil site attacks the Sinhalese regime. Thus, the terrorist sites do not concentrate only on information concerning their organizations; direct attack of the enemy is the most common strategy of the Internet terrorists.[9]

However, most terrorist groups avoid references on their Web sites to their own violent activities. The Web sites of Hezbollah, Hamas, and al-Zarqawi and the insurgents in Iraq are exceptions to this rule; they show pictures and videos of brutal killings, executions, and bombings, offer updated statistical reports of the groups' actions ("daily operations"), and keep count of the number of "dead martyrs," along with the number of "killed enemies" or "killed collaborators." But while some terrorist sites avoid or at least minimize their organization's violent record, most terrorists on the Internet highlight two "positive" issues: freedom of expression and political prisoners. Why? "Terrorists aim at Western audiences who are sensitive to the norms of freedom of expression and emphasize the issues that provoke sympathy in democratic societies. Restricted expression by political movements is contrary to the fundamental and sacred principles of democracy. The strong emphasis given to this issue in democratic societies helps terrorist organizations—which don the innocent cap of a 'nonviolent political group'—embarrass the governments against which they are struggling. This tactic works particularly well on the stage of the Internet, the symbol of absolutely free communication."[10]

Another common theme is that of political harassment and political detentions. Terrorist Web sites frequently emphasize the antidemocratic measures used by the authorities or the enemy. In doing so, they attempt to malign the authorities and to demonize the enemies. They also send a message to their own constituents and supporters, to neutral audiences, and even to their enemies. For example, the insurgents in Iraq use their Internet propaganda to demonize the Americans to the Iraqi people, the Arab communities in the world, the more neutral European states, and even the Americans themselves.

Most terrorist sites publish online the organization's communiqués, official announcements, and the speeches and declarations of their leaders, founders, and ideologues. Some of the material is recycled, previously distributed via the conventional media and other communication channels. Almost all the sites offer online "gift shops": visitors can purchase or download for free posters, books, videos, pictures, audiocassettes and discs, stickers, badges, symbols, and calendars. As we will see later, some Web sites are used for the distribution of practical terrorist manuals and guidebooks, turning these sites into virtual training camps.

The Rhetoric of Moral Disengagement on Terrorist Sites

What is the rhetoric of terrorist sites? A useful theory guiding our study of terrorist cyberrhetoric has been Albert Bandura's theory of selective moral disengagement.[11] Although this general theory of the rhetorical attempt by communicators to disengage or distance themselves from their own use of violence was not devised with terrorist discourse in mind, it is nevertheless a useful analytical tool for examining terrorist rhetoric. Terrorists' need to justify their violence in terms of some higher societal need can be explained by social cognitive theory; how they justify this behavior can be understood using the psychological concept of moral disengagement. According to this theory, people generally tend to refrain from behavior that violates their moral values and do not usually engage in such harmful conduct until they have justified to themselves the morality of their actions. Bandura sees the mechanism of moral disengagement as a cognitive restructuring of inhumane conduct into something benign or worthy. Several tactics can be employed toward this end:

Displacement of responsibility: This practice distorts the relationship between the individual's behavior and its outcome. Blaming the authorities, the circumstances, or even the victims themselves decreases one's own responsibility. To obscure or minimize their active role in the harm done, the aggressors can present their actions as having arisen from social pressures and then claim that they themselves are consequently not responsible for the actions. Thus, the use of violence can be attributed to compelling circumstances and is therefore not the aggressor's free choice.

Diffusion of responsibility: Personal responsibility can also be minimized by distribution of responsibility. The aggressors can divide their duties, so that no individual task is too terrible, although the entirety is deadly. Blaming group decisions is another way to diffuse the responsibility: "When everyone is responsible, no one is responsible."

Dehumanization of targets: People find violence easier if they do not see their victims as human beings. The victimization caused by one's actions can be minimized by highlighting the impersonal character of the attacks, by focusing on the targets' symbolic meaning, and by stripping the victims of human attributes. Dehumanization causes the victim to be viewed as subhuman, not as a person with feelings and qualities.

Use of euphemistic language: Language can play an important role in moral disengagement. Sanitizing, euphemistic language can be used to mask aggressive or violent behavior. Euphemistic language is often used to present aggression as a tolerable act and to reduce personal responsibility for it. For example, al Qaeda always refers to the 9/11 events as attacks on symbols of American power, wealth, and consumerism, but never as the killing of some 3,000 innocent people. Euphemism is an injurious weapon, enabling people to behave much more cruelly than they could if their violent actions were not given a sanitized label.

Making of advantageous comparisons: Responsibility for harmful conduct can be reduced by comparing the action to more harmful behavior. This practice involves emphasizing the far worse actions attributed to the "enemy" or the "other" (e.g., comparing a terrorist group's symbolic attack on a military post to the mass murder conducted by a strong and well-equipped army).

Distortion of sequence of events: Another common practice is to distort the sequence of the events (i.e., arguing that the terrorist act was only in response to a former action of the enemy, the government, the army, or the other). Al Qaeda's argument after the 9/11 attacks was that its actions were only a retaliation for U.S. aggression in the Middle East and Africa.

Attribution of blame: The aggressors can blame the victims for their fate. Terrorists often portray their victims in the most dehumanized and demonic images to justify their attacks. The victims are blamed and accused of causing the attacks, while the aggressors' actions are presented as retaliatory or defensive.

The analysis of rhetoric on terrorist Web sites shows that all these tactics are used, especially when discussing the use of violence. The most popular theme is the displacement of responsibility. Violence is presented as an inevitability forced upon the weak as their only means for dealing with a strong and oppressive enemy. The blame is thus attributed to others (the U.S. president, the Zionist nation, the corrupt West, the infidels). This tactic is often accompanied by diffusion of responsibility. According to Bandura, Islamic extremists construe their jihad as self-defense against tyrannical, decadent infidels who despoil and seek to enslave the Muslim world.[12] Bin Laden portrays his global terrorism as serving a holy imperative. On his Web sites he argues, "We will continue this course because it is part of our religion and because Allah, praise and glory be to him, ordered us to carry out jihad so that the word of Allah may remain exalted to the heights." Bandura concludes:

> Through the jihad they are carrying out Allah's will as a "religious duty." The prime agency for the holy terror is displaced to Allah. Bin Laden bestializes the American enemy as "lowly people" perpetrating acts that "the most ravenous of animals would not descend to." Terrorism is sanitized as "The winds of faith have come" to eradicate the "debauched" oppressors. His followers see themselves as holy warriors who gain a blessed eternal life through their martyrdom.[13]

Another rhetorical structure related to "legitimizing" the use of violence is the demonizing and de-legitimization of the enemy. The members of the movement or organization are presented as freedom fighters, forced against their will to use violence because a ruthless enemy is crushing the rights and dignity of their people or group. The enemy of the movement or the organization is the real terrorist, many sites insist, and "Our violence is dwarfed in comparison to his aggression" is a routine slogan. Terrorist rhetoric tries to shift the responsibility to the opponent, displaying his brutality, his inhumanity, and his immorality. The violence of the "freedom" and "liberation" movements is dwarfed in comparison with the cruelty of the opponent. Terrorist sites rely heavily on sanitizing language. Through the power of euphemism, even mass killing of innocent victims loses much of its repugnancy. This also serves the tactic of advantageous comparison, as Bandura argues: "Terrorists see their behavior as acts of selfless martyrdom by comparing them with widespread cruelties inflicted on the people with whom they identify. The more flagrant the contrasting inhumanities, the more likely it is that one's own destructive conduct will appear benevolent."[14]

The fifth rhetorical tactic in Bandura's list is for terrorists to emphasize "their own" weakness in contrast to the state, army, or other powerful foe. The organizations attempt to substantiate the claim that terror is the weapon of the weak. As noted earlier, despite the ever-present vocabulary of "the armed struggle" or "resistance," terror sites avoid mentioning or noting how they victimize others. On the other hand, the actions of the authorities against the terror groups are heavily stressed, usually with words such as "massacre," "slaughter," "murder," "genocide," and the like. The organization is constantly being persecuted, its leaders are sub-

ject to assassination attempts, its supporters are massacred, its freedom
of expression is curtailed, and its adherents are arrested. This tactic,
which portrays the organization as small, weak, and hunted down by a
powerful enemy or a strong state, turns the terrorists into the underdog.
This tactic relates also to the distortion of sequence tactic, whereby
terrorists present their actions as a response to prior attacks and violence
by their enemies. Bandura argues, "The merchandising of terrorism is
not accomplished by a few unsavory individuals. It requires a worldwide
network of reputable, high-level members of society, who contribute to
the deathly enterprise by insulating fractionation of the operations and
displacement and diffusion of responsibility."[15] The Internet is an efficient tool for modern terrorists to achieve the needed moral disengagement from, and the displacement and diffusion of responsibility for,
their violent and destructive actions.

A good example of terrorist rhetoric is found on the Chechen rebels'
Web site, Kavkaz-Tsentr. An article posted on it in late 2003 justified
attacks by suicide bombers in Russian cities as being the Chechen people's right to self-defense. It claimed that the actions were attacks on "the
enemy's backyard," not acts of terrorism. The article noted that the
Chechens had endured pain and suffering for twelve years and that "the
time has come to die together." The following is an extract:

> The actions of the martyrs cannot be justified, say assorted
> public figures and heads of state who send telegrams with con-
> dolences to [Russian president Vladimir] Putin. For the sake of
> justice, we should say that not all countries send their condo-
> lences to the murderers. Still, there are a lot of those who mourn
> and condemn. According to their logic, the Chechen nation
> must die magnanimously and in silence, without disturbing the
> respectable appearance of the "civilized world" and without hin-
> dering the Kremlin butchers' killings. The Chechens do not
> have the right to stain with their blood streets of the Russian
> cities which are bases of the aggressor's army. You want to shed
> blood in Chechnya—please, as much as you want. But only
> Chechen blood. But shedding blood of the occupiers is terror-
> ism. Russian tank driver, with intestines of Chechen children on
> its caterpillar track, and the pilot of a low-flying warplane shell-
> ing a bus with women and infants, are just unscrupulous about
> the use of force. A Chechen fighter firing at an armored column
> or a Chechen widow blowing herself up together with the pilots

who have murdered her children are terrorists and cannot be justified. . . . The Chechen nation has the right to die but no right to defense.

Finally, some of the terrorist sites are replete with the rhetoric of nonviolence, messages of love of peace, and support for a nonviolent solution. Although these are violent organizations, many of their sites claim that they seek peaceful solutions, diplomatic settlements, or arrangements reached through international pressure. Terrorist rhetoric on the Internet tries to present a mix of images and arguments in which the terrorists appear as victims forced to turn to violence to achieve their just goals in the face of a brutal, merciless enemy devoid of moral restraints.

The misleading character of terrorist Internet propaganda is well illustrated by the Web site of the Japanese Aum Shinrikyo, which pretends to be a New Age organization concerned solely with spreading spiritual well-being. This cult/terrorist group was established in 1987 by Shoko Asahara, with the aim of taking over Japan and then the world:

> Its organizational structure mimics that of a nation-state, with "ministries" and a "pope secretariat." Followers are controlled by a mix of charisma and coercion. On March 20, 1995, Aum members carried six packages onto Tokyo subway trains and punctured the packages with umbrella tips, releasing deadly Sarin gas that killed twelve persons and injured more than 5,000. Japanese police arrested Asahara in May 1995, and he was tried and sentenced. At the time of the Tokyo subway attack, the group claimed to have 9,000 members in Japan and up to 40,000 worldwide. Its current strength is unknown. The cult operates in Japan but previously had a presence in Australia, Russia, Ukraine, Germany, Taiwan, Sri Lanka, the former Yugoslavia, and the United States.[16]

Under the new leadership of Fumihiro Joyu, Aum is now attempting a resurrection. In an effort to change its image, the group has changed its name to Aleph (the first letter in the Hebrew alphabet, thus implying a new start). Aleph's new Web site is quite advanced and sophisticated. It uses a New Age design—soft blue tones, calming water, and the symbol of the peace dove dominate the home page and complement its title, "Liberation of the Soul, the Age of Benevolence." The main part of the front page provides links to general information about Aum: official announcements from its public relations department, a research center focusing on a scientific-spiritual civilization, a library, an exercise routine, Aum-related incidents, and an "Appeal for Charity Contributions." Except for the "Aum-incident" link, at first glance the site appears very unassuming—just a New Age religion believing it has a "far-reaching and profound doctrine."

The Aum-incident link is a press release stating an apology, from Fumihiro Joyu as the group's new representative, for the 1995 Tokyo subway attacks, and an outline of "drastic reform." Joyu says that he is a former board member of the old organization but was not involved in the attacks, and he continues to apologize for the event and assures the public that Aleph is doing its own investigation. He admits that certain former members of the organization, including the leader, were involved, and he says the current organization is committed to reforms, such as changing its name to Aleph, discarding certain parts of its teachings, and making current members sign an oath never to kill or commit mass murder. However, even though Joyu admits that Aum's leader, Shoko Asahara, was at fault, he never goes so far as to reject Asahara. He abhors the acts but not the leader, who "was a kind of genius in meditation." The press release attempts to show everyone that the organization has changed wholeheartedly, but it is clear that it has not. The organization is unwilling to dissociate itself completely from, or even condemn, those involved in the attack, and has allowed Asahara to retain a position of leadership.

The new representative also makes a plea to the public and the authorities not to persecute Aleph for the actions of the old group, though at the same time he feels that the laws targeting Aum Shinrikyo are unconstitutional. The group fears that the authorities will violate its human rights if it is forced to give the authorities a list of its membership. Again, the group's members are trying to make themselves look sympathetic and reformed, and, like many terrorists, they see themselves as persecuted and make appeals to the public to come to their aid. The theme of repentance continues throughout the Web site. According to the "About this Web site" page, the purpose of the page is to make Aleph "understood and accepted by the society" by disclosing information about the group and its reforms. The "Appeal for Charity Contributions" says that in repentance for the subway attack, members of Aleph will also donate money to the victims of 9/11, as well as to victims of the war against terrorism, including Afghan refugees and the poor in Islamic society, in order to prevent the spread of terrorism. To do this, the group asks that other organizations help in its endeavor.

Target Audiences

Whom do the Internet terrorist sites target? Are they appealing to current and potential supporters, to the international community, or to their enemies (namely, the public who is part of the opposing socio-political community in the conflict)? An analysis of site content suggests they are attempting to target all three audiences. Outreach to supporters is evident by the items offered for sale, including printed shirts, badges, flags, and video- and audiocassettes. The slogans and text on these sites, or on portions of the sites, also appeal strongly to the supporter public. Of course, the sites in local languages target these audiences more directly than do the English and other-language versions. These sites include much more detailed information about recent activities of the organizations, and elaborate detail about internal politics and relationships between local groups.

In addition to their supporters, terrorist groups also target the international "bystander" public and Web surfers who are not involved in the conflict. Basic information about the organization and extensive historical background material (with which the supporter public is presumably familiar) is presented for the benefit of this audience. Most terrorist sites also offer versions in several languages in order to increase their international audience. For example, the ETA site offers information in Spanish, German, French, English, and Italian; the MRTA site offers Japanese, Italian, English, and Spanish versions; and the IMU site offers information in Arabic, English, and Russian. Judging from the content of many of the sites, the international media constitute another bystander target audience. Organizations often place press releases on their sites. For example, one of Hezbollah's sites invites journalists to interact with the organization's press office via e-mail.

Approaches to the "enemy" audiences are not as clearly apparent from the content of many sites. However, the desire to reach this audience is evident by the efforts made on some sites to change public opinion in enemy states, weaken public support for the governing regime, stimulate public debate, and demoralize the enemy. The Internet is often used by terrorists to deliver threats and messages to enemy governments and populations as well. In June 2004, for example, al Qaeda posted an online threat to Americans and to Western airlines through a warning to Muslims:

> We are hereby renewing our call and warning to our Muslim brothers against associating [mingling] with the Crusaders: Americans, Westerners, and all the Polytheists in the Arab Peninsula. Muslims must keep away from them, their residences and compounds, and all their means of transportation. . . . We do not wish for any of our Muslim brothers to bring it upon himself, and allow his killing by keeping company with the enemy that must be fought. We have no other lawful choice but to fight and exterminate them. Everything related to those Crusaders: Compounds, bases, means of transportation, especially Western and American airlines—will soon be the target of our future operations with the help and assistance of God, in our course for the Jihad that we shall continue in the upcoming period in particular.[17]

This statement was issued on an Islamic Web site used as al Qaeda's mouthpiece and in several Arabic-language jihad forums. It was part of a general warning advising Muslims to distance themselves from Americans and other non-Muslims in order to avoid the coming attacks. The message was posted by an individual with a history of providing credible information regarding the activities of al Qaeda in Saudi Arabia. The group he represented, al Qaeda in the Arabian Peninsula (or Arabian Island), is the same group that conducted attacks on oil facilities and on the Oasis Residential Complex in Saudi Arabia during 2004.

Very often a terrorist group's communication is intended for multiple targets. A good example of such multitarget messages on the Internet is the al Qaeda videotapes posted on the Net in October 2003 that included the wills of the May 12, 2003, suicide bombers in Riyadh. The video has six parts, some in English and some in Arabic, and is meant to convey different messages to different audiences. The following are excerpts from the will of the bombers' commander, Muhammad bin Shazzaf al-Shahri, also known as Abu Tareq al-Asswad:

> Brothers in Islam, *Jihad* is one of the commandments of Islam
> and a solid pillar of this religion. . . . *Jihad,* which has earned
> the label of "the peak of Islam," is the sign of the glory and
> grace of Islam and of the Muslims, and no Muslim doubts that
> *Jihad* for the sake of Allah is one of the greatest command-
> ments of our religion, a commandment that has preserved the
> existence, the glory, and the honor of the [Muslim] nation. . . .
> The governments and regimes ruling the Muslim countries
> today are nothing more than examples of clear and overt col-
> laboration with the enemies of the religion of Allah, in order to
> remove the religious law of Allah from the Muslims. . . . See the
> Americans and the other polytheists going about the land of
> the two holy places [i.e., Saudi Arabia] as if it were one of their
> states. See their bases everywhere, their fighter planes, their
> tanks, their air defenses, their central command on the land of
> Muhammad, and as if nothing happened, when we ask about
> it, [we are] told: They have come to serve us. . . . To those who
> lose sleep over *Jihad,* and who make efforts to silence our rifles,
> we say: "Our *Jihad* will continue, if Allah wills it, and our finger
> is on the trigger." If Allah wills it, we will not stop fighting
> them ceaselessly.[18]

These words are aimed at Muslims in Arab countries. They try to
raise sympathy, support, and understanding while relying on religious
sources. They also try to broaden the cleavage between certain Arab
regimes and the common people. For example, al-Shahri declares that
"these governments based their regimes and their laws on dissociation
from all the values and principles of religious law." And he accuses the
Saudi rulers of collaborating with Allah's enemies—the Americans.
However, the American public is also a target audience, as the following
statements reveal:

> What we are doing today is a deed against the enemies of Allah,
> the Americans, and the others in the land of the two holy places,
> and it is in compliance with Allah and with the call of his mes-
> senger [Muhammad], who said: "Expel the polytheists from the
> Arabian Peninsula." It is support for our oppressed brothers
> everywhere. Oh Americans, wait for us. We have brought slaugh-
> ter upon you . . . in which the *Jihad* warriors and the *Shahids*
> marched, on the path they have cushioned with body parts, irri-
> gated with blood, and paved with skulls. . . . Wait for us, oh
> Americans, we have brought slaughter upon you.[19]

Similarly, Hazem al-Kashmiri, also known as Abu Umar al-Ta'ifi, addresses fellow Muslims as well as the hated Americans and the Saudi rulers in his will:

> I address my message to [the sons of] the Islamic nation and say to them: I swear by Allah that the Jews and the Christians will not leave the Arabian Peninsula unless by *Jihad,* as the ancients expelled them. Do not denigrate yourselves and do not underestimate your abilities. Grasp your weapon and kill the Jews and the Christians wherever they are to be found. You are the offspring of the companions of the Prophets . . . who broke the noses of the Jews and the Christians, and stepped with their feet on the kings of Persia and Byzantium. . . . I have a message to the American soldiers [in English]: For the American soldiers we say: You have to know that your government had become a big evil, killing innocent people, destroying homes, stealing our money, and holding our sons in jail. We promise that we will not let you live safely, and you will not see from us anything else just bombs, fire, destroying homes, cutting your heads. Our *Mujahideen* is coming to you, very soon, to let you see what you didn't see before.[20]

The Internet can also be used to harm the credibility of enemy media, enemy officials, and the establishment. For example, in May 2000, Chechen rebels claimed that they had shot down a Russian SU-24 jet fighter-bomber. The Russians tried to discredit the story, but the rebels posted on their Web site (www.kavkaz.org) pictures of their fighters holding up parts of the plane's wreckage. As a result, the Russian authorities had to admit that the claim was true.[21]

The Phoenix of the Internet: Al Qaeda's Web Sites

> *We were underestimating the amount of attention [al Qaeda] was paying to the Internet.*
> —Roger Cressey, chief of staff of President Bush's Critical Infrastructure Protection Board[22]

The Attraction of the Internet for al Qaeda

Al Qaeda (Arabic for "The Base") traces its roots to 1980s Afghanistan.[23] Three years following the 1979 Soviet invasion of the country, Osama bin Laden traveled to Afghanistan to join the anti-Soviet resistance. Shortly after, he established his own military camps, and then in 1988 established al Qaeda, at first not as a terrorist organization but as a network of foreign soldiers who had come to Afghanistan, so that the soldiers' relatives could track them. Al Qaeda also channeled money to the Afghan resistance. In 1989, when the Russians withdrew from Afghanistan, bin Laden returned to Saudi Arabia; however, the Saudi government placed him under house arrest and then forced him to move to Sudan. While in Sudan, bin Laden formed alliances with militant groups from Egypt, Pakistan, Algeria, and Tunisia and sent fighters to Chechnya and Tajikistan. In 1996, under U.S. pressure, Sudan forced bin Laden and other members of al Qaeda to leave, and they moved to Afghanistan, where they openly lived until the U.S. attacks on the Taliban in 2001.[24]

Given the transnational makeup and illicit nature of al Qaeda's operations, the Internet has complemented the organization's "fuzzy" structure and served its needs handily. The Net is becoming a major weapon in al Qaeda's bid to win supporters to its cause, keep its decentralized structure, galvanize its members to action, and raise funds. As Middle East expert Paul Eedle argues:

> The Web site is central to al Qaeda's strategy to ensure that its war with the U.S. will continue even if many of its cells across the world are broken up and its current leaders are killed or captured. The site's function is to deepen and broaden worldwide Muslim support, allowing al Qaeda or successor organizations to fish for recruits, money and political backing. The whole thrust of the site, from videos glorifying September 11 to Islamic legal arguments justifying the killing of civilians, and even poetry, is to convince radical Muslims that, for decades, the U.S. has been waging a war to destroy Islam, and that they must fight back.[25]

A widespread network of Web sites is used to feed directions and information from those at the top of al Qaeda to supporters and sympathizers around the world. Lectures, taped announcements, videos of terrorist attacks, guidebooks, and manuals are disseminated through al

Qaeda's Web sites, forums, chat rooms, and online bulletin boards.[26] With Net access spreading swiftly across the Middle East, the audience for the online campaign is steadily growing. According to Eedle, "The Internet is an ideal tool for a network like al-Qaeda. It is not a matter of a few radical-sounding messages posted on the odd bulletin board; it's a very wide array of Internet sites and message boards. . . . Al Qaeda has much wider ambitions than just setting off explosives. It is trying to mobilize the whole Muslim world against the West."[27] Many of the sites associated with al Qaeda gain credibility by demonstrating in various ways their close links with the organization. Certain "fingerprints" in graphics and text clearly indicate whether the sites indeed have ties with al Qaeda.

Evidence of direct links between al Qaeda and some of the Web sites is sometimes subtle, but in many cases there is little doubt that this group is the source of the material. For example, Sulaiman abu Ghaith, an almost-official speaker for al Qaeda, claimed responsibility for the November 2002 attacks in Mombasa on a Web site of al Qaeda supporters in the United Kingdom even before his statement appeared on al Jazeera television. Al Qaeda openly acknowledges the importance of the Internet as a propaganda tool:

> Due to the advances of modern technology, it is easy to spread news, information, articles and other information over the Internet. We strongly urge Muslim Internet professionals to spread and disseminate news and information about the Jihad through e-mail lists, discussion groups, and their own Web sites. If you fail to do this, and our site closes down before you have done this, we may hold you to account before Allah on the Day of Judgment. . . . We expect our Web site to be opened and closed continuously. Therefore, we urgently recommend any Muslims that are interested in our material to copy all the articles from our site and disseminate them through their own Web sites, discussion boards and e-mail lists. This is something that any Muslim can participate in, easily, including sisters. This way, even if our sites are closed down, the material will live on with the Grace of Allah.[28]

The Anti-Defamation League of B'nai Brith report *Jihad Online: Islamic Terrorists and the Internet* concludes, "The online propaganda strategy of al Qaeda, like its approach to online planning and coordination, takes advantage of the anonymity and flexibility of the Internet.

Unlike other Islamist terrorist groups, al Qaeda relies on semi-official sites instead of official sites to spread its message."[29] Al Qaeda's sites are maintained by group members and by supporters who are in direct contact with the members. Many sites are registered or hosted in Europe, Asia, or even the United States. The use of American hosts should not surprise anyone: according to a July 2004 survey, 76 percent of Islamic terrorist Web sites are hosted by U.S. companies.[30] Many of these Web sites are openly anti-American and anti-West. For example, the Azzam Publications site states: "The Muslims know that America only wants to fight Islam and to liquidate everyone who acts according to the Islamic Shariah, because America knows that the biggest danger to it and for the Jews is Islam and its believers." It features more than four dozen celebratory biographies of "Foreign Mujahideen Killed in Jihad"[31] and promotes the book edited by the convicted mastermind of the 1993 World Trade Center attack, Sheikh Omar Abdel Rahman, and another written by bin Laden's mentor, Abdullah Azzam. The al-Maqdese site markets the book called *Strengthening the Legitimacy of the Ruin in America,* which uses Islamic juridical arguments to justify the September 11 attacks.

Al Qaeda's Dynamic Presence on the Net

One weapon against terrorists' use of the Internet is direct assaults on their Web sites; however, all efforts to prevent or minimize al Qaeda's use of the Internet have proved unsuccessful. In the late 1990s, when this project began, al Qaeda had one Web site (www.alneda.com). Today, though the original site was hacked, al Qaeda is present on more than fifty Web sites. If an al Qaeda site is taken offline by a counterterrorism agency, by the Internet service provider hosting it, or by hackers, it will reemerge on the server of another service provider. Alneda.com was registered in Singapore and appeared on Web servers in Malaysia and Texas before it was removed at the request of U.S. officials. Then it changed its name and URL every few days, forced to move from server to server by citizens who complained to the ISPs hosting the sites. Then, in late 2002, al Qaeda lost the Internet domain name: it expired and was acquired by a private citizen. The Alneda site operators tried to reappear by using various server accounts that had no associated domain name. When that failed, they started posting the Alneda site as a "parasite."

Sheikh Yousef al-Ayyeri, who operated this site, exploited a known "bug" in a program called cPanel found on many Web servers. This flaw allowed him to install his site as a "parasite" on an existing and legitimate site. Thus, the Alneda site was posted on the hijacked Web site until someone noticed and got the ISP to remove the illegal site. When it was removed, the process started again. This pattern of Alneda's presence on the Net began at the end of September 2002 and continued until April 2003.

In April 2003 al Qaeda's Web site reemerged, this time named "Faroq," flying the banner of Alneda. Although the new site and other al Qaeda sites moved regularly, various informal means were used to pass on details of the sites' new locations, including via e-mails, chat rooms, and announcements or links on other groups' Web sites. The new Web site, faroq.com, began as an al Qaeda site focusing primarily on fighting the United States in Iraq but then transformed itself into a more general site, including reposting content from the original Alneda site. Another al Qaeda Web site was that of the Center for Islamic Studies and Research. Abu Ghaith posted on this site a three-part article titled "In the Shadow of the Lances." The same Web site published an article by bin Laden deputy Ayman al-Zawahiri. Al-Zawahiri's message was a declaration of war on the United States and the Western world. Here are some of his main arguments (translated from Arabic by MEMRI):

> ### Why We Fight the U.S.
> What happened to America is something natural, an expected event for a country that uses terror, arrogant policy, and suppression against the nations and the peoples, and imposes a single method, thought, and way of life, as if the people of the entire world are clerks in its government offices and employed by its commercial companies and institutions.
>
> ### The Entire Earth Must Be Subjected to Islam
> The [divine] rule is that the entire earth must be subject to the religion of Allah—not to the East, not to the West—to no ideology and to no path except for the path of Allah.
>
> ### The Blow against the U.S. Will Come from Where Least Expected
> America must prepare itself; it must go on maximum alert . . . because, Allah willing, the blow will come from where they least expect it. . . . America, with the collaboration of the Jews, is the

leader of corruption and the breakdown [of values], whether moral, ideological, political, or economic corruption.

Islamic Law Allows Reciprocation against the U.S.

If by religious law it is permitted to punish a Muslim [for the crime he committed]—it is all the more permitted to punish a *Harbi* infidel [i.e., he who belongs to Dar Al-Harb, "the domain of disbelief"] in the same way he treated the Muslim.

We Have the Right to Kill Four Million Americans

We have not reached parity with them. We have the right to kill four million Americans—two million of them children—and to exile twice as many and wound and cripple hundreds of thousands. Furthermore, it is our right to fight them with chemical and biological weapons, so as to afflict them with the fatal maladies that have afflicted the Muslims because of the [Americans'] chemical and biological weapons.[32]

Al Qaeda's Cyberpropaganda

Al Qaeda's propaganda arm responds to every major event, attempting to benefit from disasters or scandals. Even the blackout in the Northeast and Midwest of the United States in the summer of 2003 was referenced in al Qaeda's communications: Al Qaeda's Abu Hafs Brigades posted online their announcement claiming responsibility for "Operation Quick Lightning in the Land of the Tyrant of this Generation," referring to the blackout.[33] This was the third communiqué by this group: in previous postings they accepted responsibility for the downing of an airplane in Kenya and for the bombing of the Jakarta Marriott Hotel on August 5, 2003. The new communiqué stated that the operation "was carried out on the orders of Osama bin Laden to hit the pillars of the U.S. economy" as "a realization of bin Laden's promise to offer the Iraqi people a present."[34] The included text warned:

> Let the criminal Bush and his gang know that the punishment is the result of the action, the soldiers of God cut the power on these cities, they darkened the lives of the Americans as these criminals blackened the lives of the Muslim people in Iraq, Afghanistan and Palestine. The Americans lived a black day they will never forget. They lived a day of terror and fear . . . a state

of chaos and confusion where looting and pillaging rampaged the cities, just like the capital of the caliphate Baghdad, and Afghanistan and Palestine were. Let the American people take a sip from the same glass.[35]

Another online channel used to promote the ideological legitimacy of global jihad is the Web site of al Qaeda's Center for Islamic Studies and Research. This Web site has published the bimonthly virtual magazine *Sawt al-Jihad*, or *The Voice of Jihad.*[36] The magazine focuses on the use of violence as jihad's only way.[37] An "editorial" by Sheikh Naser al-Najdi titled "Belief First: They Are the Heretics, the Blood of Each of Them Is the Blood of a Dog" calls for the killing of every American:

> My fighting brother, kill the heretic; kill whoever his blood is the blood of a dog; kill those that Almighty Allah has ordered you to kill . . . Bush son of Bush . . . a dog son of a dog . . . his blood is that of a dog. . . . Shut your mouth and speak with your other mouth—the mouth of the defender against his attacker. Rhetoric might cause retreat.[38]

Another article is by Abu Abdallah al-Sa'di, titled "Explosion Is Not the Way to Reform." Al-Sa'di justifies using terrorist attacks (or, in his words, "explosions") as a part of the war of jihad:

> This is the element that shook the armies of the Cross, and turned the life of the Jews into hell. . . . Why should we be surprised? Our times require such amazement. If people are too afraid to respond to the call for Jihad what should they do when their scholars are planting in them the seeds of disgrace and irrigate them with humiliation and collapse? They cover it with disguise of "wisdom and tranquility," telling them "explosion is not the way for reform."[39]

In January 2004, the ninth issue of *Sawt al-Jihad* was released online.[40] This issue presents commentary on one of bin Laden's speeches by Louis Attyiat-Allah, an al Qaeda ideologist. It also takes a clear stance supporting jihad in the debate over waging armed jihad within Saudi Arabia. Attyiat-Allah's online article criticizes al Jazeera television for broadcasting only a segment of bin Laden's speech and also describes a possible future attack on the same scale as 9/11:

The truth is that for a long time now, I was raising a simple yet specific and clear question to some people who have connections in al Qaeda, asking them if there is going to be a second, bigger attack. From the answers, some of the next attack's features were gathered, and the following are the most prominent:

- It will be an innovative attack, in the sense that it will be completely unexpected, and impossible for them [the West] to even think about or picture its way of action, for it is unimaginable in the normal way.

- It will be bigger, in the sense that the loss from which America and the Western World will suffer [will be bigger], because it will be very big and immeasurable.

- Due to its greatness, it will change the global power balance.[41]

The same issue includes a special section targeting women and attempting to recruit women for terrorist attacks. An article titled "Um Hamza, an Example for the Woman Holy Warrior" tells the story of a female martyr, the late Um Hamza, as told by her husband: "Um Hamza and Martyrdom: Um Hamza was very happy whenever she heard about a martyrdom operation carried out by a woman, whether it was in Palestine or Chechnya. She used to cry because she wanted a martyrdom operation against the Christians in the Arabian Peninsula."[42] The article also carries a copy of a letter handwritten by Um Hamza shortly before her death.

On August 26, 2004, al Qaeda launched its online women's magazine:

> The publication, called Al-Khansa, is named after an early Islamic poetess who wrote eulogies for Muslims who died while fighting the "infidels"—and claims the former leader of al-Qaeda in Saudi Arabia, Abd-al-Aziz al-Muqrin, was one of its founders. Al-Muqrin was killed by Saudi security forces earlier this year. The web site also gives advice on raising children to carry on the Jihad, how to provide first aid for a family member injured in combat and descriptions of physical training women need to prepare themselves for fighting. The main goal of the magazine seems to be teaching women married to Islamists how to support their husbands in their violent war against the non-Muslim world. One of its first articles reads: "The blood of our husbands and the body parts of our children are our sacrificial offering."[43]

On May 23, 2004, al Qaeda released online issue 17 of *The Voice of Jihad*.[44] This issue was in color and had fifty-four pages discussing various topics, such as the execution of "Madrid-type" attacks in the United States and pending attacks in Saudi Arabia. The issue begins with a recap of world events from a fundamentalist jihad perspective and focuses on the abuse of Iraqi prisoners at Abu Ghraib prison. It presents the video-taped execution (termed "slaughter") of the U.S. citizen Nicholas Berg as "payback" for the abuse of prisoners. The article argues that the video of Berg has ignited an antiwar sentiment among Americans and has exerted a pressure on the U.S. government to end the occupation.

Al Qaeda's Web Sites of Support

The UK-based Muslim al-Muhajiroun organization has a Web site affil-iated with al Qaeda, run by Sheikh Omar Bakri Mohammed.[45] On its Web site, the organization calls itself "the voice, the eyes, and the ears of the Muslim people." On the home page, between a section on Ramadan and an announcement for a conference, is a link to an article titled "Al Aqd Al Amaan: The Covenant of Security." Al-Muhajiroun explains that Muslims in the West live under a covenant of security, which prohibits them from fighting anyone with whom they have a covenant of security. Since other Muslims have no covenant with the *kuffar* (nonbelievers) in the West, they are allowed to attack them, "whether in retaliation for constant bombing and murder taking place all over the Muslim world at the hands of the non-Muslims, or if it [is] an offensive attack in order to release the Muslims from the captivity of the *kuffar*."[46] The site also glo-rifies terrorists by referring to them as "the magnificent contemporary Mujahideen and martyrs." Although the text claims that Muslims could not have been behind the 9/11 attacks, it then praises the hijackers: "For them [non-Muslims], attacks such as the September 11th Hijackings is a viable option in Jihad, even though for the Muslims living in America who are under covenant, it is not allowed to do operations similar to those done by the magnificent 19 on the 9/11."

The bottom half of the site's home page is a menu leading to numer-ous links in both English and Arabic: "Home," "About Us," "Books," "Fatwa," "Leaflets," "Audio-Video," "E-mail," "Activities," "Links," "al-Jihad," "al-Khilafah" (Islamic state), and "al-Tawheed" (the belief that there is no god but Allah). According to the "About Us" section, al-Muhajiroun sees its purpose as to "[call] society to Islam, commanding society" to do the will of Allah, to "revive the Islamic Ummah from the severe decline that it had reached, and to liberate it from the thoughts, systems and laws of kufr (infidels) as well as the domination and influence of the kufr states." It also aims to restore the Islamic state (Khilafah) so that rule by what Allah revealed returns. The entire site follows this self-appointed duty. The books that it sells cover religious matters, argue for an Islamic state, and rail against democracy, secularism, Judaism, Christianity, and non-Muslims in general. Some of the language is quite degrading and hateful to non-Muslims: "The *kuffar* (by nature) have very shallow mentalities"; "Christianity and Judaism are falsified religions, with a promise from Allah of eternal damnation"; "This book . . . gives an Islamic solution to the Cancer known as America." Al-Muhajiroun also sells DVDs, VHS tapes, cassette tapes, and downloadable audio files that advocate jihad and the building of an Islamic state, maintain that Islam and capitalism are incompatible, and provide guidance on religious issues and life.

One of al Qaeda's supporting organizations, S.O.S. (Supporters of Shareeah), has a very modern and sophisticated Web site.[47] This is the site of Abu Hamza al Masri, the imam of the Finsbury Park mosque in London, who was arrested in the United Kingdom in May 2004. He faces eleven terrorism charges, including hostage taking and trying to set up a terrorist training camp in the United States. The United States, Yemen, and Egypt are demanding his extradition. According to Yotam Feldner's study, "From his headquarters in London, Abu Hamza sends funds and volunteers to fundamentalist Muslim terror organizations across the world. While his sons and other supporters were under arrest in Yemen on suspicion of terror activity, Abu Hamza began a campaign to recruit and train British Muslims."[48] According to the *Christian Science Monitor,* the Supporters of Shareeah Web site published an announcement for the "Islamic camp" held in the Finsbury Park mosque during December 24–26, 1998.[49] The ad, illustrated with a picture of a hand grenade, described the camp as offering "military training for brothers, self-development skills, martial arts, map reading, etc." Abu Hamza argued that the camp, which was attended by thirty young men, would "distract them from television and the obscenity of Christmas."[50]

The Web site of the Supporters of Shareeah is very professional, combining advanced computer graphics and "flash" (online multimedia) technology. On the introduction page, the heading "Echoes of Truth" and the image of a lightning bolt accompany the Web site's name in Arabic and English. In accordance with its S.O.S. abbreviation, the intro to the English-language Web site plays a rhythmic song in Arabic while the following words flash across the screen: "Our planet is in danger. Families are breaking apart. AIDS is widespread. Poverty is increasing. Children are being slaughtered. The time has come to save our planet from destruction. The time has come to support Shareeah." The lightning on the intro page and the words, their movement, and the music all combine to create an atmosphere of energy, urgency, anxiety, and doom. As visitors can see once they enter the site, the messages are directed against the West, the United States, and secular rule. On the English-language home page the main features are the image, along the top, of traditionally dressed, armed Muslims and the light blue link to the latest *khutbah* (sermon) from Abu Hamza. Along the side of the Web page is a menu allowing the viewer to choose from the following: "Home," "About S.O.S.," "Our Projects," "Audio-Video," "Books-Articles," "Discussion Board," "Question 'n Answer," "Catalogue," "News," "Contact Us," and "Links."

The text maintains that to support Islamic law one has to support "the various groups of Mujahideen . . . and learning from the lives of those who have become Shaheed in the struggle to establish the Shareeah of Allah." This appears to be a call to support Islamist terrorists and possibly suicide terrorists *(shaheed)*. At the bottom of the page is the link "How can I join the Supporters of Shareeah? Read now!" What follows is not a sign-up form but a rule of conduct, such as being righteous, supporting the establishment of Islamic law and rejecting those who reject it, reading and listening to the books and tapes of S.O.S., and so on. The site provides a flash video file that is "a glimpse of what it is like to be in Iraq." It presents a series of still pictures of dead bodies and the injured in hospitals, many of which are from al Jazeera. The pictures are quite graphic—many beyond anything the American and European news media ever show—and are shocking and disturbing. The video ends with the words "The only solution—Al-Jihad, in the cause of Allah." The site's interactive question-and-answer section includes this exchange:

QUESTION: Even though the Jews and the Christians are *kuffar*, there are some among them that mean well and have good intentions. There have been people that have died like Mother Theresa, Princess Diana and other celebrities that have done a lot of good for people like the sick, poor and so on. Does Allah accept their deeds or not?

ANSWER: Allah, Glorified and Exalted, indeed only accepts the deeds of the righteous. But no doubt there are some righteous people among the *kuffar* in their deeds and the acts of charity that they do. . . . The likeness of those who are *kuffar* in their Lord, their deeds are like ashes, on which the wind blows on harshly. They will not be able to get anything from what they earned.

QUESTION: I would like to make Hijrah but I am afraid that the *kuffar* will come in and rape and torture us. I feel the need to have weapons and help the Mujaahidin. It is possible for a Muslim sister to be up in the mountains with the Mujaahidin?

ANSWER: In both of the above, al-Masri advises that they should go, but women must continue the fight in ways that are decent and Islamically sound.[51]

Numerous Web sites are used by, linked to, or associated with al Qaeda, and despite all attempts to ban or destroy the Internet presence of bin Laden and his supporters, their presence and activities on the Net have only become more conspicuous, more significant, and more sophisticated.

FARC's Web Sites

The sophisticated Web sites of FARC, the Revolutionary Armed Forces of Colombia, are an impressive example of media-savvy Internet use by a terrorist group.[52] In contrast to al Qaeda's shadowy, dynamic, versatile, and often vicious Web sites, the FARC sites are more "transparent," stable, and mainly focused on information and publicity. Thus, we will examine the various content included on FARC Web sites rather than focus on the sites' dynamics. FARC was established in 1964 as the military wing of the Colombian Communist Party. It is organized along military lines, and its dossier includes murder, kidnapping, bombing and mortar attacks, extortion, hijacking, and both guerrilla and conventional military actions against the Colombian authorities. FARC often targeted foreign citizens as hostages for ransom and has well-documented ties to networks of narcotics trafficking, including cultivation, sales, and distribution.

FARC's Web sites appear in six languages: Spanish, English, Italian, Portuguese, Russian, and German. The initial page of the main site in Spanish is very well designed: the graphics are bright and crisp and instantly portray FARC's struggle against the Colombian government, employing a map of Colombia and a colorful picture of two members of FARC, a young man and woman, looking up and far off into the jungle, the man's arm around the shoulder of the woman, and bearing the title "Desde Marquetalia Hasta la Victoria" (From Marquetalia until Victory). Marquetalia is the town in which FARC started its campaign in 1964. The group's name is prominently displayed both as acronym and in full: FARC-EP and Fuerzas Armadas Revolucionarias de Colombia—Ejército del Pueblo. "Ejército del Pueblo" means "Army of the People." Therefore, with its name and hopeful, colorful images, FARC immediately presents itself as a champion of the people, as do most guerrilla and terrorist groups. Beneath the main graphic is a menu containing the choices: "Home" *(Inicio)*, "Woman" *(Mujer)*, "Culture" *(Cultura)*, "Bolivarian Movement" *(Movimiento Bolivariano)*, "This Is Colombia" *(Asi Es Colombia)*, and "University Page" *(Página Universitaria)*. Below that is another menu:

- New Releases *(Novedades)*
  - Communiqués
  - Conjecture
  - Interviews *(Entrevistas)*
  - This Is Colombia
  - Calendar
  - Anniversary of the FARC-EP

- Documents
  - Our History *(Nuestra Historia)*
  - Laws *(Leyes)*
  - Dialogues
  - Plenary Session
  - Other Opinions

- Resistance
  - National Resistance[53]
  - International Resistance[54]

The visitor can choose from various topics and move to other Web pages, but the main menu ("Home," "Woman," "Culture," and so on) remains on top, while links to the other three sections ("New Releases," "Documents," and "Resistance") are added above that as a drop-down menu, allowing the visitor to navigate easily through the Web site from any page. The English-language site (www.farcep.org/pagina_ingles/) is structured differently. There the main images are an outline of North and South America along with the title "Colombia in America," FARC's name in English, and its initials and crest. Along a side menu, the site is divided into the following sections, all accessible as links:

- *Communiqués*

  This link is aimed at the Colombian people and the international community. The text, in the form of press releases, condemns the Colombian government as illegitimate and fascist, communicates to the government or comments on any negotiations (or the lack thereof), denies responsibility for violent acts, or affirms FARC's principles (including peace and democracy).

- *Resistance*

  This page contains articles on FARC's actions and motives. Themes and topics include blaming and condemning the government, promoting human rights, and offering reflections on peace, culture, economic reform, and history.

- *Articles*

  Articles are from various sources condemning the Colombian government as untruthful, fascist, and "terrorist," arguing against the United States and its interventionist policies, and criticizing the state-controlled media and the false perception of FARC as a narcoterrorist group.

- *Our History*

  This link presents FARC as a group persecuted by the government and the United States, highlighting its heroic fight for thirty-six years to bring about democracy and social equality for the people of Colombia.

The history page still reads, "36 years for Peace and National Security." FARC was founded in 1964, so this page has not been updated for several years.

- *Documents*

  The site provides information about "the Colombia reality in general and in particular the reality of FARC" to the nation and the international community in order to justify the group's fight against a "belligerent" government and to show that the group supports human rights. These "protocols" deal with the structure and nature of the organization and how it, as a legitimate army, will behave in accordance with the Geneva Conventions.

- *Plenum*

  Statements consist of a political declaration calling for Colombians' support and for the United States to stop its support of "Plan Colombia," FARC's rejection of the Colombia-U.S. extradition treaty, and its support of the legalization of drug consumption in order to stop drug trafficking.

- *Dialogues*

  Articles on this page discuss the social issues of unemployment; money for housing, production, and jobs; substitution of legal crops for illegal ones; and proposals for peace.

- *Fariana Life*

  Articles about life in the FARC include titles such as "The Hardest Thing Is Leaving the Kids," "Women in the FARC Guerrilla," "Love beneath the Intimacy of the Mosquito Netting," and other human-interest stories.

- *MBNC*

  This page is an appeal from the Bolivarian Movement for the New Colombia (MBNC) to the people to join the movement and FARC in fighting a corrupt regime and to create a new, democratic Colombia that is independent of the United States.

- *Laws*

  One "law" announces that FARC will "collect the TAX FOR PEACE from those persons or corporations whose wealth is greater than $1,000,000.00 US" (obviously justifying extortion), and the other mandates that those who have stolen public goods or money will return the money, pay a fine, and be incarcerated.

Much of the information is the same in the various languages. There are, however, some unique features on the Spanish site. The link to Calendar 2003 contains graphics of a calendar and a poster for the Bolivarian Movement, which includes a picture of Simón Bolívar and a quote from him: "There is no better way to achieve liberty than to fight for it." The plenary session page on the Spanish site has pictures of FARC leaders and "documents and greetings to the central General Staff of the FARC-EP," which contains FARC's political declaration, its law to tax the rich, its proposal to legalize drugs, and its rejections of the extradition treaty. There are also "greetings" aimed at nearly every possible domestic constituency. "This Is Colombia" is another unique section. Using advanced flash graphics, it provides the visitor with information about Colombia and its current state of affairs, along with an interactive flash graphic of the Colombian map and images of people, Simón Bolívar, mountains, a government building, and a FARC rally, and leads to the following links:

- Amerindian Colombia—provides information about precolonial native Colombians, state-sponsored persecution and their resistance to it, and FARC's promise of equality for them in the future
- African Colombians in the National History
- Prerevolution and Wars for Independence—shows insurrectional movements and social mobilization, including Simón Bolívar's fight for independence, as an important part of Colombian contemporary history
- Protest and Social Mobilization in the 19th and 20th Centuries
- Worker and Peasant Struggles (*Luchas Obreras y Campesinas*)
- Bipartisanism and Political Alternative Options—gives a historical overview of the government's totalitarian and undemocratic tactics
- State Terrorism and Armed Insurgency—charges that the government is responsible for the violence in Colombia and defends armed insurgency as a valid struggle against a repressive and violent regime

The sections on women and culture also add an emphasis not stressed in the English-language site, most likely because the main Web site is aimed at local Colombians and possibly other Latin Americans, to whom these issues would be important. The culture section in particular is not about Colombian culture but provides information that serves to inspire supporters, to promote a Colombian community under FARC, and to glorify the life and struggle of the guerrillas. The section headings are "Fariana Life," "Country Songs," "Guerrilla Stories" *(Cuentas Guerrillas)*, "Images," and "Videos." Images include pictures of landscapes, animals, people, and indigenous artifacts and painted representations of freedom and the struggle for freedom, including Picasso's *Guernica*. Videos include images of life in FARC, the FARC guerrilla as the friendly neighbor, and members of FARC being welcomed in villages and helping the villagers.

FARC has other Web sites, too. One of them is *Resistencia Nacional*, the quarterly magazine of the Secretary of the Central Army Staff of FARC.[55] The background of the home page is based on the Colombian flag, but the stripes appear more jagged, possibly symbolic of a country in turmoil or, in FARC's view, ruled by an unjust government. In the upper left corner is the crest seen on the FARC Web site. According to the side menu to the left, the magazine has information on the political-military structure of the organization and contains documents, Fariana music, contacts, a gallery of photos, previous editions of the magazine, and FARC radio. The "Contacts" link opens an e-mail,[56] and the "Radio" link provides a list of frequencies for Radio Resistencia within the various FARC commands around the country. The music section includes links to FARC's hymn as well as songs titled "Involve Yourself in the Story," "Song of Pablo," "Countryman" (as in rural dweller or peasant), "Dreams of Liberty," "What More Can Leave," "Guerrillas," "Recommendations," "The Conflicts of My Mother Country," "Rap of the Ambush," "Chambelona," and "Flattery," which are all available in Realplayer and mp3 formats. Below the songs is a section called "Thus the Guerrilla Songs Are Born," which describes the songs as revolutionary songs that allow FARC members to sing about the injustices that they say still exist today, and that explain their political platform.

FARC also puts out an international edition of the magazine, named *The Resistance*.[57] This Web site, in Spanish, publishes a quarterly with the cover showing an emotionally fraught graphic of a person engulfed in flames, crouching over and lifting up a tiny skeleton, with the caption "We repudiate the imperial aggression!" The site has a link for e-mail and several links framed as a menu:

- Editorial: "New government: Democratic, independent, and sovereign"
- Guest Columnist: "Our motherland is America"
- Political Conjecture: "Gringos to the exchange," "Fascist dictator," "Will the dictator learn?" "Exchange is necessary," "Interview: The clandestine Communist Party speaks out about referendum," and "Antisocial politics"
- Human Rights: "They are political prisoners"
- Economy: "We propose to save the people"
- Women: "The FARC-EP, the house of all"
- World: "Assault on Iraq: History repeats itself"
- Our History: "Chronicle of 39 years of struggle"
- Culture: "Guerrilla poems"
- Other Opinions: "Clear stories" (an editorial against U.S. intervention)

Similar in content to the main FARC site, this magazine is meant to appeal to Spanish-speakers on a variety of issues—from the group's views on the Colombian government and U.S. policy in Colombia and the world to other issues, such as women, human rights, and the economy—that matter to possible supporters. The sections on women and human rights also target foreign audiences, such as human rights activists, in order to gain support. In addition, the poems from the culture section, as well as the information on Fariana life on the main Web site, not only disseminate opinions and information but also make the FARC guerrillas seem more human, allowing people to sympathize more easily with them and their cause.

Hamas and Hezbollah Internet Propaganda

Hamas

This new wave of Internet use by Islamist groups has been a strategy of the Palestinian Hamas since the mid-1990s. Hamas was one of the first terrorist groups to make effective use of the Net, including online publishing of its London-based main publication, *Filastin al-Muslimah*. Hamas ("zeal" in Arabic; also an acronym for Harakat al-Muqawima al-Islamiyya, Islamic Resistance Movement) was established in 1988 by Sheikh Ahmad Yassin as the armed wing of the religious Palestinian Muslim Brotherhood (Ikhwan al-Muslimin) in Gaza, for which Yassin was then serving as a preacher. The movement's August 1988 charter declares that all Palestine is Islamic trust land and calls for the destruction of Israel through militant action. Hamas's political wing produces propaganda, distributes leaflets, raises funds, recruits new members, and controls mosques. Its intelligence wing, which was created for internal policing and control (including the killing of collaborators), later merged with its military wing, the Ezzedeen al Qassam Brigades. The military wing has been responsible for many attacks against Israeli civilians and soldiers, including shootings, numerous suicide bombings, car bombings, and stabbing attacks. In September 1989 Hamas was designated as an illegal terrorist organization by the government of Israel. The U.S. State Department officially designated Hamas as a foreign terrorist organization in 1996.

Hamas uses a network of Web sites targeting many populations. Its official Web site (www.palestine-info.com) is in six languages: Arabic, French, Russian, Malaysian, Farsi, and Urdu. The emblem of Hamas, always present on its Web sites, depicts the al-Aqsa Mosque in Jerusalem, with Palestinian flags and religious slogans arrayed in semicircles on either side. At the pinnacle of the al-Aqsa Mosque on Hamas's Web sites is a map of Palestine according to the vision of Hamas: it encompasses all the territory of Israel as well as the Palestinian Authority–controlled areas of the West Bank and Gaza. Hamas is a part of the Islamic awakening movement, and this awakening calls for the liberation of Palestine. In its charter Hamas declares, "For our struggle against the Jews is extremely wide-ranging and grave, so much so that it will need all the loyal efforts we can wield, to be followed by further steps and reinforced by successive battalions from the multifarious Arab and Islamic world, until the enemies are defeated and Allah's victory prevails."[58]

Hamas acknowledges conducting terrorist attacks. Indeed, in its online communiqués it claims responsibility for suicide bombings and other attacks, while the attacks themselves are listed and described on the official Internet site of the movement, the Palestine Information Center, in both Arabic and English in a document titled "Sijil al-Majid" ("The Record of Glory").[59] Since its first suicide attack, in 1994, Hamas had to bestow legitimacy on suicide bombings, since mainstream Islam forbids suicide. On its Web sites, Hamas often cites the fatwas (Islamic theological rulings) of Sheikh Yusuf al-Qaradawi, who legitimizes suicide bombings based on his own radical interpretation of Islamic rules. Al-Qaradawi's fatwa titled "Hamas Operations Are Jihad and Those Who [Carry It Out and] Are Killed Are Considered Martyrs" is also posted on the Palestinian Information Center site. Following al-Qaradawi, Hamas discourse refers to those who commit suicide bombings not as suicide bombers but as *shuhada,* or "martyrs," and to the suicide bombings as *amaliyat istishadiya,* or "acts of martyrdom." Numerous Web pages carry the pictures, names, and dates of actions of these *shuhada,* including praise for their courage, devotion, and commitment.

One of Hamas's Web sites is designed to target children: the site presents, in comic-book style, stories that encourage children to engage in jihad and become martyrs. An excerpt from one of the stories on this Web site reads: "Our expectations will not be fulfilled until we fight and kill the Jews, especially as we are standing east of the river [of Jordan] with the Jews still standing west of the river of Jordan; and until the rock and the tree says, 'woe Muslim, woe subjects of Allah, here is a Jew [hiding] behind me. Come and kill him!' "[60]

The military wing of Hamas, the Ezzedeen al Qassam Brigades, has its own Web site (www.alqassam.info), used mainly for recruitment and as a virtual monument for the dead *shuhada.* The suicide bombers are promised that on the Day of Judgment they will face no reckoning for their sins, and that on the Day of Resurrection they will be able to take seventy of their relatives to heaven and will have at their disposal seventy-two virgins. They are also told that their families will be provided for. On May 29, 2002, the Web site Islam Online[61] posted an interview with Salah Sh'hadeh, commander of the Ezzedeen al Qassam Brigades, who was later assassinated by Israel. The following are excerpts from the interview:

> QUESTION: How do you choose who will carry out a martyrdom operation?
>
> SH'HADEH: The choice is made according to four criteria: First, devout religious observance. Second, we verify that the young man complies with his parents' wishes and is loved by his family, and that his martyrdom will not [adversely] affect family life— that is, he is not the head of the family and he has siblings, as we will not take an only child. Third, his ability to carry out the task assigned [to] him, and to understand its gravity; and fourth, his martyrdom should encourage others to carry out martyrdom operations and encourage Jihad in the hearts of people. We always prefer unmarried [men]. It is the regional leadership of the military apparatus of the Hamas movement that proposes his candidacy, and then decides whether to accept him.
>
> QUESTION: How do you account for the stream of youths [coming] to join the ranks of perpetrators of martyrdom operations? And does this attest to [mental] health or to escape from the frustration and disappointment among the Palestinians?
>
> SH'HADEH: The stream of youths [who seek to] attain martyrdom shows [mental] health and the awareness of Palestinian society, and is not a mistake or an escape from a situation of despair or frustration. Many people come to Jihad, and they are willing to lay down their souls—which is the most precious thing a man has. There is a vast difference between someone who sacrifices money or an offering and someone who sacrifices his soul for the sake of Allah to bring happiness to the nation, and to remove its torment and distress. Nevertheless, we cannot provide everyone with a martyrdom operation because the targets are limited and the enemy positions we want to reach are highly fortified. If some of the youths do not follow the military apparatus's instructions, and [set out on operations on their own] without being linked officially to this apparatus, this proves that the [entire] nation has become a nation of Jihad on the threshold of liberation, and that it rejects humiliation and submission.
>
> QUESTION: How does the military apparatus choose a target?
>
> SH'HADEH: We have surveillance groups whose role is to monitor Israeli and settler patrols and the movement of the enemy on

the border. We utilize every breach we find in the enemy's security fence. Afterwards we define the target and the nature of the assault on it, whether it is a settlement, a military post, a military vehicle, or anything else. The target is filmed, and then [the video] is shown to a committee appointed by the General Staff of the Military Operations. After the target is approved, the martyrdom operation's perpetrator is trained. . . . Then the operation is ready to go, after a group of experts approves the plan and determines the factors for its success or failure.

QUESTION: What about killing Israeli citizens?

SH'HADEH: We do not target children, the elderly, and places of worship, although these places of worship incite to murdering Muslims. Similarly, we have not targeted schools, because we do not give orders to kill children. The same goes for hospitals, although this is easy for us, and attainable. We act according to the principles of Jihad to which we adhere. Our motto is: "We are not fighting the Jews because they are Jews, but because they occupy our land. We are not fighting them because of their religion but because they have usurped our land. If we kill a child it is not intentional . . ."

QUESTION: What about the organizational structure of the Iz al Din al Qassam Brigades?

SH'HADEH: In general, the brigades are a small army subject to political decisions, like any [other] army in the world. It has all the kinds of divisions and structures that an army has. We are soldiers. The political apparatus does not tell us, "Do such and such" and "Carry out this or that operation"; the political apparatus is sovereign over the military apparatus, and a decision of the political [echelon] takes precedence over the decision of the military [echelon], without intervening in military operations. The success of an operation is not defined by the number of enemy dead, but by the extent to which our Jihad fighters managed to reach the target, and by the operation's execution. Good planning is vital for the operation's success. The number of dead depends on the will of Allah.[62]

Hamas's Web sites, such as the Palestinian Information Center, the London-based Return Center, and the Qassam Brigades site, have always been used to promote the group and not any specific individual. (The Lebanese Hezbollah, under the leadership of Sheikh Hasan Nasrallah, followed a very different philosophy, operating Web sites devoted to the leader personally.) However, Reuvan Paz, who monitors Islamist Web sites, argues that this pattern is changing.[63] Hamas's founder and former leader, Sheikh Yassin, had no special presence in the movement's Web sites (except for an online biographical book about him in the books section). And yet a significant change in this policy occurred with the opening, on April 5, 2003, of a personal Web site of Abd al Aziz al Rantisi (www.rantisi.net), who later became the leader of the Islamic movement after Sheikh Yassin was killed in 2004. The Web site, active even after al Rantisi's own death, was hosted by an American server.[64]

According to Paz, a consistent theme of the Hamas Internet propaganda is its focus on the United States:

> Attacks by Hamas leaders, Yasin, al Rantisi, Mahmoud al-Zahhar, Isma'il Abu Shanab, or Ibrahim Maqadmeh, against the United States have been part of Hamas' messages in recent years, especially since the direct campaign in the United States against foundations linked or controlled by Hamas in the field of fundraising and money-laundering. The American support for the Israeli policy in the Palestinian territories under the present administration, the war in Iraq, and the American occupation there, have naturally brought about more sharpened language. From time to time there were declarations of Hamas leaders, including Sheikh Yasin, which could be interpreted as direct threats to attack American interests. Yet, in interviews with Arab and foreign media, Hamas leaders hurried to deny any intention to operate out of the Palestinian arena and Israel, and focused on the on-going armed struggle against Israeli targets by suicide operations.[65]

In an article posted in March 2003 under the title "Bush Suffers from Religious Mania Not Security One," al Rantisi argued, "We really wish for the emergence of an Islamic resistance on Iraqi soil, that would know how to defeat the United States, through a daily exhausting with the help of all the Muslims . . . so the United States would dig its own grave in Iraq with God's help."[66] On April 6, 2003, al Rantisi published another online article, titled "Why Shouldn't We Attack the United States?," wherein he suggested several ways the Muslims could retaliate and attack the United States. He stated, "The divine equation is to refer our enemies in the same manner they treat us. . . . Therefore there is no wonder if we fight those who fight us and make peace with those who live in peace with us and stop attacking us. . . . What should we do if the enemy attacks us like he did in Iraq, Sudan, or Libya and other Arab and Islamic countries? Obviously we should attack him according to the divine equation. This is the moral and national duty . . . but above all the religious one."[67] On his Web site, al Rantisi claimed that the Islamic people can carry out effective attacks against the United States in several ways, including economic jihad, propaganda campaigns, and tourist boycotts, yet he does also suggest the use of terror against the United States:

> While the Americans caused us to lose our sense of security in Palestine, Afghanistan, Iraq, the Philippines, Chechnya, Kashmir, and elsewhere, by attacking us directly or by supporting our enemies, we should retaliate by terror against the United States. We cannot let who attacked us live safely. The Americans are using in each Islamic country the most modern weapons of mass destruction invented by their satanic mind. They are agitating the governments they control for oppressing and eliminating our Muslim youth. They fight the Muslims economically. . . . They are experts in humiliating the Muslims, even on the TV channels, as occurred in the Nazi Zionist prison of Guantanamo, and as happens nowadays in Iraq. The American propaganda presented every Muslim as a terrorist wanted in each part of the world.
>
> Why wouldn't we run after them as they do with us? Why wouldn't we terrorize them as they do with us? We are capable of doing so. Don't we have the right to turn our bodies into human bombs, as long as we have no weapons of mass destruction, with which they kill our kids? As long as these murderers do not acknowledge that they cannot secure themselves by depriving our safety, we will not be safe.[68]

Hezbollah

Hezbollah, meaning "Party of God," is a Lebanese group of Muslim Shiite militants that has developed into a political party and a major force in Lebanon's society. Hezbollah was formed in 1982 as a response to the Israeli invasion of Lebanon: Shiite Muslims with the assistance of Iranian Revolutionary Guards formed the new organization to combat the Israeli forces. Hezbollah follows the ideological inspiration of the Iranian revolution and Ayatollah Khomeini. Led by Secretary General

Hasan Nasrallah, this organization opposes the West, seeks to create a Muslim fundamentalist state modeled on Iran and to liberate Jerusalem and ultimately eliminate Israel, and has advocated the ultimate establishment of Islamic rule in Lebanon. Though closely allied with Iran, Hezbollah has also been assisted by Syria. The Hezbollah emblem portrays a hand raising a machine gun against a background of the Earth, and the slogan comes from the Koran: "Only Allah's congregation shall be victorious."

Since its establishment Hezbollah's policy has been based on global terrorism directed mainly against Israeli and U.S. targets, blending political and religious motives. This organization relies on an international network of supporters recruited mainly from Shiite Muslim communities worldwide, including the United States, Europe, and South America. This network serves several purposes: gathering information; fundraising; maintaining "latent cells"; and activating "high-quality" attacks in various places in the world, as has already happened twice in Argentina. Hezbollah's activities include many anti-U.S. and anti-Israeli terrorist attacks, some with a heavy toll of victims. These include the suicide bombings of the U.S. embassy and U.S. Marine quarters in Beirut (October 1983) and the bombing of the U.S. embassy in Beirut (September 1984).[69] The group was responsible for the kidnapping and detention of U.S. citizens and other Westerners in Lebanon in the 1980s. Three members of Hezbollah, Imad Mughniyah, Hasan Iz-al-Din, and Ali Atwa, are on the FBI's list of most-wanted terrorists for their part in the 1985 hijacking of TWA flight 847, in which a U.S. Navy diver was murdered. Hezbollah was involved in numerous attacks on Israeli targets as well, from shelling towns in northern Israel to suicide bombings, kidnappings, and other assaults.

A media-savvy organization, Hezbollah operates radio and television station al-Manar and was one of the first terrorist organizations to establish and operate a large network of linked Web sites in several languages, including English and Arabic. Jenine Abboushi Dallal, in her study "Hizballa's Virtual Civil Society," states that the Internet became a useful tool for this organization to form a virtual community and even a virtual civil society.[70] "This has been achieved through increasingly sophisticated and compelling uses of the new media and information technologies,"[71] she argues, pointing to Hezbollah's use of the Net to reach out to

and connect constituencies both in Lebanon and overseas. She emphasizes the interactive nature of this medium, which has allowed development of "transnational media forms that do not conform to nor are in
dialogue with dominant global cultural forms."[72]

The official Web site of Hezbollah is the Central Press Office. This is
an impressively designed, advanced, regularly updated site in English
and Arabic.[73] It presents political declarations, public statements, transcripts of speeches given by Sheikh Nasrallah, photos, songs celebrating
jihad, and a collection of videotapes to be viewed or downloaded.
Another important Web site is that of the Islamic Resistance Support
Association (moqawama.org). It has numerous links—"News," "Views,"
"Martyrs," "Wounded," "Letters," "Statistics," "Gallery," "Cartoons,"
"Military Operations," and more. Other Web sites of Hezbollah are in
Arabic, English, German, and French. The Arabic versions of the sites
differ from those in other languages, both in text and in design. The
Arabic site contains more content, is more aggressive and militant, and,
unlike the other versions, repeatedly refers to Israelis as "Nazis." Accord-
ing to the report *Jihad Online,*

> The "Islamic Resistance Support Association" site complements
> the "Central Press Office" site. Throughout this site, the term
> Israel appears in quotation marks, reflecting the belief of
> Hezbollah that Israel does not, in fact, actually exist. The site
> documents the activities of the group with videos of its rallies
> and military operations, daily reports describing its attacks on
> Israeli targets, and an encyclopedia of its "martyrs"—suicide
> bombers and others killed in the fight against Israel—complete
> with photos of them and information about their families. In
> order to justify its violent activities, Hezbollah posts "legal"
> documents on the site that validate "armed resistance."[74]

Hezbollah also operates the al-Manar Web site.[75] Established in 1991,
al-Manar television operates with an annual budget of approximately
$10 million. On its Web site the station describes itself as "the first Arab
establishment to stage an effective psychological warfare against the
Zionist enemy."[76] The al-Manar Web site offers video broadcasts of the
television station as well as transcripts from the station's English news.
One of the text documents found on the Web site presents the conspiracy theory that 4,000 Jews purposely did not go to work at the World
Trade Center on September 11, 2001, because they knew of the attack

in advance. Hezbollah also uses the al-Nour site, representing the organization's radio station with streaming and downloadable broadcasts of five Arabic daily radio news programs, and the personal Web sites of Sheikh Nasrallah, which present the pictures, lectures, and declarations of Sheikh Nasrallah, including threats directed at the United States and Israel. In 1998, on the fiftieth anniversary of Israel's inception, Sheikh Nasrallah's posted message was on "the bitter and distressing historical catastrophe of the establishment of the state of the grandsons of apes and pigs—the Zionist Jews—on the land of Palestine and Jerusalem." He closed his declaration with these words: "We reaffirm the slogan of the struggle against the Great Satan and call, like last year: 'Death to America.' To the murderers of the prophets, the grandsons of apes and pigs, we say: 'Death to Israel.'"[77]

Hezbollah's English-language Web site is called Moqawama, or "Resistance."[78] This is the English-language site of the Islamic Resistance Support Association. The site does not rely heavily on graphics but has a professional, organized appearance on the home page. The main image is religious and violent in nature, depicting both the al-Aqsa Mosque and armed militants. Sections include the "Israeli Occupation," with subsections titled "Reality," "Background," "Characteristics," "Israeli Aggressions," "Features," and "Views in Zionism." The "Resisting the Occupation" section has subsections titled "Background," "Views," "Military Operations," "Martyrs," "Hostages," and "Wounded." There are additional links to pages such as "Daily Report," "Gallery," "Caricatures," "Readers' Letters," "Contributions," "Articles and Opinions," and "Statistics" (about "operations" per month, from 1999 onward). The site presents views in news-style daily briefs, contributions from "intellectuals and cultured peoples," and articles from respected U.S. news media such as the *Washington Post* and NBC News. The articles describe the aggressions of the enemy Israel, and Hezbollah's rightful resistance to "Zionist occupation"; celebrate suicide bombers as "martyrs" and discuss their families and their "military operations" against Israel; and include topics such as marriage, women's equality in Hezbollah, and a Hezbollah hospital, showing "the softer side of jihad." The site presents itself as a journalistic Web site, and the group as a supporter of Hamas. The articles on women, marriage, and the hospital are meant to have broadbased appeal, including to Westerners who view the site; however, the site's strong support for Hamas and the use of terms such as "martyrs" and "military operations" and the articles about these show that the site is at least closely linked with Hezbollah.

Targeting Children

The Internet is very popular among children and youth. Terrorists know this and are using the Internet increasingly to target children. One of Hamas's Web sites, al-Fateh ("The Conqueror"), is updated every other week and is designed for children, with a cartoon-style design and colorful children's stories. The Web site's title promises "pages discussing Jihad, scientific pages, the best stories, not be found elsewhere, and unequalled tales of heroism." The al-Fateh site has a link to the official Hamas site. Among its attractive graphics, drawings, children's songs, and stories ("The Thrush," "The Troubles of Fahman the Donkey," texts written by children themselves, and so on), the site also posts messages promoting suicide terrorism. Thus, in October 2004, the Web site presented a picture of the decapitated head of young Zaynab Abu Salem, a female suicide bomber. On September 22, 2004, she detonated an explosive belt at a soldiers' hitchhiking stop in Jerusalem, killing two border patrol policemen and wounding seventeen civilians. The text accompanying the horrible picture praises the act, arguing that she is now in paradise, a *"shaheeda"* like her male comrades: "The perpetrator of the suicide bombing attack, Zaynab Abu Salem. Her head was severed from her pure body and her headscarf remained to decorate [her face]. Your place is in heaven in the upper skies, oh, Zaynab, sister [raised to the status of heroic] men."[79]

The same Web site, among its cartoons and children's stories, posted the last will of a Hamas suicide bomber who, on June 1, 2001, carried out a suicide bombing attack at the Dolphinarium, a teen club in Tel Aviv. The attack resulted in the deaths of twenty-one Israeli civilians, most of them teenagers, with eighty-three wounded. In his online will, the suicide bomber writes to "the Engineer, Yahya Ayyash" (a Hamas terrorist who was an expert in constructing bombs and explosive belts until he was killed by the Israelis): "You taught us . . . that the true heroes are those who write the history of their people in blood. . . . I will turn my body into shrapnel and bombs, which will chase the children of

Zion, will blow them up and will burn what is left of them. . . . There is nothing greater than killing oneself on the land of Palestine, for the sake of Allah."[80]

Hezbollah also targets children and adolescents. In 2003, Hezbollah began online promotion of a computer game simulating terrorist attacks on Israeli targets. The computer game, called Special Force, was developed by the Hezbollah Central Internet Bureau, and its development, according to a report in Lebanon's *Daily Star,* took two years.[81] The producers of Special Force point out that the game, which places the player in various Hezbollah operations against Israelis, is based on actual Hezbollah battles with Israeli forces. Special Force can be played in Arabic, English, French, or Farsi and is available on the Web site (www.specialforce.net/english/indexeng.htm). The violent game also features a training mode in which participants can practice their shooting skills on Israeli prime minister Sharon and other Israeli political and military figures. A "high score" earns a special certificate signed by Sheikh Nasrallah and presented in a "cyberceremony." At the end of the game the players are presented with a special display of Hezbollah "martyrs"— fighters killed by Israel. On the game's cover and in the online version is this message to users: "The designers of Special Force are very proud to provide you with this special product, which embodies objectively the defeat of the Israeli enemy and the heroic actions taken by heroes of the Islamic Resistance in Lebanon. Be a partner in the victory. Fight, resist and destroy your enemy in the game of force and victory." Mahmoud Rayya from Hezbollah told the *Daily Star* that the decision to produce the game was made by the group's leaders. "In a way," he added, "Special Force offers a mental and personal training for those who play it, allowing them to feel that they are in the shoes of the resistance fighters."[82]

The IRA Splinter Groups

The Irish Republican Army (IRA) is rooted in Ireland's struggle for independence from the United Kingdom in the early twentieth century and is devoted to the integration of Ireland as a complete and independent nation. In 1969 the IRA split into two groups: the "officials," the majority group, advocating a united socialist Ireland but rejecting terrorist activities, and the "provisionals" (PIRA), the minority group, supporting terrorism as a necessary measure to obtain the desired freedom and uni-fication. Following the split, the provisionals began a terrorist campaign in Northern Ireland, and in 1972 they extended their campaign to Eng-land, where in 1974 they bombed a Birmingham pub, killing nineteen people. The British Parliament reacted with the Prevention of Terrorism Act, outlawing the IRA in Britain. In 1979 the IRA assassinated Louis Mountbatten, a British statesman and the uncle of Prince Philip, Duke of Edinburgh, and attempted to assassinate Prime Minister Margaret Thatcher in Brighton, England.

In 1994 the IRA declared a cease-fire and raised hopes for peace. Sinn Fein, the legal, political arm of the IRA, even began participating in talks with the United Kingdom in 1995. However, a renewed wave of terror-ism and bombings caused a halt in the negotiations. Following the IRA's announcement of a new cease-fire in July 1997, Sinn Fein was allowed to rejoin peace talks that resulted in a peace accord known as the Good Friday Agreement of April 1998. There were various objections to the Irish peace process, and as a result, three splinter groups emerged: the Real IRA, the Continuity IRA, and the Irish National Liberation Army. These groups were formed by hard-liners who challenged the negotia-tions being pursued by the IRA and its political wing, Sinn Fein. By continuing terror activities, these groups hoped to harm Northern Ire-land's problematic peace process.

Both the Real IRA (RIRA) and the Continuity IRA are designated as terrorist groups by the U.S. State Department. The Real IRA, how-ever, is considered by British, American, and Irish authorities as the most dangerous of the three splinter groups.[83] RIRA was established by several IRA "army executives" who resigned to protest the IRA's sup-port of the peace process. The group is relatively small and has suffered heavy losses from the Irish police. RIRA recruited about 30 experi-enced activists from PIRA, and its estimated membership varies from about 70 to 175. RIRA was involved in thirty attacks in Northern Ire-land and six in London, including an unsuccessful attempt to blow up a Thames River bridge, and bombings at BBC Television and MI6 intelligence headquarters. RIRA also claimed responsibility for the deadliest terror strike in Northern Ireland's history: the August 1998 car bombing in the town of Omagh, which killed 29 people and wounded more than 300.

Another splinter group is the Continuity IRA, believed to be responsible for the 1987 bombing in Enniskillen, Northern Ireland, which
killed eleven Protestants. The Continuity IRA has conducted several
bombings and assassinations since 1994, most of them targeting Protestants. Least active of the splinter groups is the Irish National Liberation
Army. This group is also responsible for several attacks on Protestant
targets, including the killing of a loyalist terrorist leader, Billy Wright, in
Northern Ireland's Maze prison in December 1997.

RIRA is using the Internet in rather mysterious ways: an Internet
Web page run by RIRA, which can be accessed only with a password,
details the security operation for Prince William while he attended
St. Andrews University.[84] The site describes where the prince and his
bodyguards would be staying, and the electronic security system being
installed in his quarters. It also describes places where William could be
"overlooked at extremely accurate range" and where a potential attacker
could hide. RAND's Bruce Hoffman said, "Someone has clearly taken
some time and trouble to check this out. On one level it is good news for
the security services, as they now know what the terrorists know. However, it also has to be said that everyone else knows now as well. The Real
IRA enjoys spreading propaganda like any other terrorist group, but the
password element to this suggests that it is more of a communication
between operatives than anything else."[85]

Although the Web site belongs to an organization calling itself the
"Scottish Separatist Group," a political wing of the SNLA (Scottish
National Liberation Army), it is posted in the United States by a
California-based businessman and therefore breaks no UK law. The
SNLA's former leader, Adam Busby, is believed to have formed ties to
RIRA through contacts in the United States. According to Myra Philp
and Dennis Rice, "British security sources said the site was run
by the Real IRA. The Web page, linked to a site called Ireland's Own
Forum, also reveals details of the Queen's movements. Security experts
said it was perfectly feasible that the Scottish group was acting as the
eyes and ears of the Real IRA in preparation for a possible attack on
the Prince."[86]

In October 2001, the FBI closed down an American Web site that
allegedly supported RIRA. The site, called IRAradio.com and run by
New York residents John McDonagh and Travis Towle, broadcast a

weekly radio program called *Radio Free Eireann.* The site was closed by
an order of the FBI under suspicion that it was in support of RIRA.
According to the British *Guardian,* "Travis Towle, the owner, claimed
that the FBI asked his internet service provider to stop giving web space
to the site or face having its assets seized as a backer of terrorism."[87] A
message on the Web site explained the closure: "President Bush recently
signed a new law that lets the FBI, CIA & OHS seize assets without any
notice and/or any real reasonable evidence of any company or person
that helps, supports, or does anything that can be called or labeled terrorism or is found to be connected to terrorism in any way or means
possible."[88]

Like all other groups on the U.S. list of terrorist groups, RIRA is not
allowed to raise funds in the United States, and those who support this
group can be prosecuted and jailed. According to Maura Conway's
report to the Foreign Policy Association, "It is believed that American
supporters send hundreds of thousands of dollars to the RIRA each year
and that these funds are used to purchase explosives and weapons, in the
former Yugoslavia and elsewhere. The designation extends to the group's
fund-raising arm, the 32 County Sovereignty Movement, and a related
group, the Irish Republican Prisoners' Welfare Association."[89] The
IRAradio.com site claimed not to support terrorism, but as Middleton
argued, "A quick look at its source code makes one wonder why it features 'bombs,' 'blowing up british,' 'down with the brits,' 'freedom,' and
'unrepentant fenian bastards' in the meta tags."[90] Jimmy Burns noted on
the Web site of the National Irish Freedom Committee,

> John McDonagh's weekly propaganda show on *Radio Free Eireann*
> and its Web site spread political statements of dissident republi-
> cans and generates financial support "of tens of thousands of dol-
> lars" to a separate prisoner welfare association, called CABHAIR
> (Irish Republican Prisoners Dependants Fund) which shares
> offices with Republican Sinn Féin in Dublin. While officially
> allied to Republican Sinn Féin, the political arm of the Continuity
> IRA, another breakaway terror group, Mr. McDonagh has also
> provided a postal address for "letters of support" to be sent to
> Michael McKevitt, one of the alleged leaders of the Real IRA now
> facing trial in Dublin on terrorist charges.[91]

In turn, McDonagh argued that funds can be sent to Ireland via addresses on the Internet that cannot be identified with any proscribed organization and that lie outside U.S. jurisdiction: "We are averaging 20,000 hits a day on our Web site—that makes it a potential vehicle for fundraising."[92]

Amazon.com, the online bookstore, was also used by RIRA. In 2000, Amazon found that the 32 County Sovereignty Movement—the political wing of RIRA—had posted a link to the Amazon.com Web site on its own site. All the revenues from sales by this site (some 3 to 5 percent of sales prices), were donated to the Irish Republican Prisoners' Welfare Association. Amazon, after discovering this, removed the 32 County Sovereignty Movement from its associates' program and deleted all links with the Web site.[93]

In January 2004, the Irish authorities closed down a RIRA Web site: this site was selling online RIRA T-shirts and other memorabilia items of this group. The site used redesigned logos of Celtic, Coca-Cola, Nike, and UEFA (European football association) to promote RIRA. Despite the use of commercial logos, the items for sale included an AK-47 thong and a "RIRA Belfast Brigade" lunch box. It is worth noting that RIRA used a booby-trap bomb in a lunch box in the terrorist attack that killed David Caldwell in Derry in August 2002. RIRA argued that this Web site should be taken as a joke, but the Alliance Party of Northern Ireland welcomed the site's closure with this statement: "This Web site might have started as a joke, but it is a very sick one. To glorify terrorism in this way is demeaning to the victims of violence. But to offer a RIRA lunch box for sale after having used one to disguise a booby trap bomb that killed a civilian is simply disgusting. You would think after the furor over the Sinn Fein Web site that lessons would have been learned."[94]

The Iraqi Underground on the Web

In late 2003 a new radical Islamic Web site appeared, presenting al-Jama'a al-Salafiya al-Mujahida (The Society/Group of Jihad-Launching Followers of the Way of the [Islamic] Founding Forefathers).[95] The group was then a new Iraqi Sunni resistance organization targeting U.S. troops, according to Jonathan Halevi's report released by the Jerusalem Center for Public Affairs.[96] "Al-Salafiya al-Mujahida is seen to be offering a radical Islamic platform that contains many points in common with al-Qaeda," says Halevi. "It views Americans not just as modern crusaders waging a religious war in the name of Christianity against Islam, but as an infidel people who believe in a new infidel religion—democracy—that is striving to achieve world hegemony."[97] In this context, Halevi's report states that it is important to be aware of this new radical Islamic group: "Al-Jama'a al-Salafiya has positioned itself as a fighting opposition, seeking to block American moves in Iraq designed to establish a pro-Western government, and to bring about the removal of American forces by means of armed struggle."[98] Since the United States is presented as having declared total war on Islam, al-Jama'a al-Salafiya sees the 9/11 attacks not as terrorism but rather as "blessed" actions that brought hope and vitality to the awakening of Islam throughout the world.

The official Web site of al-Jama'a al-Salafiya is devoted to the religious writings and preaching of Saudi religious scholars (e.g., Sulayman bin al-Ulwan, Ali al-Khudayr, Hamud bin Uqla al-Shuaybi, Omar Abd al-Rahman, and Abu Muhammad al-Maqdisi). These edicts approve of suicide attacks, present jihad as the only way to fight the infidels, and support the view of *al-wala* (belief in Islam) and *al-bara* (war on the infidels) as the basic elements of the Islamic religion. The Web site presents links to several Web sites of al Qaeda and the Islamic Taliban from Afghanistan and to Internet forums of radical Islamic groups.

The al-Jama'a al-Salafiya Web site is a typical jihadist site with identified elements of the global jihad Web sites. It resembles the Alneda Web site (the original site of al Qaeda), which serves as a model to many radical Islamic groups, and has the common Islamic declaration: "There is no God but God, and Muhammad is the messenger of God." The site also has several pages, including: "Our Faith," "The Main Page," "Hymns," "News," "Islamic Teachings," "Songs," "Books," and flash images. The most impressive page is a collection of Islamic books: *The First Gate [or Part] of Jihad; The Gate of Faith [Aqidah]; The Gate of Jurisprudence [Fiqh];* and *The Gate of Religious Sects and Schools [Firaq, Madhahib].* The page "Our Belief and Our Tactics" (Aqidatuna wa-Manhajuna) makes statements that reflect the inner division between the Sunni and Shiite communities in Iraq, declaring that the Shiite Muslims are a sect of *kuffar* and *riddah* (apostasy), which is to say that they are worse than nonbelievers and thus are to be persecuted and executed.

In addition to conveying the religious and ideological views of the group, the Web site of al-Jama'a al-Salafiya serves as a practical propaganda channel for winning recruits. It carries numerous announcements claiming the group's responsibility for attacks against U.S. forces in Iraq, showing blurry videos of alleged attacks on U.S. forces. The videos began appearing in late 2003, as the United States escalated attacks and round-ups of suspects to break the resistance. With religious chanting as a soundtrack, one grainy video shows a purported attack on a U.S. Humvee, with a voiceover by a man identified as Adel, who calls suicide bombings "the greatest deed a man can do." Similar videos have been used by al Qaeda and Hezbollah to trumpet the terrorist cause and rally support.

In 2004 a new Web site, www.ansar-sonnah.8m.com, emerged, representing the Ansar al Sunna group—jihadists fighting against the United States in Iraq, and a branch of the Ansar al Islam movement (included on the U.S. State Department list of terrorist organizations). Ansar al Islam grew out of the post-9/11 unification of several militant Islamist groups active in the mountains of northern Iraq, near the Iranian border. On September 20, 2003, in an online message on the Net, Ansar al Sunna officially declared its existence. The new organization united Kurdish Ansar al Islam operatives, foreign al Qaeda terrorists, and newly recruited Iraqi Sunnis. According to Michael Rubin, "Ansar al-Islam adheres to a rigid Salafi ideology. Its founding declaration states that 'jihad in Iraq has become an individual duty of every Muslim after the infidel enemy attacked the land of Islam' and that its members 'derive their jihad program and orders from the instructions of the holy Koran and the Prophet [Muhammad]'s Sunna (tradition).' The goal of Ansar al Sunna is to achieve in Iraq 'the Muslims' hope of an Islamic country where Islam and its people are strong.' "[99]

Ansar al Sunna has carried out numerous attacks since October 2003. In February 2004 it released a propaganda video claiming 285 attacks and 1,155 people killed. In one action, in February 2004, the group conducted two suicide attacks in the northern Iraqi Kurdish city of Arbil, killing at least 105 who had gathered for a major Muslim festival.

In their statement, posted on a Web site, the group said, "Two of our martyr brothers attacked the two dens of Satan in Arbil. . . . Our joy on Eid al-Adha [Feast of the Sacrifice] was boosted by this attack against the agents of Jews and Christians."

The Ansar Web site (www.al-ansar.biz) received worldwide attention in May 2004 when it posted the video of the shocking beheading of American civilian Nick Berg by a group of masked persons headed by Abu Musab al-Zarqawi, the insurgent leader in Iraq whose Tawhid and Jihad group is called by some "al Qaeda 2.0." The video was released on the Ansar al Sunna Web site and within minutes was downloaded by a host of other jihadist Web sites. The gruesome video started with Berg, sitting in a chair and making the following statement: "My name is Nick Berg; my father's name is Michael; my mother's name is Susan. I have a brother and sister, David and Sarah. I live in Philadelphia." Then the video showed masked men standing behind Berg. After reading a statement from al-Zarqawi (or maybe read by him), they pulled Berg from the chair, put a large knife to his neck, and beheaded him in front of the camera, shouting, "Allahu Akbar!" The al-Zarqawi statement read on the video targeted both Americans and Iraqis. Most of the text addressed "the Islamic nation." The following are segments of the statement, translated from Arabic:

> The Islamic nation! Does any excuse for waiting remain? How the free Muslim sleeps, with his eyelids closed. And he sees that Islam is slaughtered and can be seen bleeding its dignity. And the shameful pictures and the news of the evil humiliation of the Islam people men and women in [Abu] Ghareb prison then where the jealousy and where the zeal and where the anger about the Allah's religion and where the jealousy for the Muslims sanctities and where the revenge for the honors of Muslims and Muslims is in the crosses prisons.[100]

Al-Zarqawi has tried to channel the anger of the Iraqis and Muslims following the torture and humiliation of Iraqis in Abu Ghraib prison by U.S. military personnel and contractors. He reminds them of pride, he provokes feelings of humiliation, and he calls them to wake up. He also addresses the U.S. public, aware of the shock waves to follow the grisly execution:

> As for you, the Roman dog Bush, I hope you are displeased and
> we wait for you, with God's help tough days and you and your
> soldiers today who trod Iraq's land will regret it. . . . We demand
> of the American and will take revenge for the blood of our
> brothers in and Iraq and elsewhere. . . . We tell you to know that
> the coffins will arrive to you one coffin after another, as your
> people are slaughtered in this way.[101]

According to Robert Leiken and Steven Brooke, al-Zarqawi is far
from a newcomer to slaughter and was involved in the Madrid bombings, too:

> Al-Zarqawi's lieutenant, a 36-year-old Moroccan named Amer
> el Azizi, planned the Madrid terrorist bombing of trains and is
> the living link between al Qaeda, the al-Zarqawi network, and
> the Moroccan immigrant cell that set the Madrid bombs. Azizi
> also organized and presided over the 2001 meeting in Spain
> where Mohammed Atta and al Qaeda leaders put the finishing
> touches on the September 11 plan. Al-Zarqawi has been associ-
> ated with other groups besides his own group, the Tawhid. Most
> notorious is Ansar al Islam, a largely Kurdish organization oper-
> ating out of Northern Iraq.[102]

Al-Zarqawi uses the Internet extensively. He targets various audiences
via the Net, ranging from U.S. soldiers to Muslims in Iraq and other
Arab countries. In his posted online messages, al-Zarqawi often threatens
U.S.-led forces: On May 2, 2004, for example, al-Zarqawi claimed that
his "heroic Mujahideen have killed more than 200 soldiers from the
coalition of the crusaders. . . . We have torn up their bodies in several
places: at the UN in Baghdad, coalition forces in Kerbala, the Italians in
Nasirijah, American forces on the al-Khalidiya bridge, U.S. intelligence
agents at the Hotel Chahine and the presidential palace in Baghdad,
the CIA at the Hotel Rachid, Polish forces at Hilla. God has privileged
you and humiliated at your hands the mightiest power in history."[103]
Al-Zarqawi's online messages also target various groups in Iraq. In his
online announcements, he ruthlessly criticizes the Iraqi Shiite Muslims,
referring to them as "a Trojan horse used by the enemies of the nation"
to take over Iraq, naming them "idolaters" and "traitors" and calling his
followers to "sharpen your swords and burn the ground under the

invaders' feet. Fight the Americans, fight the rejectionists [Shiites] and the agents and hypocrites."[104]

Al-Zarqawi is also using the Internet to communicate with al Qaeda leadership and operatives. In January 2004, Iraqi Kurds intercepted a message from al-Zarqawi to bin Laden. In this message, one of many, al-Zarqawi offered bin Laden a chance to expand al Qaeda's involvement in Iraq by inciting conflict between Iraq's Shiite and Sunni populations. Al-Zarqawi offered bin Laden a choice: "If you agree with us . . . we will be your readied soldiers, working under your banner, complying with your orders, and indeed swearing fealty to you publicly and in the news media. . . . If things appear otherwise to you, we are brothers, and the disagreement will not spoil [our] friendship."[105] Then, on October 18, 2004, al-Zarqawi posted online a declaration of allegiance to bin Laden. The statement said that al-Zarqawi's Tawhid and Jihad group and al Qaeda had been in communication "eight months ago" and that "viewpoints were exchanged" but that the dialogue was then interrupted. Then "God soon blessed us with resumption in communication, and the dignified brothers in al Qaeda understood the strategy of Tawhid and Jihad." The statement addressed bin Laden as "the sheik" and said that Zarqawi would obey bin Laden's commands: "We will listen to your orders," it said. "If you ask us to join the war, we will do it and we will listen to your instructions. If you stop us from doing something, we will abide by your instructions."[106] The statement also cited a Koranic verse calling for Muslim unity and stated that al-Zarqawi considered bin Laden "the best leader for Islam's armies against all infidels and apostates."

In March 2005 an online forty-three-page magazine named *Zurwat al-Sanam (The Tip of the Camel's Hump)* was posted on a Web site by Abu Maysara al-Iraqi, the person considered the "media coordinator" for al-Zarqawi's group:

> Saved as an attachment, it has appeared on at least two extremist Islamic Web sites that have previously posted al-Qaida statements and claims of responsibility. Mainly a rehash of letters, tracts and texts that have previously appeared on the Internet, the magazine includes a vow of fealty from al-Zarqawi to Osama bin Laden and a pledge to keep fighting. It also includes excerpts from a bin Laden letter commending al-Zarqawi's fighters. The letter appears to be a patchwork of past speeches made by bin Laden. Al-Zarqawi pledged allegiance to bin Laden last year in a

letter posted on the Internet. In an audiotape aired later on the
Al-Jazeera television network, bin Laden endorsed al-Zarqawi as
his deputy in Iraq. The letter from bin Laden appearing in the
magazine refers to al-Zarqawi as the "emir" of al-Qaida in Iraq
and calls on people to "obey him."[107]

In the article "What the Terrorists Have in Mind," published in the
October 27, 2004, *New York Times,* Daniel Benjamin and the present
author wrote, "To get a sense of the jihadist movement's state of mind, we
must listen to its communications and not just the 'chatter' collected by the
intelligence community. Today, the central forum for the terrorists' discourse is not covert phone communications but the Internet, where Islamist
Web sites and chat rooms are filled with evaluations of current events, discussions of strategy, and elaborations of jihadist ideology."[108] Analyzing the
Iraqi insurgents' Web sites, we discovered "a drastic shift in mood in the
last two years. Radicals who were downcast and perplexed in 2002 about
the rapid defeat of the Taliban in Afghanistan now feel exuberant about the
global situation and, above all, the events in Iraq."[109] For example, an article in one of the numerous issues of al Qaeda's *Sawt al-Jihad* argues that
the strategic chaos the United States is now involved in is greater than the
Soviet Union's mess in Afghanistan during the 1980s. In his Web site, al-
Zarqawi states:

> There is no doubt that the American losses are very heavy
> because they are deployed across a wide area and among the
> people and because it is easy to procure weapons, all of which
> makes them easy and mouth-watering targets for the believers.
> But America did not come to leave, and it will not leave no mat-
> ter how numerous its wounds become and how much of its
> blood is spilled. It is looking to the near future, when it hopes to
> disappear into its bases secure and at ease and put the battlefields
> of Iraq into the hands of the foundling government with an
> army and police that will bring the behavior of Saddam and his
> myrmidons back to the people. . . . Praise be to God, we have
> made good strides and completed important stages. As the deci-
> sive moment approaches, we feel that [our] body has begun to
> spread in the security vacuum, gaining locations on the ground
> that will be the nucleus from which to launch and move out in
> a serious way, God willing.[110]

Benjamin and the author found repetitive arguments on the insurgents' Web sites:

> Among the recurrent motifs on the Web are that America has blundered in Iraq the same way the Soviet Union did in the 1980's in Afghanistan, and that it will soon be leaving in defeat. "We believe these infidels have lost their minds," was the analysis on a site called Jamaat ud-Daawa, which is run out of Pakistan. "They do not know what they are doing. They keep on repeating the same mistake." For the radicals, the fighting has become a large part of a broader religious revival and political revolution. Their discussions celebrate America's occupation of Iraq as an opportunity to expose the superpower's "real nature" as an enemy of Islam that seeks to steal the Arab oil patrimony. "If there was no jihad, Paul Bremer would have left with $20 trillion instead of $20 billion," one Web site declared.[111]

More important, the U.S. war and presence in Iraq are considered to be the best propaganda themes for the jihadists and, Benjamin and the author believe, other groups and organizations are responding to their call: for example, the Pakistani Sunni extremist group Lashkar e-Tayba (meaning "Army of the Pure") appears to be shifting its longtime focus on Kashmir toward Iraq and anti-American campaigns. In its Web site, LeT calls for sending holy warriors to Iraq to take revenge for the torture of Iraqis at Abu Ghraib prison as well as for "dishonoring our mothers and sisters" and "the rapes of Iraqi Muslim women." LeT describes "an army of 8,000 fighters from different countries" that will join the insurgency in Iraq.

Assessing the Impact

It is not easy to assess the real impact and effectiveness of terrorist uses of the Internet. For one thing, there is no source of reliable data on the degree of exposure to terrorist Web sites: some sites have "numerators" indicating the number of visitors to the site, but these numbers of hits provided by the operators of terrorist Web sites are not reliable. The operators or their supporters can easily inflate the numbers, and our scan of these numerators revealed questionable numbers of hits (e.g., 3 million hits are claimed by the Zapatista Web site). Moreover, there are no surveys or studies of public exposure to these Web sites. Even the claims of responsibility for acts of terrorism issued via the Internet are hard to verify, permitting multiple claims.

Several indicators, however, are being used in attempts to assess the effectiveness of terrorist Web sites in terms of their communicative impact. In order to examine terrorist Web sites' effectiveness, Maura Conway applied the coding scheme[112] developed by Rachel Gibson and Stephen Ward in their article "A Proposed Methodology for Studying the Function and Effectiveness of Party and Candidate Web Sites."[113] Although Gibson and Ward focus on political party and candidate Web sites, they foresee their schema as having broader applicability to the sites of other political actors, such as "Internet groups, municipal governments, and civic or community-based pro-democracy advocates."[114] Although Gibson and Ward do not specifically refer to terrorist organizations, Conway judged their general schema to be applicable to these sites as well. This coding schema seeks to gather evidence pertaining to basic questions applicable to all political Web sites, including how effectively the sites deliver their contents. The schema facilitates the comparison of sites based on indicators for information and communication flows; these include the presence or absence of contact information, bulletin boards, chat rooms, online stores, donation mechanisms, multimedia, and so on.

To assess the success of the terrorist Web sites, Conway applied a scale based on six basic components: presentation, appearance, accessibility, navigability, freshness, and visibility.[115] Presentation and appearance refer to the "glitz factor." Gibson and Ward broke this component down into two subcategories: flashiness (graphics emphasis) and dynamism (multimedia properties). Using these measures, Conway concludes that the effectiveness of the sites varies widely, with some being quite slick and information-heavy (such as sites by Hamas, Kach, LTTE, and NPA) and others "thin" and outdated (such as sites by Aleph and FARC). However, the overall scores of success are relatively high, at least from the "information provision" perspective: "In terms of information provision, the sites were an unmitigated success. A majority of the sites contained large volumes of information about the groups' history, heroes, founders, mindsets, and motivations that would be difficult for most people to access without the aid of the Internet. If information provision

was clearly the primary function of the sites, then promotion of participation was a close second."[116]

Besides the direct measurement of the sites' effectiveness, there are
several indirect indicators of impact:

Proliferation and expansion: The proliferation of terrorists' presence
on the Net is an indication of their evaluation of the medium's effectiveness. Today all terrorist groups are in one way or another (and
often in more than one way) on the Net. They maintain chat rooms,
forums, and Web sites; they e-mail their messages (including threats,
claims of responsibility for attacks, and announcements) using the
Net; and they use the Net for various purposes from propaganda to
recruitment and fund-raising. Tsafati and the author's exploratory
studies in the late 1990s documented about twelve terrorist Web sites.
Only eight years later, our database grew to over 4,300 Web sites, a
proliferation rate of about 4,500 percent per year.

Testimonies of terrorists: The terrorists themselves often acknowledge
the importance of the computer-mediated campaign. A good example
is the following declaration by Ibrahim Nasser al-Din, a Hezbollah
leader: "By means of the Internet Hezbollah has succeeded in entering the homes of Israelis, creating an important psychological break-
through."[117] Similar declarations about the importance of modern
communication technologies were made by other terrorists, including
bin Laden, Hamas's al Rantisi, Hezbollah's Nasrallah, al-Zarqawi, and
others. Another example comes from al Qaeda's *Sawt al-Jihad* magazine. The February 2004 issue highlights the importance of propaganda, especially through the use of the Internet. And as an illustration of their campaign's success, al Qaeda operatives refer to their
online video, *Badr al-Riyadh.* The SITE Institute, a Washington,
D.C.–based terrorism research group that monitors al Qaeda's Internet communications, stated that issue 11 of *Sawt al-Jihad* reported
"that between three and four hundred thousand people downloaded
the movie from the Internet in less than five days, parts of the video
were broadcast by various TV news channels, and the video was also
copied 'in great numbers' on video cassettes and distributed all over
Saudi Arabia."[118] In May 2005, the Global Islamic Media, al Qaeda's
Internet site, posted an article discussing the use of new media in

jihad and how it has supported al Qaeda's propaganda efforts. The article ends with the note, "There must be financial support for media and let us be the fuel of this battle."[119]

Effect on individuals: Following the terrorist attacks on two packed nightclubs on the Indonesian resort island of Bali on October 12, 2002, the Indonesian police arrested and interrogated Imam Samudra, who was subsequently convicted as the field coordinator of these attacks. According to the BBC report, "Imam Samudra listed 13 reasons for the attack, including revenge for what he called 'the barbarity of the US army of the cross and its allies England, Australia and so on . . . to take revenge for the pain of . . . weak men, women and babies who died without sin when thousands of tones [*sic*] of bombs were dropped in Afghanistan in September 2001 . . . during Ramadan. . . . To carry out a [*sic*] my responsibility to wage a global jihad against Jews and Christians throughout the world." Samudra admitted that he had formed his convictions from reading the works of Islamist writers such as the Egyptian Muslim Brotherhood activist Sayyid Qutb, as well as articles posted on certain radical Internet sites. According to terrorism expert Kumar Ramakrishna, "Samudra's admission that he had been influenced by what he himself had absorbed from the Internet underscores the real danger that Al Qaeda . . . through numerous Internet sites, is becoming an ideology that many young, Southeast Asian Muslims, increasingly conscious of their membership in, and obligations to, the transnational, global Islamic community or *ummah,* are finding emotionally powerful."[120]

Maxime Brunerie, aged twenty-five, who attempted to murder French president Jacques Chirac in a "Jackal"-style assassination attempt in Paris on July 14, 2002—Bastille Day—was similarly influenced by Web sites of right-wing extremist groups. French police found a message from him on an English-language Web site calling on readers to turn on the television on Sunday. The message, signed "Maxime," announced, "Watch the TV This Sunday, I will be the star."

Al Muhajiroun, located in London's Finsbury Park mosque, is an influential jihadist organization well known for its anti-Western ideas and activities and for preaching global jihad and Islamic extremism to young British Muslims, both at Finsbury Park and on its Web site.

Among those who have been exposed to al Muhajiroun's Web site were Richard Reid, the so-called shoe bomber, who was convicted in the United States of trying to carry out a suicide attack on a plane in 2001, and also two Pakistani-born British citizens, Asif Mahmud Hanif, twenty-two, and Omar Khan Sharif, twenty-seven, who, in April 2003, committed a suicide attack in a Tel Aviv bar, killing three and injuring more than fifty. In a videotape released a year later (on the Web sites of Hamas), the two are shown quoting from the Koran and from various statements posted by al Muhajiroun. Omar Bakri Mohammed, the emir (religious leader) of al Muhajiroun, said, "These two brothers have drawn a divine road map, one which is drawn in blood. We pray to God to accept our brother [*sic*] as a martyr. I am very proud of the fact that the Muslims grow closer everyday, that the Muslim land is one land and there is no more nationalism or Arabism."[121]

"Chatter" of followers and sympathizers: Surfing Web sites of supporters and followers of terrorist groups reveals the importance of terrorist Web sites. Supporters' "discussions" often refer to these terrorist Web sites, cite from them, direct to them, praise them, or refer to their contents. As an example, here is an exchange on the Islamic Awakening chat room, from February 27, 2002:

> ABDULLAH: Assalamu Alaikum. Does anyone know where you can find videos of jihad online? There was a site that had videos of the Chechen jihad on RealVideo, but unfortunately I can not seem to find it any longer?
>
> JEZZAKAMULLA KHAIR: Assalamu Alaikum. Thanks for the reply, but the videos at azzam have been down for quite some time, and it doesn't seem like they are coming back. The site I was referring to actually allowed you to download the videos. But am unsure of its location . . .
>
> JEZZAKAMULLA KHAIR: Walikumsallam! There is a site kavkaz.org which allowed to download but its been upgrading now.
>
> ABDULLAH: Assalamu Alaikum. Yes, Kavkaz was an excellent site for vids, but unfortunately, the video section seems to be on indefinite construction, wa Allah A'lam. Omar . . . I tried connecting to

http://connect.to/q8, but it gives me Permission Denied. Is there a password needed for the site?

UMM: Salaam, right-click this link to download and watch it! A chechen mujaahid slits the throat of a Russian soldier!!! [See http:// koti.mbnet.fi/~zeeze/videos/rusthroat.mpg.]

It's much better with the volume up! Had the color version, but can't find it now. Any info would be appreciated. Wa-salaam, Umm.

ABU JIHAAD (UMAR): Assalamu'alaikum, Masha'Allaah, slaughtered alive.

Another example, as found on January 20, 2004, in a forum at www .taliyah.org, home of the revolutionary messianic Shiite Vanguard of the Mahdi, reveals how surfers direct one another to Web sites on weapons, anarchist cookbooks, and so on:

ABDULLAH: Salaam. I wonder what any of u think of the following that I found on the net: http://www.ninja-weapons.com/Books/ Anarchist_Books/ post back soon! Abdullah

GUEST: As-salaamu alaykum. I dont think those books are worth your money nor your time. I'd suggest you check out Paladin Press instead. [URL address included]

NEED-AL HAAQ: Salaam. thanks for the paladin press link. are their books any good? any other good sites? what about http://www .ninja-weapons.com/ in general—good stuff?

GUEST: what can I do about training with certain weapons, I have a grip of felonys. is it illegal to train with these type of weapons. let me know your feed back on a private message if you wish . . .

Media usage of terrorist Web sites: Modern terrorists are communicating their messages to the conventional media via the Internet. Al Qaeda operatives send warnings, claim responsibility for various acts, publicize bin Laden's messages and fatwas, and explain their motives by using e-mails, Web sites, forums, and chat rooms. Journalists are using these announcements, quoting from them, analyzing them, and publishing them. The Internet has thus become a "bridging" channel between modern terrorists and the mass media (and, consequently,

the public). The increasing use of the Internet by reporters and journalists serves the terrorist to create a "two-step flow" of information:
terrorists to journalists via the Internet to the public.[122] Following the
Madrid train bombings in March 2004, journalists were desperately
scanning the Internet for claims of responsibility. This author, for
one, was approached by several journalists and news agencies seeking
any clues to the identity of the perpetrators of the attack. And indeed,
within a day such an announcement, by a group affiliated with al
Qaeda, was e-mailed to an Arab newspaper in London. ETA, the
Basque separatist movement that was initially blamed by Spanish
authorities, was doing the opposite by disavowing any part in this act,
and they, too, used Internet Web sites to launch their denial campaign. Most of the communication between modern terrorists and
the mass media and the public is computer mediated, and the journalists as well as the terrorists are utilizing all forms of this virtual
channel (e-mail, announcements on Web sites, and downloaded video
and audio) to serve their particular needs.

Opinions of experts and researchers: All experts on modern terrorism
agree that the Internet is an effective and important tool of contemporary terrorists. They point to the impact on followers, the evidence
on increased recruitment and incitement, and the Internet's growing
attraction for terrorists. "Just as the fax machine served a critical role
in the dissemination of early pro–bin Laden propaganda in the Saudi
kingdom during the early 1990s, the internet has become a primary
means of communication for al-Qaeda," says Evan Kohlmann, a
senior terrorism analyst at the Investigative Project, a Washington-
based counterterrorism think tank.[123] The RAND Corporation's John
Arquilla, David Ronfeldt, and Michele Zanini claim, "The Internet is
becoming an integral component of such [terrorist] organizations."[124]
Bruce Hoffman sees the Internet as an effective propaganda tool,[125]
while Shyam Tekwani says, "The Web has brought 'propaganda to the
people,' free of the economic barriers and regulatory controls that put
the traditional media off limits."[126] Tekwani, who studied the Liberation Tigers of Tamil Eelam (LTTE), says, "The LTTE was quick to
grab the opportunity to tell its own side of the story with the
emergence of the Internet. The Internet has emerged as the single

most important weapon in the arsenal of Tamil militants and is an important means for the Tamil diasporas to keep abreast of events in the homeland."[127]

The pull of terrorist Web sites: The al Qaeda–linked Web site that first posted the video of Nicholas Berg's beheading was closed down on May 13, 2004, two days after the gruesome execution, by Acme Commerce, the Malaysian company that hosted it—because it could not handle the traffic. Alfred Lim, senior officer of Acme Commerce, said his company was not aware that the site may have been connected to terrorism or to executions: "If it [Acme Commerce] had, the company would likely have shut it down earlier." Lim added, "Acme Commerce disabled the site Thursday morning because it had attracted a sudden surge of massive traffic that is taking up too much bandwidth and causing inconvenience to our other clients."[128] Edited versions from the video that do not show Berg's beheading but were downloaded from the Web site were presented in television news broadcasts and on newspaper front pages all over the world. In May and June 2004 other al Qaeda groups also posted on the Net the videos of the beheadings of Americans Nick Berg and Paul Johnson. It is probably impossible to measure accurately how many people watched the videos using the Internet. But on the Google search engine, "Nick Berg" was the second most popular request in May 2004, following only "American Idol." In June 2004 the most popular request in Google was for "Paul Johnson."

While terrorists are clearly communicating their message on the Internet, almost anyone who has used the Internet understands that its capabilities extend well beyond mere communications, to include financial transactions, marketing and solicitations, and so on. These activities, like so many daily exchanges on the Internet, remain unseen on the surface, until searched for, and only then does the full scope of terrorist activities on the Internet become apparent. The next chapter will highlight some of those instrumental activities.

4

Instrumental Uses of the Internet for Terrorism

Oh Mujahid [holy warrior] brother, in order to join the great training camps you don't have to travel to other lands. Alone, in your home or with a group of your brothers, you too can begin to execute the training program. You can all join the Al Battar Training Camp.
    —*Al Battar* (the online manual of al Qaeda), vol. 1

TERRORISTS EMPLOY THE INTERNET for a variety of instrumental, as well as communicative, purposes. Indeed, it is possible to identify no fewer than seven different, albeit sometimes overlapping, instrumental uses. Some of these parallel the uses to which everyone puts the Internet—information gathering, for instance. Some resemble the uses made of the medium by traditional political organizations—for example, raising funds and coordinating actions. Others, however, are much more unusual and distinctive—for instance, hiding instructions, manuals, and directions in coded messages or encrypted files.

Data Mining

The Internet may be viewed as a vast digital library. The World Wide Web alone offers more than a billion pages of information, much of it free— and much of it of interest to terrorist organizations. For instance, terrorists can learn from the Internet about the schedules and locations of targets such as transportation facilities, nuclear power plants, public buildings, airports and ports, and even counterterrorism measures. Dan Verton, in his book *Black Ice: The Invisible Threat of Cyber-Terrorism,* explains: "Al Qaeda cells now operate with the assistance of large databases containing details of potential targets in the U.S. They use the Internet to collect intelligence on those targets, especially critical economic nodes, and modern software enables them to study structural weaknesses in facilities as well as predict the cascading failure effect of attacking certain systems."[1]

Numerous tools are available to facilitate such data collection, often called "data mining," including search engines, e-mail distribution lists, and chat rooms and discussion groups. Many Web sites provide search tools for mining information from online archives and databases. Word searches of online newspapers and journals can likewise generate useful information for terrorists; some of this information may also be available in the traditional media, but online searching capabilities allow terrorists to capture it anonymously and with very little effort or expense. A personal computer of an al Qaeda operative captured in Afghanistan was found to contain all the structural features of a dam, and it was used to simulate catastrophic damages caused by the dam's failure.[2] According to Secretary of Defense Donald Rumsfeld, speaking on January 15, 2003, an al Qaeda training manual recovered in Afghanistan tells its readers, "Using public sources openly and without resorting to illegal means, it is possible to gather at least 80 percent of all information required about the enemy."[3]

In February 2002 an audit for a major U.S. financial institution by the security-consulting firm Stroz Associates outlined the extent to which the company's Web site exposes it to potential attacks by al Qaeda and other terrorist organizations. Eric Feinberg, managing director of the financial firm, said that "the amount of sensitive data uncovered by Stroz Associates at various corporate Web sites is startling. Many Web sites constitute a gold mine for potential attackers. The audits have found descriptions of physical locations of backup facilities, the number of people working at specific facilities, detailed information about wired and wireless networks, and specifications on ventilation, air conditioning, and elevator systems. Other sites give graphical representations of floor plans, cabling connections and ventilation ductwork."[4] Consequently, the FBI's National Infrastructure Protection Center (NIPC) issued a warning to all companies and government agencies to secure their Web sites and protect the sensitive information on critical infrastructure systems stored on those Web sites.

The Web site operated by the Muslim Hackers Club (a group that, U.S. security agencies believe, aims to develop software tools for launching cyberattacks on Western targets) featured links to U.S. sites that purport to disclose sensitive information such as code names and radio frequencies used by the U.S. Secret Service. The Muslim Hackers Club Web site offers tutorials in creating and spreading viruses and devising hacking stratagems, undertaking network sabotage, and developing codes; it also provides links to other militant Islamic and terrorist Web addresses. Specific targets that al Qaeda–related Web sites have discussed include the Centers for Disease Control and Prevention in Atlanta; FedWire, the money-movement clearing system maintained by the Federal Reserve Board; and facilities controlling the flow of information over the Internet.

Like many other Internet users, terrorists have access not only to maps and diagrams of potential targets but also to imaging data on those same facilities and networks that may reveal counterterrorist activities at a target site. Terrorists can use the Internet to learn about counterterrorism measures or the vulnerabilities of such measures. For example, according to Timothy Thomas, in his article on cyberplanning, "Recent articles reported on attempts to slip contraband items through security checkpoints. One report noted that at Cincinnati's airport, contraband slipped through over 50 percent of the time. A simple Internet search by a terrorist would uncover this shortcoming, and offer the terrorist an embarkation point to consider for his or her next operation. . . . Exposing the targeting techniques of law enforcement agencies allows the terrorist to alter his or her operating procedures."[5]

In April 2004 it was reported in the Israeli press that Hezbollah had managed to penetrate computers of senior Israeli journalists and access sensitive information from them and even listen to phone conversations.[6] The break-in was exposed during the interrogation of Alam Koka, a senior Fatah al-Aqsa Brigades operative from Samaria. Koka was convicted by an Israeli court and sentenced to eighteen years in prison. Koka told his interrogators about his contacts with Hezbollah's computer experts, from whom he learned about penetrating computerized systems. According to Koka, he learned how to use Italian software that enables breaking into computers through their connection to the Internet. Then Koka was given several computer addresses of Israeli journalists, and he broke into the personal computer of one senior Israeli journalist and the computerized mailboxes of other journalists. The information Koka downloaded from the computers and the conversations he taped online were sent to his operator.

Terrorists can find on the Net valuable information on how to acquire radioactive material to make a dirty bomb, the routes used to transport high-level radioactive waste, and how to find an antitank weapon to attack a nuclear shipment. For example, an official Web site of the state of Nevada, www.state.nv.us, contains a special guide with nineteen pages, twenty-seven figures, and seven tables.[7] The information was posted there legitimately, as a report presented to a counterterrorism training symposium in 1996. The report was prepared by a transportation consultant and an instructor at a university criminal justice department as part of Nevada's campaign against using a Nevada site to store high-level nuclear waste. However, the report gives a detailed review of the methods used for shipping high-level nuclear waste, the highways and railways used for transportation, and even the weapons that can be used to attack such shipments. In a terrorist's hands, the report becomes a real threat. According to the Internet Haganah organization, terrorists already have found it: on the Islamist almoltaqa.org site, in the section on how to construct explosives, there is a link to the Nevada site.[8]

Networking the Terrorists

Most terrorist groups in the past have had a hierarchical pyramid structure similar to those of modern corporations or military organizations. They typically had a leader or various councils or ministries of senior officials, midlevel managers, and low-level operatives. However, postmodern terrorists prefer the loose network structure, or "leaderless resistance," since they believe that a hierarchical structure is more vulnerable when facing state intelligence.[9] Bruce Hoffman of RAND describes modern terrorism moving to "flat, segmented networks instead of the pyramidal hierarchies and command-and-control systems (no matter how primitive) that have governed traditional insurgent organizations. The insurgency in Iraq is taking place in an ambiguous and constantly shifting environment, with constellations of cells and individuals gravitating toward one another—to carry out armed attacks, exchange intelligence, trade weapons, and engage in joint training—and then dispersing, sometimes never to operate together again."[10]

In the loose network structure, group members are organized into cells that have little or no contact with other cells or with a central control or headquarters. Leaders do not issue orders to the cells but rather distribute information via the media, Web sites, and e-mails that can be distributed and accessed anonymously. The advantage of this operational structure is that surveillance, penetration, or capture of operatives does not lead the intelligence agency to other cells or to the central control structure. Furthermore, cell members can be dispersed quickly and the organization dismantled when one member is captured, due to the flexible, ad hoc nature of the organization.[11] Terrorism experts John Arquilla, David Ronfeldt, and Michele Zanini point to the emergence of new forms of terrorist organizations attuned to the information age and contend, "Terrorists will continue to move from hierarchical toward information-age network designs. More effort will go into building arrays of transnational internetted groups than into building stand alone groups."[12] Drawing on CIA testimonies, a paper submitted by the National Communications System (NCS) similarly concludes: "Many terrorist groups have undergone a transformation from strictly hierarchical organizations with designated leaders to affiliations of loosely interconnected, semi-independent cells that have no single commanding hierarchy, like Hamas and the bin Laden organization. Through the use of the Internet, loosely interconnected groups without clearly designated leaders are able to maintain contact and communication."[13]

Al Qaeda, for example, is a notably and deliberately decentralized, compartmentalized, flexible, and loosely knit network. According to Paul Smith, "Al Qaeda has traditionally operated with an informal horizontal structure, comprising more than 24 constituent terrorist organizations, combined with a formal vertical structure. Until the U.S. intervention in Afghanistan, al Qaeda acted in a manner somewhat resembling a large charity organization that funded terrorist projects to be conducted by preexisting or affiliate terrorist groups."[14] But after the

U.S. assaults on al Qaeda's strongholds in Afghanistan, the organization changed its format to a rapidly changing multicellular transnational structure spanning the entire globe. One French terrorism expert, who compared al Qaeda to a constantly changing virus, claimed, "If you have good knowledge of the [al Qaeda] network today, it's not operational tomorrow."[15]

According to Zanini and Edwards, "What has been emerging in the business world is now becoming apparent in the organizational structures of the newer and more active terrorist groups, which appear to be adopting decentralized, flexible network structures. The rise of networked arrangements in terrorist organizations is part of a wider move away from formally organized, state-sponsored groups to privately financed, loose networks of individuals and subgroups that may have strategic guidance but that, nonetheless, enjoy tactical independence."[16] Zanini and Edwards classify terrorists' organizational structures into traditional and new-generation groups: Traditional groups date from the late 1960s and early 1970s; the majority were relatively bureaucratic and relied mainly on autonomous cells, but these cells were organized by a hierarchy of command with little horizontal coordination. The new-generation groups (e.g., Hamas, the Palestinian Islamic Jihad, Hezbollah, Algeria's Armed Islamic Group, the Egyptian Islamic Group, and al Qaeda) are loosely organized networks that rely less on hierarchical structure and more on shared horizontal networking. To varying degrees, many modern terrorist groups share the pattern of the loosely knit network: decentralization, segmentation, and delegation of authority. These features of postmodern terrorism make computer-mediated communication an ideal tool of coordination, information exchange, training, and recruitment.

Several reasons explain why modern communication technologies, especially computer-mediated communications, are so useful for modern terrorists in establishing and maintaining networks. Zanini and Edwards suggest several factors: "First, new technologies have greatly reduced transmission time, enabling dispersed organizational actors to communicate and coordinate their tasks. . . . Second, new technologies have significantly reduced the cost of communication, allowing information-intensive organizational designs such as networks to become viable. . . . Third, new technologies have substantially increased the scope and complexity of the information that can be shared, through the integration of computing with communications."[17] Also, the Internet connects not only members of the same terrorist organization but also members of different groups. For instance, dozens of sites exist that express support for terrorism conducted in the name of jihad. These sites and related forums permit terrorists in places such as Chechnya, Palestine, Indonesia, Afghanistan, Turkey, Iraq, Malaysia, the Philippines, and Lebanon to exchange not only ideas and suggestions but also practical information about how to build bombs, establish terror cells, and carry out attacks. "Thus, information-age technologies are highly advantageous for a netwar group whose constituents are geographically dispersed or carry out distinct but complementary activities. In addition, information technology (IT) can be used to plan, coordinate and execute operations. Using the Internet for communication can increase speed of mobilization and allow more dialogue between members, which enhances the organization's flexibility, since tactics can be adjusted more frequently."[18] The Internet-based communications enable terrorists to be connected from almost any country in the world. Some analysts have argued that modern terrorists may have a reduced need for state support thanks to communication technologies that allow them to operate with a greater degree of secrecy and safety.[19]

Recruitment and Mobilization

Without recruitment terrorism cannot survive and develop. Recruitment provides the killers, the suicide bombers, the kidnappers, the executioners, the engineers, the soldiers, and the armies of modern terrorism. As Bruce Hoffman argues: "Al Qaeda's resiliency and longevity are predicated not on the total number of Jihadists that it might have trained in the past but on its continued ability to recruit, to mobilize, and to animate both actual and would-be fighters, supporters, and sympathizers."[20]

Marc Sageman studied the background, recruitment, indoctrination, and other characteristics of more than 150 terrorists from four major subgroups of al Qaeda: the Central Staff of Osama bin Laden, the Core Arabs, the Maghreb Arabs, and the Southeast Asians (primarily from the Philippines, Indonesia, and Malaysia).[21] His book *Understanding Terror*

Networks highlights the role of social networks in the modern recruitment of terrorists. The study documents the role of kinship and social networking as a means of recruiting operatives, providing social and psychological security, and radicalizing and mobilizing supporters. For example, he found that 68 percent of the sample of terrorists had jihadist friends or had joined as groups, while 20 percent had close relatives already in the jihad. Sageman argues that recruitment is a bottom-up, self-selecting process rather than a top-down, "seek out and recruit" process. Thus, his findings emphasize the war for the hearts and minds of these hundreds of thousands of prospective terrorists.

The Internet can be used to recruit and mobilize supporters to play a more active role in terrorist activities or causes. In addition to seeking converts by using the full panoply of Web site technologies (audio, digital video, and so on) to enhance the presentation of their message, terrorist organizations capture information about the users who browse their Web sites. Users who seem most interested in the organization's cause or who seem well suited to carrying out its work are then contacted. Sophisticated methods are used by terrorists to refine or customize recruiting techniques on the Net. According to Zanini and Edwards,

> Using some of the same marketing techniques employed by commercial enterprises, terrorist servers could capture information about the users who browse their web sites, and then later contact those who seem most interested. Recruiters may also use more interactive Internet technology to roam online chat rooms and cyber cafes looking for receptive members of the public, particularly young people. Electronic bulletin boards and user nets can also serve as vehicles for reaching out to potential recruits. Interested computer users around the world can be engaged in long-term "cyber relationships" that could lead to friendship and eventual membership.[22]

The Internet also provides a useful tool to reach the conventional media (television, radio, press). For example, the wave of hostage beheadings in Iraq was followed by the posting on Web sites of gruesome footage of the killings. These postings were then picked up, sometimes within minutes, by television networks and news agencies all over the world. This creates a new type of symbiosis between Internet terrorists and some television networks, allowing publicity-seeking terrorists such as al-Zarqawi to stage cruel executions that will be channeled to world media through Internet Web sites, carrying their manifestos, declarations, and calls for action.

In addition, some would-be recruits use the Internet to advertise themselves to terrorist organizations. In 1995, as reported by Dan Verton in *Black Ice,* Ziyad Khalil enrolled as a computer science major at Columbia College in Missouri. He also became a Muslim activist on the campus, developing links to several radical groups and operating a Web site that supported Hamas. Thanks in large part to his Internet activities, he came to the attention of bin Laden and his lieutenants. Khalil became al Qaeda's procurement officer in the United States, arranging purchases of satellite telephones, computers, and other electronic surveillance technologies and helping bin Laden communicate with his followers and officers. Similarly, in February 2004, Spc. Ryan G. Anderson, a U.S. National Guardsman, was arrested and charged with "aiding the enemy by wrongfully attempting to communicate and give intelligence to the al Qaeda terrorist network." Anderson had converted to Islam five years before his arrest. He was held after allegedly offering military information through an Internet chat room. He thought the people he was contacting were Muslim terrorists, but in fact they were FBI agents running a sting operation. CNN reported that the information the suspect was trying to sell concerned protective equipment for armored vehicles deployed in Iraq. An investigation of Usenet discussion forums by *National Review Online* reporter Michelle Malkin yielded some interesting clues about Anderson:

> Using the e-mail address wensler@wsunix.wsu.edu, Anderson posted prolifically to a strange and volatile variety of Internet newsgroups, including forums for gun enthusiasts, skinheads, cinema, games, Islam, and Arabic culture. He offered opinions on everything from the movie *Starship Troopers* to sniping weapons and presidential politics. Putting aside the chronic misspellings, the 154 messages are an instructive glimpse into the mind of an immature American youth with a potentially dangerous longing to belong. . . . On September 26, 1997, Anderson—now with a new, adopted Muslim name, Amir, posted to soc.culture.arabic: "Salaam Alaaykum all, I am a Muslim convert studying at Washington State University for an Asian History Major, my focus is on Arabic nations. . . ." In October

1997, apparently reacting to news of the release of a Hamas
spiritual leader by Israel in a three-way prisoner swap brokered
by Jordan's King Hussein, Anderson offered a conspiracy theory
posted to soc.culture.somalia, soc.culture.palestine, alt.religion.
islam and alt.culture.somalia: "Is it possible Mossad replaced the
Sheik entirely? With the amount of knowledge they have on
people, I wouldn't put it entirely beyond them to be able to sub-
stitute an imposter."[23]

In September 2004 Anderson was found guilty on all five counts of
trying to help the al Qaeda terrorist network. In many other cases, however, terrorist organizations go looking for recruits rather than waiting
for them to present themselves. The SITE Institute, a terrorism research
group that monitors al Qaeda's Internet communications, has provided
chilling details of a high-tech recruitment drive launched in 2003 to
recruit fighters to travel to Iraq and attack U.S. and coalition forces
there: "potential fighters are bombarded with religious decrees and anti-
U.S. propaganda as well as training manuals on how to be a terrorist.
Willing recruits are also being given specific instructions on how to go
to Iraq through a maze of secret chat rooms."[24] Rita Katz, the SITE
Institute's director and author of the book *Terrorist Hunter,* says, "Al
Qaeda's use of the Internet is amazing. We know from past cases—from
captured al Qaeda fighters who say they joined up through the Internet—that this is one of the principal ways they recruit fighters and suicide bombers."[25]

On June 6, 2003, a message appeared on the Arabic message board
"himmame," hosted by Lycos in the United Kingdom. The message,
posted by Abu Thur, a computer programmer in Malaysia, read:

Dear Brothers,
I have already succeeded with the grace of Allah and his help, to
go to Kurdistan for Jihad through one of the brothers in this
forum. Praise be to Allah, I have fought there, by the grace of
God and his bounty. But Martyrdom was not granted to me,
and therefore I ask Allah to give me more lifetime and to make
my deeds good. I ask anyone who has the capacity to organize
for me to go to another Jihad front to correspond with me.[26]

A similar message was posted on the "Jihad Echo" message board by
Asad Allah, an Egyptian based in Malaysia: "I told myself that if I am

already here (in Malaysia), I might as well fulfill my Jihad, far away from the Egyptian authorities. . . . I failed to contact or get to know someone who might help me with fulfilling Jihad here. Should I go back [to Egypt]?"[27]

An illustrative exchange in a secret al Qaeda chat room took place in early September 2003 and was reported in the *New York Post:*

> An unknown Islamic fanatic, with the user name "Redemption Is Close," writes: "Brothers, how do I go to Iraq for Jihad? Are there any army camps and is there someone who commands there?" Four days later he gets a reply from a mystery man with the user name "Merciless Terrorist." "Dear Brother, the road is wide open for you - there are many groups, go look for someone you trust, join him, he will be the protector of the Iraqi regions and with the help of Allah you will become one of the Mujahidin." "Redemption Is Close" then presses for more specific information on how he can become a jihad fighter in Iraq. "Merciless Terrorist" sends him a propaganda video and instructs him to download software called Pal Talk, which enables users to communicate with each other by voice on the Internet. That will lead him to an impossible-to-monitor "talking chat room," where he can get details on how to sign up for jihad in Iraq.[28]

Many terrorist Web sites stop short of enlisting recruits for violent action but do encourage supporters to show their commitment to the cause in other tangible ways. "How Can I Help the Struggle: A Few Suggestions," ran a heading on the Kahane Lives Web site; "Action Alert: What You Can Do" is a feature on the Shining Path's Web site. The power of the Internet to mobilize activists is illustrated by the response to the arrest of Abdullah Ocalan, leader of the Kurdish terrorist group PKK. When Turkish forces arrested Ocalan, tens of thousands of Kurds around the world responded with demonstrations within a matter of hours—thanks to sympathetic Web sites urging supporters to protest.

In the summer of 2002, Israeli police arrested three Jerusalem Arabs linked to Hamas who allegedly planned to carry out a mass poisoning of clients in a Jerusalem café. One of the three, Othman Kiania, was employed as a chef at the restaurant and planned to mix poison in the drinks. His partners were Sufian Abdo and Mussa Nasser, who ran a Hamas Internet forum. According to the *Jerusalem Post,* "Abdo had

contacted various members of Hamas via e-mail early this year, expressing his willingness to take part in terrorist activities. For the next eight
months, he and Nasser kept in contact with Hamas officials, providing
them with the name of an Egyptian engineer who could help them
develop Kassem rockets and raise funds for Hamas. In July, Abdo told
them he wanted to carry out a suicide bombing to avenge the death of
Salah Sh'hadeh [a well-known Hamas leader]. They suggested he carry
out a mass poisoning at a large Jerusalem cafe, and he agreed."[29] They
were tracked down and arrested by Israeli security agents just a day before
executing the plan.

The use of the Internet by radical Muslim terrorists was formally
approved by Sheikh Abdul Aziz al-Alshaikh, the grand mufti of Saudi
Arabia and the highest official cleric in the country. In December 2002
the Saudi Information Agency obtained a fatwa issued by the grand mufti
approving cyberterrorism. This special fatwa appeared in the religious
magazine *Al-Dawa,* published in Riyadh in question-and-answer form:

> QUESTION: If there were websites on the Internet that are hostile
> to Islam, and broadcasting immoral materials, is it permissible
> for me to send it viruses to disable and destroy these websites?
> Abdul Aziz Saleh Al-Morashid—Erqa.
>
> ANSWER: If these websites are hostile to Islam and you could
> encounter its evilness with goodness; And to respond to it, refute
> its falsehood, and show its void content; that would be the best
> option. But if you are unable to respond to it, and you wanted
> to destroy it and you have the ability to do so, it's ok to destroy
> it because it is an evil website.[30]

Following the publication of this fatwa, Saudi hackers started to attack
FBI and Pentagon Web sites. In an interview with one of these hackers,
published in the *Al-Riyadh* newspaper on September 5, 2001, he reported
attacking more than one thousand Web sites in the United States, including many official government Web sites.

In an article titled "The Globalization of Islamic Suicide" published
in the Saudi paper *Al-Yawm* on May 12, 2005, the journalist Sawsan al-
Sha'er describes how extremist jihadist and Islamist groups are using
advanced communication technologies to recruit suicide bombers:

Today, the centers for recruiting [suicide bombers] are no more than websites or satellite television channels, to which the youth connect from internet cafés, scattered throughout our Arab world, that have boosted the still-active traditional recruitment centers concealed in the mosques in far-flung villages. . . . I myself have visited many Jihad websites, and I have seen the extent of the degradation of the minds and lives of the youth, and I see how adults are profiteering from them. Things became worse when the websites began disseminating emails with murderous pictures and ideas that turn a man into a ticking bomb— as if these websites are stores selling weapons without [restriction] by laws or regulations.[31]

Instructions and Online Manuals

"My dear brothers in Jihad," a surfer who identified himself as Abu Jendal wrote on the Internet site of the Ezzedeen al Qassam Brigades (the Hamas militant wing), "I have a kilo of acetone peroxide. I want to know how to make a bomb from it in order to blow up an army jeep; I await your quick response."[32] The answer appeared on the same Web site an hour later: "My dear brother Abu Jendal, I understand that you have 1,000 grams of *Om El Abad*. Well done! There are several ways to change it into a bomb . . ." (*Om El Abad*, "the mother of Abad," is the Hamas nickname for the improvised explosive TATP—triacetone triperoxide). The respondent, using the name Abu Hadafa, explained in detail how to use the homemade explosive as a roadside bomb and added a file that shows how to prepare detonators for the bomb.

Terrorists may use the Internet to provide information to fellow terrorists, including maps, photographs, directions, codes, and instructions on using explosives. The World Wide Web is home to dozens of sites that provide information on how to build chemical and explosive weapons. Many of these sites post *The Terrorist's Handbook* and *The Anarchist's Cookbook,* two well-known manuals that offer detailed instructions on how to construct a wide range of bombs. Another manual, *The Mujahadeen Poisons Handbook,* written by Abdel-Aziz in 1996 and published on the official Hamas Web site, details in twenty-three pages how to prepare various homemade poisons, poisonous gases, and other deadly materials for use in terrorist attacks. The manual includes the following example of instructions on using cyanide. Some of the details are purposely incomplete, so that the recipe cannot actually be used.

> Cyanides
>
> Name: Potassium Cyanide Chemical
>
> Appearance: Deliquescent crystalline salt
>
> Lethal Dose: ********
>
> Time to Death: 3-4 minutes
>
> Preparations: 1. Add ** gm of *****—found in printing shops to 3 gm of ******** or 3 gm of *****, and grind them both together in a beaker. 2. Heat: until it turns black 3. Put about ** ml of ***** into the beaker and mix. Allow the mixture to cool. 4. Filter. The KCN is dissolved in the water. 5. To obtain the powder form, evaporate the water. Precautions: Even though neither ***** nor ***** is poisonous, you MUST wear gloves and a gas mask during preparation and handling of cyanides. Do not touch it even with a gloved hand. Inhalation of its odor will lead to headaches, dizziness, fever and stomach pain. If by mistake it touches the mouth, give huge amounts of water and induce vomiting. Keep away from acid.
>
> Notes: It is notorious as an intensely powerful poison. By mouth, by injection or by skin. This is the most powerful chemical poison. If using skin penetration, you must dissolve in olive oil as it will penetrate the skin and hide the smell to some extent. It can also be use in most face creams—especially *****—for easy skin penetration.

This kind of information is sought out not just by sophisticated terrorist organizations but also by disaffected individuals prepared to use terrorist tactics to advance their idiosyncratic agendas. In 1999, for instance, a young man named David Copeland planted nail bombs in three different areas of London: multiracial Brixton, the largely Bangladeshi community of Brick Lane, and the gay quarter in Soho. Over the course of three weeks, he killed three people and injured 139. At his trial, he revealed that he had learned his deadly techniques from the Internet, downloading *The Terrorist's Handbook* and *How to Make Bombs: Book Two.* Both titles are still easily accessible. In 2000, the British *Guardian* ran a search for the keywords "terrorist" and "handbook" on the Google search engine and found nearly 4,000 matches that included references to guidebooks, manuals, and instruction books.[33] When we repeated the search in May 2005, 7,900 such sites were found.

In Finland in 2002, a brilliant chemistry student who called himself "RC" discussed bomb-making techniques with other enthusiasts on a Finnish Internet Web site devoted to bombs and explosives. Sometimes he posted queries on topics such as manufacturing nerve gas at home. Often he traded information with the site's moderator, whose messages carried a picture of his own face superimposed on Osama bin Laden's body, complete with turban and beard. Then RC set off a bomb that killed seven people, including himself, in a crowded shopping mall. The Web site frequented by RC, known as the Home Chemistry Forum, was shut down by its sponsor, a computer magazine. But a backup copy was immediately posted again on a read-only basis.

The report "How to Bomb Thy Neighbor: Hamas Offers Online 'Academy'" describes an Internet course, launched by Hamas, on the production and assembly of explosives:

> Hamas, which claims responsibility for the lion's share of Palestinian suicide bombing attacks, has established an Internet site that offers Muslims instructions in the production of bombs, rockets and light aircraft. . . . The site, called "Military Academy," offers 14 lessons in bomb-making as part of what the Islamic group said is a campaign to expand the pool of bombmakers. The courses include lessons on the production of a belt filled with explosives that can be worn by a suicide bomber. Other courses demonstrated how to manufacture RDX plastic explosives, material that is said to be difficult to detect. The Hamas online course also provides instructions on preparing regular bombs as well as methods to identify targets. . . . The Hamas site is interactive and those taking the course can correspond with the movement's bomb instructors. But the military wing warned that those who miss one lesson will not be allowed to continue the course.[34]

In 2004 al Qaeda started publishing online its virtual training manual *Al Battar;* however, in 2002 a full-volume computerized manual had already been found by the Manchester (UK) Metropolitan Police during a search of an al Qaeda member's home. The manual was translated into English and published online by the United States Department of Justice.[35] The public version is wisely selective since, as declared there, "it is only providing the following selected text from the manual because it does not want to aid in educating terrorists or encourage further acts of terrorism." Lesson twelve in the manual is titled "Information Gathering Methods" and includes the following suggestions:

> Information needed to be gathered through covert means is of only two types:
>
> First: Information about government personnel, officers, important personalities, and all matters related to those (residence, work place, times of leaving and returning, wives and children, places visited).
>
> Second: Information about strategic buildings, important establishments, and military bases. Examples are important ministries such as those of Defense and Internal Security, airports, seaports, land border points, embassies, and radio and TV stations.
>
> During the process of gathering information, whether about governing personalities or establishments, the person doing the gathering must take the following security measures. . .[36]

Another "lesson" describes recruitment methods and even details "Types of Agents Preferred by the American Intelligence Agency (CIA)," distinguishing between (a) "Foreign officials who are disenchanted with their country's policies and are looking towards the U.S. for guidance and direction," (b) "The ideologist who is in his county but against his government and is considered a valuable catch and a good candidate for the CIA," and (c) "Officials who have a lavish lifestyle and cannot keep up using their regular wages, or those who have weaknesses for women, other men, or alcoholic beverages." Lesson four describes "Weapons: Measures related to buying and transporting them." In another part detailing safety measures, the "married brothers" are warned that they "should observe the following: (a) Not talking with their wives about Jihad work, and (b) The members with security risks should not travel with their wives. A wife with an Islamic appearance (veil) attracts attention." Other "lessons" relate to hiding places, using false documents, communication among "brothers," traveling (including instructions on what to do "when your travel to Pakistan is discovered"), meetings, "in case of being captured," and more.

In December 2004, a militant Islamic chat room posted a twenty-six-minute video clip with instructions on how to assemble a suicide bomb vest, along with a taped demonstration of its use on a model of a bus filled with passengers.[37] According to a SITE Institute report,

> The highly detailed video, of high quality and polished presentation, proceeds in several sections: required materials (explosives, shrapnel, triggers, vest); assembly instructions; instructions for mounting the belt on the body of the would-be suicide bomber; and testing of the belt's destructive impact. . . . Finally, in what is perhaps the video's most chilling sequence, a testing ground for the explosive belt is used, complete with mock victims arranged in a pattern mimicking a crowded bus, and (separately) with victims arrayed at varying removes from the explosion in order to gauge the lethality of the explosive impact at different distances.[38]

According to NBC terror analyst Evan Kohlmann, the video would be extremely valuable to terrorists and especially to those who attack U.S. troops in Iraq: "The video was accompanied by a note that explained it was there for the purposes of aiding the brothers, the fighting brothers, in cities in central Iraq."[39]

In April 2005 a jihadist Web site posted instructions on the use of the Stinger missile, providing the Stinger's detailed specifications, such as length, diameter, weight, speed, and height and distance reached. The posting included illustrations of the missile and the proper placement of the launcher to target an airplane. The text even congratulated those who successfully downed U.S. helicopters: "I would like to congratulate the brothers who shot down two helicopters in Iraq and Chechnya. The shooting down of helicopters by the mujahideen happens regularly, with the Grace of Allah."[40]

The Internet can also serve as a virtual training camp. The American attacks on al Qaeda terrorist training camps in Afghanistan forced the terrorists to move some of their operations to the Internet. As a result, al Qaeda uses the Internet not just to coordinate operations and launch attacks, but also to train, indoctrinate, and recruit, turning the Internet into what experts call an "online terrorism university." "It is not necessary . . . for you to join in a military training camp, or travel to another country. . . . you can learn alone, or with other brothers, in [our arms] preparation program," claimed al Qaeda leader Abu Hadschir al Muqrin, cited in *Der Spiegel Online*.[41]

In 2004 al Qaeda launched its online *Al Battar Training Camp. Al Battar* takes its name from the "Sword of the Prophets," currently housed in the Topkapi Museum in Istanbul. The online *Al Battar* appears bimonthly, and each issue is devoted to practical instructions in specific terrorist practices, including assassinations, intelligence gathering, kidnapping, bombs and explosives, guns and ammunition, fighting in cities, use of poisons, and so on. The purpose of *Al Battar* is stated in the introduction to its first issue:

> Preparing [for jihad] is a personal commandment that applies to every Muslim. . . . Because many of Islam's young people do not yet know how to bear arms, not to mention use them, and because the agents of the Cross are hobbling the Muslims and preventing them from planning [jihad] for the sake of Allah— your brothers the Mujahideen in the Arabian peninsula have decided to publish this booklet to serve the Mujahid brother in his place of isolation, and he will do the exercises and act according to the military knowledge included within it. . . . The basic idea is to spread military culture among the youth with the aim of filling the vacuum that the enemies of the religion have been seeking to expand for a long time. Allah willing, the magazine will be simple and easy, and in it, my Muslim brother, you will find basic lessons in the framework of a military training program, beginning with programs for sports training, through types of light weapons and guerilla group actions in the cities and mountains, and [including] important points in security and intelligence, so that you will be able . . . to fulfill the religious obligation that Allah has set upon you.[42]

The first issue also features a detailed article on the Kalashnikov rifle and an article by Sheikh al-'Ayyiri himself on the importance of physical training of the mujahedeen. Another article in this issue reminds the mujahid brother that he does not have to travel to foreign countries to "join the great training camps" but can begin the training program right at home, either alone or with a group of brothers.

The sixth issue of *Al Battar*, published online in April 2004, focused on such practical issues as cell organization, armaments training, and even wilderness survival training. But this specific issue referred also to the Madrid bombings of March 2004. An analysis of the editorial in this issue reveals:

> The issue starts with an editorial praising the militants who carried out the attacks in Madrid on March 11. The article places the blame for the attacks on the Spanish decision to join with the coalition in Iraq. It contains various historical references to the days when Spain was Andalusia and was under the control of the Islamic Caliphate. It makes explicit references to injustices perpetrated against Islamic civilian populations in the Palestinian territories, Chechnya, Afghanistan and Iraq, Turkey, Morocco, Saudi Arabia, Russia, the United States, and Spain, and states that Spain has received its punishment for joining with the infidels.[43]

In May 2004, the tenth issue of *Al Battar* appeared on the Net.[44] The main focus of this issue was kidnapping and hostage-taking operations. The text describes two types of kidnappings: "secret" and "public" ones. Then there is a long discussion of negotiations about the fate of hostages. The first part presents the motives for kidnappings:

> Reasons for detaining one or more individuals by an enemy:
>
> i) Force the government or the enemy to succumb to some demands.
>
> ii) Put the government in a difficult situation that will create a political embarrassment between the government and the countries of the detainees.
>
> iii) Obtaining important information from the detainees.
>
> iv) Obtaining ransoms. Such was the case with the brothers in the Philippines, Chechnya, and Algiers. Our brothers from Muhammad's Army in Cashmere received a two million dollar ransom that provided good financial support to the organization.
>
> v) Bringing a specific case to light. This happened at the beginning of the cases in Chechnya and Algeria, with the hijacking of the French plane, and the kidnapping operations performed by the brothers in Chechnya and the Philippines.[45]

Planning and Coordination

Terrorists use the Internet not only to learn how to build bombs but also to plan and coordinate specific attacks. Al Qaeda operatives relied heavily on the Internet in planning and coordinating the September 11 attacks. To preserve their anonymity, the al Qaeda terrorists used the Internet in public places and sent messages via public e-mail. It is easy to use the Internet without being traced: many public facilities such as universities, libraries, and Internet cafés provide free access to the Net. The al Qaeda operatives used *hawalas,* or storefront money exchanges, for their Internet access (the U.S. government raided and shut down many of these *hawalas* in November 2001) and searched the Internet to find flight times and routes. Their leader, Mohammed Atta, even made his plane reservations online.

In May 2004, detailed plans to assassinate Saudi Arabia's minister of the interior, Prince Nayef bin Abdel Aziz, were discovered in a Web site of al Qaeda operatives in Saudi Arabia.[46]

> The plans, authored by Abu Hajar Abdel Aziz al-Moqrin, the leader of al Qaeda in Saudi Arabia and the man who claimed responsibility for the May 29, 2004, attack on the residential complex in Saudi Arabia, outlined Prince Nayif's itinerary, manner, and route of travel, personal security, and planned method of attack using rocket-propelled grenades. The detailed plans were found in Issue 11 of Camp al Battar, a well known military-style training manual referenced by terrorists and published regularly on an elusive Internet forum.[47]

Selected segments, translated from Arabic text, give the following instructions:

> The target: Nayef Bin Abdel Aziz. He will attend a reception of external security personel in a secret visit of the queen at King Khaled International Airport.
>
> Residence address: the Gardens—several palaces (the present palace in Arqa, also the Mother's palace, and several other palaces that he frequents).
>
> Daily routine: He goes to sleep shortly before dawn, and goes to the ministry some days at 7 o'clock at night until eight thirty, resting in the evenings, and attending parties, and private meetings.
>
> Number of guards: 8 persons.
>
> Typed of armament: light. The guards can be targeted as they descend from the car; they are near but not too close. The guarding crew varies the route at times. The target changes its car. Mostly uses the same car, which is not easy to approach since the highways are closed.
>
> Route information: From Arqa palace to the airport, 40 kilos.

Route Description: From Arqa, take the western circular, then the northern circular, then the airport highway, with the probability of moving onto other roads.

Schedule: The departure time: at six at night. The arrival time: 25 minutes after 6.

The first stage: the specification of the target. This stage is complete.

The second stage: the collection of the information. This stage is complete also.

The third stage: Determining the way of killing (the explosives), and it will be with the explosions in the procession during the passing of the procession at the bottom of the bridge linking the northern circular and the eastern one, and on the sides of the highway at the turn, beginning with the emergence of the group of confirmation and the destruction, with the assurance of killing them, or it may be carried out with the use of anti-armament missiles.

Hamas activists in the Middle East use chat rooms to plan operations, with operatives exchanging e-mail to coordinate actions across Gaza, the West Bank, Lebanon, and Israel. Instructions in the form of maps, photographs, directions, and technical details of how to use explosives are often disguised by means of steganography, which involves hiding messages inside graphic files. Sometimes, however, instructions are delivered concealed in only the simplest of codes. Hidden pages or phrases can contain coded instructions for terrorist operatives and supporters who know the password to access those pages. Sometimes codes are displayed openly.[48] As one report noted, "Al Qaeda uses prearranged phrases and symbols to direct its agents. An icon of an AK-47 can appear next to a photo of Osama bin Laden facing one direction one day, and another direction the next. The color of icons can change as well. Messages can be hidden on pages inside sites with no links to them, or placed openly in chat rooms."[49] Moreover, it seems that terrorists do not need to use sophisticated methods such as steganography to communicate efficiently and secretly on the Net:

Shortly after Sept. 11, questions swirled around steganography, the age-old technique of hiding one piece of information within another. A digital image of a sailboat, for instance, might also invisibly hold a communique, a map or some other hidden data.

A digital song file might contain blueprints for a desired target. But the troubling truth is that terrorists rarely have to be technically savvy to cloak their conversations. Even simple, prearranged code words can do the job when the authorities do not know whose e-mail to monitor or which Web sites to watch. Interviews conducted by al-Jazeera, the Arab television network, with the terror suspects Khalid Shaikh Mohammed and Ramzi bin al-Shibh (both have since been arrested), suggested that the Sept. 11 attackers communicated openly using prearranged code words. The "faculty of urban planning," for instance, referred to the World Trade Center. The Pentagon was the "faculty of fine arts."[50]

Mohammed Atta's final message to the other eighteen terrorists who carried out the attacks of 9/11 is reported to have read: "The semester begins in three more weeks. We've obtained 19 confirmations for studies in the faculty of law, the faculty of urban planning, the faculty of fine arts, and the faculty of engineering."[51]

The Internet allows terrorists to use virtual communication to lure victims and to plan the place and timing of attacking them: in 2001, Amana Mona, a twenty-five-year-old Palestinian woman, admitted that she had used the Internet to lure an Israeli teen to his death.[52] Her victim, sixteen-year-old Ofir Rahum, was shot in the West Bank town of Ramallah. In order to carry out her plan to take revenge on a Jewish Israeli, Mona contacted several Israeli teenagers via chat rooms. Then she targeted Rahum, with whom she pretended to start an online romance. Finally, she suggested a face-to-face meeting in Jerusalem. When he came to meet her, she convinced him to escort her to Ramallah. There, a Palestinian believed to be a senior activist in a Palestinian terrorist faction fired dozens of bullets from his Kalashnikov rifle and killed the Israeli teenager.

The Internet can be used by terrorists even to interfere with elections. The first attempt to do this was made during the Russian elections in March 2004. According to a MEMRI report,

The www.qoqaz.com site, operated by Al-Qa'ida members in Chechnya, posted a audio recording directed to the Mujahideen in Saudi Arabia by Sheikh Abu 'Omar Al-Seif, a Saudi considered the deputy of Abu Al-Walid, who is regarded as the commander of the Jihad in Chechnya, and who is also a Saudi. Al-

> Seif's previous recording was a video, also distributed over the Internet, that documented the wills of some of the perpetrators of suicide bombings in Riyadh. In the new recording, Sheikh Al-Seif states that the aim of the Mujahideen in Chechnya is to bring about Vladimir Putin's defeat in the upcoming March 2004 elections, and calls on his supporters to refrain from carrying out attacks against the Saudi government and instead to go to Iraq to fight the Americans.[53]

The text includes this statement: "In this tape, I want to advise that it is no secret that there will be a presidential election in Russia in the coming months, and those months will be of the most significant ones. The Mujahideen are trying to escalate the operations in order to topple Putin, Allah willing. Putin is trying by any and all means to present himself during these months as a victor, in order to win the elections. These months will be difficult and important to this issue."[54]

Another example of terrorist planning via the Internet was the March 11, 2004, Madrid bombings, days before the Spanish general elections. Shortly after the Madrid attack that killed 201 people and wounded 1,240, a strategy document that had earlier been found on radical Islamic Web sites and that had identified Spain as a target came to light. Brynjar Lia, a researcher at the Norwegian Defense Research Establishment (FFI), had come upon the original online document in December 2003, three months before the bombings, on the al Qaeda Web site Global Islamic Media. Lia read the text and, interpreting it as a strategy document intended for the Islamic resistance within Iraq, filed it. Only after the Madrid bombings did FFI researchers recall the document and analyze it in more detail. Prepared by the Media Committee for the Victory of the Iraqi People (Mujahidin Services Centre), the document was dedicated to al Qaeda ideologist Sheikh Yousef al-Ayyeri, who was killed by Saudi security forces in May 2003. FFI's analysis of the text revealed:

> The main thesis proposed in the document is that America cannot be coerced to leave Iraq by military-political means alone, but the Islamist resistance can succeed if it makes the occupation of Iraq as costly as possible—in economic terms—for the United States. . . . If the *mujahidin* can force U.S. allies to withdraw from Iraq, then America will be left to cover the expenses on her own, which she cannot sustain for very long. The intermediary strategic goal is therefore to make one or two

of the U.S. allies leave the coalition, because this will cause others to follow suit and the dominos will start falling. The document then analyses three countries (Britain, Spain and Poland) in depth, with a view to identifying the weakest link or the domino piece most likely to fall first. The author provides a surprisingly informed and nuanced analysis of the domestic political map in each country. He argues that each country will react differently to violent attacks against its forces because of domestic political factors. Spain is presented as very vulnerable to attacks on its forces, primarily because public opposition to the war is almost total, and the government is virtually on its own on this issue. The author therefore identifies Spain as the weakest link in the coalition.[55]

The most interesting part of the original document is the conclusion section. There the author refers directly to Spain, the elections in Spain, the timing (March 2004) for an attack, and the form of action (several attacks or "blows"). As the author states (translated from Arabic): "Therefore we say that in order to force the Spanish government to withdraw from Iraq the resistance should deal painful blows to its forces. This should be accompanied by an information campaign clarifying the truth of the matter inside Iraq. It is necessary to make utmost use of the upcoming general election in Spain in March next year. We think that the Spanish government could not tolerate more than two, maximum three blows, after which it will have to withdraw as a result of popular pressure."[56]

Fund-Raising

Like many other political organizations, terrorist groups use the Internet to raise funds. Al Qaeda, for instance, has always depended heavily on donations, and its global fund-raising network is built upon a foundation of charities, nongovernmental organizations, and other financial institutions that use Web sites and Internet-based chat rooms and forums to solicit and gather funds. The fighters in the Russian breakaway republic of Chechnya have likewise used the Internet to publicize the numbers of bank accounts to which sympathizers can contribute. (One of these Chechen bank accounts was located in Sacramento, California.) In October 2003, a *Washington Post* correspondent reported that the FBI was probing Wahhabi Muslim Web sites and that "FBI and Treasury officials said they believe some Islamic conferences, as well as Web sites that extol radical Islam, are vehicles in the United States for recruitment and fundraising by terrorist groups."[57]

According to Timothy Thomas, the Internet is also used "to put together profiles": Internet user demographics (culled, for instance, from personal information entered on online questionnaires and order forms) allow terrorists to identify users with sympathy for a particular cause or issue.[58] These individuals are then asked to make donations, typically through e-mails sent by a front group (i.e., an organization broadly supportive of the terrorists' aims but operating publicly and legally and usually having no direct ties to the terrorist organization). Until it was modified, the Islamic Assembly of North America (IANA) had a Web site (Islamway .com) "that offered Arabic-language videos with graphic scenes of jihadist combat and called for contributions. IANA has received $3 million since 1995, according to FBI court filings; much of the contributions came from abroad. U.S. government officials are tracing the finances of IANA."[59] "It's much more than about the money they raise. It's proselytizing, recruiting and radicalizing people in this country and other places across the globe," said Matthew Levitt, a former FBI official.[60]

Hamas is another active fund-raiser on the Internet.[61] A message on the Qassam Brigades site promises "secure handling" of donations and instructs potential donors to use only "fake names" when sending an e-mail message regarding their donations. On one American Web site, one can read the personal account of a visitor at the Hamas Web site (www.qassam.org):

> I went right over to the web site to check things out and there it was, plain as day. The appeal was headlined, "A call for donation from Martyr Izz el-Deen el-Qassam Phalanxes." After quite a lot of rhetoric, the writer got down to the point: "Muslim brothers . . . all over the world . . . Martyr Izz el-Deen el-Qassam Phalanxes, your own defending phalanxes, the military wing of Hamas movement in Palestine, is calling upon you to donate with what you can to assist the cause of Jihad and resistance until the occupation is eliminated and every span of the Muslim Palestine is liberated. . . . The price of Kalashnikov bullet is $3 and the price of the Kalashnikov gun itself now is $2,000 and it was $3,500 couple of months ago, and do you know that the

price of R-B-G is $12,000 and the price of T.N.T that's used by
your mujahideen brothers is $100 a kilo, also Martyr Izz el-
Deen el-Qassam Phalanxes now manufactures Al-Qassam land-
to-land missiles in different sizes and also the anti-shields Al-
Banna bomber, Martyr Izz el-Deen el-Qassam Phalanxes also
supervises the development of fighting, defensive and attacking
weapons and other much projects must not be elaborated for
confidentiality purposes."[62]

The text also claims that the group has killed 65 percent "of what has
been killed of Zionists since the start of the Intifada (uprising) of Al-
Aqsa" and tells potential donors to send an e-mail (to an address posted
on the Web site). These e-mails are answered with instructions to transfer money to a specific person (name given), Elbatech Bank, account no.
(given) at the Arab bank, Gaza branch. The name and account number
change almost every day.

Donations for Hamas have also been raised by a Web site of a charity
organization based in Texas and named the Holy Land Foundation for
Relief and Development (HLF). As President Bush charged, "Money
raised by the Holy Land Foundation is used by Hamas to support schools
and indoctrinate children to grow up into suicide bombers. . . . [T]he
facts are clear, the terrorists benefit from the Holy Land Foundation.
And we're not going to allow it."[63] In December 2001 the U.S. government seized the assets of HLF because of its ties to terrorist activities and
to Hamas. On its Web site, HLF stated that its purpose is to stop human
suffering "through humanitarian programs that impact the lives" of "dis-
advantaged, disinherited, and displaced peoples suffering from man-
made and natural disasters."[64] Yet it also said, "Is it not out of honesty
and sincerity that we all be brothers to the martyr's widow? Should we
not stand by her and compensate her children for what they lost by their
father's martyrdom?"

On May 29, 2002, the Web site Islam Online presented an interview
with Salah Sh'hadeh, the commander of the Qassam Brigades who was later
assassinated by Israel.[65] The following are excerpts from the interview:

QUESTION: "How much does a martyrdom operation cost?"
SH'HADEH: "The cost of an operation varies. . . . Attack operations with automatic weapons cost the price of the weapon,
which hold at least 250 rounds, and of the ammunition, and the

price of about 10 hand grenades. But some of the operations cost much more and include transporting [the perpetrator] . . . buying a car, and bribing Jewish collaborators. There are operations that cost a great deal—between $3,500-$50,000, in accordance with the target."

QUESTION: "What are the obstacles that the Al-Qassam Brigades face?"

SH'HADEH: "The most significant obstacles are the scarcity of good-quality weapons, such as anti-aircraft and long-range missiles. . . . In addition, weapons prices have been raised by the bloodsucker arms dealers, so the price of an M-16 has reached $5,000, and each of its bullets now costs $1.50, and a Kalashnikov costs $2,000, and each of its bullets costs $4.00. The military apparatus has managed to meet the challenge of weapons scarcities by collecting donations from people who love supporting the path of Jihad for the sake of Allah. Similarly, the movement has succeeded in manufacturing some of the intermediate weaponry, thus reducing costs. The cost of a rocket [made by the movement] is less than 1% of its cost if we had to buy it." [Author note: the variance in the prices quoted may reflect the nature of the black market for arms.][66]

Another example of terrorist fund-raising on the Internet comes from Lashkar e-Tayba (LeT), one of the most violent terrorist groups in Kashmir, serving as the terrorist wing of the Markaz Dawa-Wal-Irshad, an Islamic fundamentalist organization of the Wahhabi sect in Pakistan. It is a well-organized and well-funded terrorist group that has trained thousands of mujahedeen, sending them to Afghanistan, Chechnya, Kashmir, Bosnia, Kosovo, Iraq, and the Philippines. The LeT's pamphlet titled "Why Are We Waging Jihad" includes calls for the "restoration" of Islamic rule over India. According to Benjamin and the present author, however, LeT "appears to be shifting its sights away from its longtime focus on Kashmir and toward Iraq. Probably the largest militant group in Pakistan, it has used its online Urdu publication to call for sending holy warriors to Iraq to take revenge for the torture at Abu Ghraib prison as well as for what it calls the 'rapes of Iraqi Muslim women.' 'The Americans are dishonoring our mothers and sisters,' reads a notice on its site. 'Therefore, jihad against America has now become mandatory.' "[67]

Visitors to the LeT Web site are asked to help with the group's efforts: "Allah gives you the opportunity to take part in the struggle for Muslim rights—Jihad," states the English-language Web site. "Even if you cannot take part physically in the Jihad, you CAN help us by the means of financial aid."[68] The readers are led to two bank accounts in Karachi, Pakistan, to which they can send donations and an e-mail address in case of questions or directions. In her book *Terror in the Name of God*, Jessica Stern describes an interview with a LeT terrorist, Ahmed: "I talk with Ahmed, the young recruit, in the car. He tells me he has a master's degree in engineering and that he is doing computer work for Lashkar e-Tayba, which uses its sophisticated Web site for fundraising and recruitment. One of its Web sites solicits funding for additional equipment. Visitors to one of the group's sites are requested 'to provide as much money as you can . . . or otherwise provide us a fast enough computer and accessories.' "[69]

The Internet was and still is a fund-raising device for al Qaeda. A 2002 report titled "Terrorist Financing," prepared by an independent task force of the Council on Foreign Relations, describes this mechanism in detail:

> Al-Qaeda's financial network is characterized by layers and redundancies. It raises money from a variety of sources and moves money in a variety of manners. . . . The most important source of al-Qaeda's money is its continuous fundraising efforts. Al-Qaeda's financial backbone was built from the foundation of charities, nongovernmental organizations, mosques, web sites, fundraisers, intermediaries, facilitators and banks and other financial institutions. . . . This network extended to all corners of the Muslim world. It included everyone from wealthy gulf Arabs, who could be solicited directly to give huge sums themselves, to the masses, who would make regular charitable donations as part of their religious obligations.[70]

In the United States, al Qaeda has received funds from numerous social charities. The U.S. government has so far frozen the assets of three charities that ran Web sites to raise money—the Benevolence International Foundation (BIF), the Global Relief Foundation (GRF), and the al-Haramain Foundation—because of evidence that those charities have funneled money to al Qaeda. The BIF, based in Illinois, was founded in the 1980s by Saudi sheikh Adil Abdul Galil Batargy, an associate of bin Laden. According to the BIF's Web site, it is "a humanitarian organization dedicated to helping those afflicted by wars. . . . BIF first provides short-term relief such as emergency food distribution, and then moves on to long-term projects providing education and self-sufficiency to the children, widowed, refugees, injured and staff of vital governmental institutions."[71] For those who want to give, the Web site provides information on how to donate and provides a form for regular monthly donations. According to the FBI, the BIF raised millions of dollars for bin Laden. It also reportedly sent $600,000 to Chechen extremists trained by al Qaeda. In addition, the BIF was linked to the 1993 World Trade Center bombing: "U.S. prosecutors allege that Enaam Arnaout, executive director of a Muslim charity known as the Benevolence International Foundation (BIF), helped Osama bin Laden's al-Qaeda terrorism network move money and equipment around the world. The court papers say evidence found in Bosnia indicates that Arnaout was a personal friend of bin Laden's and that he had relationships with several top figures in al-Qaeda."[72]

The Global Relief Foundation (GRF), also based in Illinois, describes itself on its Web site as "organized exclusively for charitable, religious, educational and scientific purposes including to establish, promote, contribute and carry out relief and charitable activities, projects, organizations, institutions and funds." The Web site carries the mission statement of the GRF, focusing on activities in four areas: "Emergency Relief," "Medical Aid," "Advancement of Education," and "Development of Social Welfare." Like the BIF's, the GRF's site has received donations online via credit cards, wire transfers, regular bank deductions, and donations of stocks. The European director of the GRF, Nabil Sayadi, was connected with Wadih al-Hage, an al Qaeda operative convicted for his role in the 1998 U.S. embassy bombings in East Africa. The report *Jihad Online* argues that "Mohammed Galeb Kalaje Zouaydi, who was arrested by Spanish authorities because he is believed to be an al Qaeda financier, transferred hundreds of thousands of dollars to GRF via Sayadi."[73]

The third Islamic foundation whose assets the U.S. government has seized is the al-Haramain Foundation, based in Saudi Arabia and active in more than fifty countries. This organization, too, claims on its Web

site that it "aims to establish the correct beliefs in the hearts of the Muslims" and to "provide aid to the Muslims who suffer from catastrophes,
disasters and calamities."[74] For interested donors, the site provides thirteen bank accounts. Although al-Haramain declares that donations are
used for humanitarian causes such as feeding the hungry and supporting
orphans and poor families, it also highlights militant messages: "We may
never get to the battlefields and be slain for the sake of Allah, even though
we ardently desire that" (from an online 1999 article). On March 11,
2002, the United States and Saudi Arabia froze the assets of the al-
Haramain Foundation, including two overseas branches: the Somali
branch had links to al Qaeda and to al-Ittihad al-Islami, Somalia's largest
militant Islamic organization, and al-Haramain's Bosnian office had ties
to Egyptian al Qaeda ally Gama'a al-Islamiyya.

In January 2004, a federal grand jury in Idaho charged a Saudi graduate student with conspiring to help terrorist organizations wage jihad by
using the Internet to raise funds, field recruits, and locate prospective
U.S. targets—military and civilian—in the Middle East. Sami Omar
Hussayen, a doctoral candidate in computer science in a University of
Idaho program sponsored by the National Security Agency(!), was
accused of creating Web sites and an e-mail group that disseminated
messages from him and two radical clerics in Saudi Arabia who supported jihad. The prosecutors argued that Hussayen launched the e-mail
group in 2000, calling on Muslims to "fight with your money, your
selves, your tongues and your prayers." However, in June 2004, the
Idaho jury found him innocent of all three terrorism charges as well as
three immigration charges. According to juror John Steger, "There was
a lack of hard evidence. There was no clear-cut evidence that said he was
a terrorist, so it was all on inference."

Another terrorist group, Hezbollah, uses its al-Manar Web site to collect funds "for the sustenance of the Intifadah." This official Hezbollah
Web site presents three bank accounts in Lebanon for money transfers.[75]
Hezbollah has three other Web sites used for fund-raising to support
social charity and military operations: the al-Shahid and al-Emdad sites,
collecting donations "for the families of Hezbollah soldiers killed in
battle," and the al-Jarha Web site, collecting money "for wounded
Hezbollah soldiers." According to the report *Jihad Online,* "The al-Jarha
site urges donors to send $25 a month, reminding them that it takes

$12,000 a year to care for an injured Hezbollah operative and his family. . . . For a minimum of $360 per year, a donor can 'sponsor' an orphan of a 'martyr.' For that money, the donor receives four letters from the orphan each year and the right to personally visit the orphan. The site also offers donors the opportunity to fund the widow of a 'martyr,' at a cost of $300 or more each year. Finally, the donor has an option to support the education of the orphan of a 'martyr' for $300 or more per year."[76]

Attacking Other Terrorists

The Internet serves also as a battlefield between and within terrorist organizations, which use the Net to conduct ideological debates or even personal disputes. One example is the case of a rivalry within al Qaeda, studied and reported by Reuven Paz.[77] It appears that from within this loosely knit organization emerged a group of young Saudi Islamists who want to play a more important role: "Many of them were students and disciples of the older groups of Wahhabi clerics and scholars who could not come to terms with the American presence on Saudi soil. In recent years they radicalized their positions and began backing up the positions of Qa'idat al Jihad, including political violence against the United States, Western culture and, in recent years, the Saudi royal regime, while providing Islamic legitimacy for these actions."[78] In 2002 they began to issue new electronic pamphlets via the Web sites of their supporters, under a new name: Qa'idat al Jihad (the Jihad base). The severe conflict between the groups within the Saudi Jihadists led to the online publication of a 460-page book titled *Osama bin Laden: Mujaddid al-Zaman Wa-Qahir al-Amrikan (Osama bin Laden: The Reformer of Our Times and Defeater of the Americans),* by the Saudi scholar Abu Jandal al-Azdi. Circulated on several Web sites, including one of the most important Web sites of the Jihadi Salafiyyah,[79] the book attempts to raise bin Laden to a new level of a major reformer or reviver, a status bestowed on only a very few scholars.

Another rivalry related to Qa'idat al Jihad also found its way to the Internet. When Israel and Hezbollah exchanged prisoners on January 29, 2004, Hezbollah and its leader, Hasan Nasrallah, were highly praised in parts of the Arab and Muslim world. This created criticism and resentment among several Arab groups and in particular among groups opposed to Hezbollah. The most serious criticism of Hezbollah, argues Paz, came from Saudi Salafi-jihadi elements that support Qa'idat al-Jihad:

> The Lebanese Shiite group has never been popular among the Salafi adherents of Global Jihad, given their fundamental hatred towards the Shi'ah. The collapse of the Ba'athist regime of Saddam Hussein and the conflict between the Shiite majority and the Sunni minority in Iraq, added additional fuel to the fire of traditional Salafi enmity towards the Shi'ah. Since the start of the attempts at establishing a new government in Iraq, Salafi web sites and forums on the Internet have stepped up their attacks against the Shi'is, Iran, and Shi'i doctrines with every possible arsenal of verbal arms. Accompanying the growing phenomenon of severe verbal attacks against the Iraqi Shiites and the Lebanese Hizballah are condemnations of Iran prevalent on several web sites, and initiated primarily by Saudi supporters of Global Jihad. Furthermore, in the past year there was a growing attempt by Saudi Salafi scholars and laymen to link the Shiites to Jews, both in history, and in present times.[80]

The most significant verbal attack, according to Paz, was the labeling of Hezbollah with the Salafi term "Hizb al-Shaytan" ("Party of the Devil"). One of the primary Salafi online forums against the non-Sunnis, primarily the Shiites—"Al-Difa an al-Sunnah" ("Defense of the Sunnah")—led the attacks with numerous writings, several of them by important Islamic writers.[81] Their Web site, described by Paz, presents articles such as "The Actions of the Murderer So-Called Shiite Mahdi," "The Crimes and Betrayals of the Shi'is throughout History," "Meetings between Shiite Clerics and Jews and Christians," and "The Scandals of Shiite Clerics and Religious Authorities," which refers to Shiite leaders such as Khomeini, Khamenei, Khoei, and Sistani, as well as Hezbollah.[82] The "Hezbollah File" on this Web site indicates why the Salafis criticize Hezbollah and Nasrallah: "The secretary general of Hezbollah portrays himself and is portrayed by others as the 'New Salah al-Din al-Ayubi,' and a superior commander at the forefront of the struggle against Israel."[83] Thus, the younger Islamists use the jihadi forums to attack Nasrallah in person and one of them even posted in the jihadi forum of al-Erhap his criticism titled "Hasan Nasrallah, Leader of Hezbollah—the Most Famous and Corrupt Traitor in the History of the Nation."[84]

Another example of using the Internet for internal disputes is found in the ninth issue of al Qaeda's *Sawt al-Jihad* online magazine, published in January 2004.[85] Most of this issue is devoted to a dispute within al Qaeda circles in Saudi Arabia regarding the al Qaeda bombings in Saudi Arabia. The text, by an anonymous author, seeks to justify the jihad in Saudi Arabia:

> My Muslim mujahid brother, can you not see Muslims killed in Afghanistan, and then in Iraq. . . . Can you not see the corpse of the children completely torn, their skulls and brains scattered all over the [television] screens? Can you not see the Muslims in this worst condition of shame, humiliation, pain, harm, and injury? Can you not see that the headquarters of the war was from the [Arabian] Peninsula and that the center of all kinds of logistical support was this land, which the Prophet, may peace be upon Him, commanded be purified from the polytheist?
>
> You have seen the war on Iraq, and you have seen how all the military powers in the land of the two holy mosques were in the hands of the Christians, including military bases, and even more—the civilian Arar airport has been changed to a military base because of its strategic location, which was indispensable in attacking Iraq.[86]

An interesting cleavage between Hamas and al Qaeda was revealed on the Hamas Web site.[87] The Palestinian Hamas movement and al Qaeda have a very complex relationship. Al Qaeda and the affiliated Salafi-jihadi and Tawhidi-jihadi groups are trying to manipulate the Palestinian problem and the Israeli-Palestinian conflict while Hamas uses the same issues for its own propaganda, recruitment, and fund-raising. Al Qaeda and its affiliates "also adopted from Hamas the *modus operandi* of suicide attacks and much of the Islamic justification for them. On the other hand, Hamas has so far tended to reject attempts to create organizational links with the global jihad, or to expand its terrorist activities beyond Israel and the Palestinian territories. . . . Hamas leaders did their best not to link their struggle in Palestine to the global Jihad of al Qaeda."[88] On May 30, 2004, Hamas published on its official Web site the following press release related to the Khobar attack in Saudi Arabia, where twenty-two people, most of them foreigners, were killed by an al Qaeda–related group during a twenty-five-hour hostage ordeal:

> The Islamic Resistance Movement Hamas declares its severe condemnation and sorrow for the criminal attack that occurred yesterday night in one of the complex of buildings in the town of Khobar in the brother kingdom of Saudi Arabia, which caused the death of dozens of civilians and innocent people. While we reject this kind of attacks, we wish to emphasize that they harm the security and peace of our countries, and the national and Islamic interests. Therefore, we call those responsible for these attacks to stop them, and preserve the interests and security of their country and nation, especially while our nation is facing external threats and challenges.[89]

In addition to using the Internet to criticize other terrorist groups, Hamas has used the Net to respond to its own critics. In January 2004 Hamas posted photos on its Internet site of Reem Raiyshi, its first female suicide bomber, posing with her two young children. Raiyshi blew herself up at a border crossing between the Gaza Strip and Israel, killing four Israelis. The terror group's posting was an attempt to answer Palestinian critics who condemned sending a mother on a suicide mission. In the pictures Raiyshi is posing in camouflage dress and the Hamas headband, holding an assault rifle and her three-year-old son, who holds a mortar shell. Sheikh Saed Seyam, a Hamas leader, claimed, "This picture shows the outrage the Palestinians have reached. This scene should urge people to ask themselves what motivates women, who are known for their attachment to their children and families, to leave them forever."[90] When the sheikh was asked why Hamas had sent a mother to her death, he answered that there are many volunteers who want to carry out attacks: "Some of them cry [to be chosen], which makes the military leadership submissive to their pressure for this honor."[91]

* * * * *

As this chapter demonstrates, the use of the Net by terrorist groups as a communication channel and propaganda tool is just the tip of the iceberg. They are using the Internet to raise funds, recruit, incite violence, and provide training. They are also using it to plan, network, and coordinate attacks. Thomas Hegghammer, who researches Islamist Web sites at the Norwegian Defense Research Establishment, says, "In a sense, [the Internet has] replaced Afghanistan as a meeting place."[92] In fact, the Internet has been described as a "virtual Afghanistan": as Paul Eedle points out, "[al Qaeda operatives] have to replace their physical bases in Afghanistan somehow and so long as there is a small number of highly trained people to lead groups, then these detailed manuals of how to write recipes for explosives are all crucial."[93] As the number of terrorist Web sites has increased, the uses to which terrorists put the Internet have diversified. Yet the Internet is not just a tool or a channel. It is also a target and a weapon. In the next chapter we will turn the spotlight on cyberterrorism.

5

Cyberterrorism
How Real Is the Threat?

Tomorrow's terrorist may be able to do more damage with a keyboard than with a bomb.
  —National Research Council[1]

For the foreseeable future, acts of cyberterrorism, such as the ones usually imagined, will be very difficult to perform, unreliable in their impact, and easy to respond to in relatively short periods of time.
  —Douglas Thomas, a professor at the University of Southern California, in testimony to a congressional subcommitte in July 2002[2]

Our nation is at grave risk of a cyberattack that could devastate the national psyche and economy more broadly than did the 9/11 attacks.
  —Carnegie Mellon University computer scientist Roy Maxion in a letter to President George W. Bush, cosigned by 50 computer scientists

Terrorists are interested in creating bloodshed and terror. The Internet doesn't rise to this level of impact in a way that a truck bomb does.
  —George Smith, coeditor, vmyths.com

CYBERTERRORISM IS COMMONLY DEFINED as the use of computer networks to sabotage critical national infrastructures (such as energy, transportation, or government operations). As modern infrastructure systems have become more dependent on computerized networks for their operation, new vulnerabilities have emerged—"a massive electronic Achilles' heel."[3] Cyberterrorism is an attractive option for modern terrorists, who value its anonymity, its potential to inflict massive damage, its psychological impact, and its media appeal. Indeed, the threat posed by cyberterrorism has grabbed the attention of the mass media, the security community, and the information technology (IT) industry. Journalists, politicians, and experts in a variety of fields have popularized a scenario in which sophisticated cyberterrorists electronically break into computers that control dams or air traffic control systems, wreaking havoc and endangering not only millions of lives but national security itself. And yet, despite all the gloomy predictions of a cybergenerated doomsday, no single instance of real cyberterrorism has yet been recorded.

Just how real is the threat that cyberterrorism poses? Because most critical infrastructure in Western societies is networked through computers, the potential threat from cyberterrorism is, at least in theory, alarming. Hackers, although not motivated by the same goals that inspire terrorists, have demonstrated that individuals can gain access to sensitive information and to the operation of crucial services. Terrorists, some argue, could thus follow the hackers' lead and then, having broken into government and private computer systems, could cripple or at least disable the military, financial, and service sectors of advanced economies. The growing dependence of our societies on information technology allows terrorists the chance to approach targets that would otherwise be utterly unassailable, such as national defense systems and air traffic control systems.

Concern about the potential danger posed by cyberterrorism is thus well founded. That does not mean, however, that all the fears that have been voiced in the media, in Congress, and in other public forums are rational and reasonable. Some fears are simply unjustified, while others are highly exaggerated. Furthermore, the distinction between the *potential* and *actual* damage inflicted by cyberterrorists has too often been ignored, and the relatively benign activities of most hackers have been conflated with the specter of pure cyberterrorism.

This chapter examines the reality of the cyberterrorism threat, both present and future. It begins by outlining why cyberterrorism angst has gripped so many people, defines what qualifies as true cyberterrorism and what does not, and charts cyberterrorism's appeal for terrorists. Then we will examine evidence both for and against Western society's vulnerability to cyberattacks based on a variety of recent studies and simulations in order to assess whether we need to be so concerned. The conclusion looks to the future and argues that the world must remain alert to real dangers while not becoming caught up in overblown fears.

Cyberterrorism Angst

The roots of the notion of cyberterrorism can be traced back to the early 1990s, when the rapid growth in Internet use and the debate on the emerging "information society" sparked several studies on the potential risks faced by the highly networked, high-tech-dependent United States. As early as 1990, the prototypical term "electronic Pearl Harbor" was coined, linking the threat of a computer attack to an American historical trauma.

Joshua Green, in his *Washington Monthly* article "The Myth of Cyberterrorism," argues, "It's no surprise that cyberterrorism now ranks alongside other weapons of mass destruction in the public consciousness . . . but there's just one problem: There is no such thing as cyberterrorism—no instance of anyone ever having been killed by a terrorist (or anyone else) using a computer. Nor is there compelling evidence that al Qaeda or any other terrorist organization has resorted to computers for any sort of serious destructive activity."[4] It seems fair to say that the current threat posed by cyberterrorism has been exaggerated. No single instance of cyberterrorism has yet been recorded; U.S. defense and intelligence computer systems are air-gapped, meaning they are not even connected to the Internet; the systems run by private companies are more vulnerable to attack but also are more resilient than is often supposed; the vast majority of cyberattacks are launched by hackers with few if any political goals and no desire to cause the mayhem and carnage of which terrorists dream. So why, then, has so much concern been expressed over a relatively minor threat?

Psychological, political, and economic forces have combined to promote the fear of cyberterrorism. From a psychological perspective, two
of the greatest fears of modern times are combined in the term "cyberterrorism." The fear of random, violent victimization blends well with the
distrust and outright fear of computer technology. An unknown threat
is perceived as more threatening than a known threat. Although cyberterrorism does not entail a direct threat of violence, its psychological
impact on anxious societies can be as powerful as the threat of terrorist
bombs. Moreover, the biggest obstacles to our understanding the actual
threat of cyberterrorism are a fear of the unknown and a lack of information, or, worse, too much misinformation.

After 9/11, the security and terrorism discourse soon featured cyberterrorism prominently. This was understandable given that more night-
marish attacks were expected and that cyberterrorism seemed to offer al
Qaeda opportunities to inflict enormous damage. But there was also a
political dimension to the new focus on cyberterrorism. Debates about
national security, including the security of cyberspace, always attract
political actors with agendas that extend beyond the specific issue at
hand—and the debate over cyberterrorism was no exception to this pattern. For instance, Yonah Alexander, a terrorism researcher at the
Potomac Institute—a think tank with close links to the Pentagon—
announced in December 2001 the existence of an "Iraq Net." This network supposedly consisted of more than one hundred Web sites set up
across the world by Iraq since the mid-1990s to launch denial-of-service,
or "DoS," attacks (such attacks render computer systems inaccessible or
inoperable) against U.S. companies. "Saddam Hussein would not hesi-
tate to use the cyber tool he has. . . . It is not a question of if but when.
The entire United States is the front line," Alexander claimed.[5] Whatever the intentions of its author, such a statement was clearly likely to
support arguments then being made for an aggressive U.S. policy toward
Iraq. No evidence of an "Iraq Net" has yet come to light.

Combating cyberterrorism has become not only a highly politicized
issue but also an economically rewarding one. An entire industry has
emerged to challenge the dangers of cyberterrorism: think tanks have
launched elaborate projects and issued alarming white papers on the
subject; many experts have testified about cyberterrorism's threats in
various forums; and private companies hired security consultants and

installed expensive protective software. After the 9/11 attacks, the federal government requested $4.5 billion for infrastructure security the following year, and the FBI now has more than 1,000 "cyber investigators."[6] According to one survey, spending on security-related technology is expected to increase over the next couple of years, leveling off at 5 percent to 8 percent of the IT budget of global companies.[7] The same report concludes: "Security spending takes up from 3 percent to 4 percent of IT budgets today; that amount, however, is expected to increase at a compound annual growth rate of between 8 percent and 10 percent through 2006, before reaching a plateau."

Before September 11, 2001, George W. Bush, as a presidential candidate, warned that "American forces are overused and underfunded precisely when they are confronted by a host of new threats and challenges—the spread of weapons of mass destruction, the rise of cyberterrorism, the proliferation of missile technology."[8] After the 9/11 attacks, President Bush created the Office of Cyberspace Security in the White House and appointed his former counterterrorism coordinator, Richard Clarke, to head it. The warnings came now from the president, the vice president, security advisers, and government officials: "Terrorists can sit at one computer connected to one network and can create worldwide havoc," cautioned Tom Ridge, director of the Department of Homeland Security, in a representative observation in April 2003. "[They] don't necessarily need a bomb or explosives to cripple a sector of the economy or shut down a power grid." These warnings certainly had a powerful impact on the media, the public, and the administration. For instance, a survey of 725 cities conducted by the National League of Cities found that cyberterrorism ranks alongside biological and chemical weapons at the top of a list of city officials' fears.[9]

The mass media have added their voice to the fearful chorus with scary front-page headlines such as the following, which appeared in the *Washington Post* in June 2003: "Cyber-Attacks by Al Qaeda Feared, Terrorists at Threshold of Using Internet as Tool of Bloodshed, Experts Say." A typical report published in the *Washington Post* represents hundreds of similar news items:

> This situation is alarming when one considers that America has
> many thousands of dams, airports, chemical plants, federal res-
> ervoirs and of course power plants (of which 104 are nuclear),

most of whose integral systems are operated and controlled by sophisticated computer systems or other automated controllers. These systems are now experiencing cyber attacks. In the second half of 2002 alone, 60 percent of power and energy companies experienced at least one severe cyber attack. Fortunately, none incurred catastrophic loss.[10]

Cyberterrorism, the media have discovered, makes for eye-catching, dramatic copy. Screenwriters and novelists have likewise seen the dramatic potential, with movies such as the 1995 James Bond feature *GoldenEye,* 2002's *Code Hunter,* and novels such as Tom Clancy and Steve R. Pieczenik's *Netforce* popularizing a wide range of cyberterrorist scenarios. The mass media frequently fail to distinguish between hacking and cyberterrorism and exaggerate the threat of the latter.

The net effect of all this attention has been to create a climate in which instances of hacking into government Web sites, online thefts of proprietary data from companies, and outbreaks of new computer viruses are all likely to be labeled by the media as suspected cases of "cyberterrorism." Indeed, the term has been so misapplied and overused that if we are to have any hope of reaching a clear understanding of the dangers posed by cyberterrorism, we must begin by defining it with some precision.

What Is Cyberterrorism?

Various groups and individuals, with a wide range of agendas, attack the Net or use the Net to attack Web sites and computerized services. Very often they are mislabeled as cyberterrorists, but there is an important distinction between the various types of everyday hackers and true terrorists. Kevin Coleman reports in *Directions Magazine*:

In the 2002 research study conducted by the Computer Crime Research Center, 90% of respondents detected computer security breaches within the last twelve months. In another more recent study conducted by CIO Online, 92% of companies have experienced computer attacks and/or breaches in the last 12 months. If that is not shocking enough, security professionals are worried about the increased sophistication of threats against computer systems. Here are some interesting statistics:

- In the first half of 2002, there were more than 180,000 Internet based attacks on business.

- Attacks against the Internet increase at an annual rate above 60%.
- The average business will experience 32 break-in attempts this week.
- Reported systems vulnerabilities and security incidents are doubling each year.
- The reported number of vulnerabilities and security incidents represent an estimated 10% of the actual total.[11]

But is this really cyberterrorism? There have been several stumbling blocks to creating a clear and consistent definition of the term "cyberterrorism."[12] First, as just noted, much of the discussion has been conducted in the popular media, where journalists typically strive for drama and sensation rather than good operational definitions of new terms. Second, it has been especially common when dealing with computers to coin new words simply by placing "cyber," "computer," or "information" before another word. Thus, an entire arsenal of terms— "cybercrime," "infowar," "netwar," "cyberterrorism," "cyberharassment," "virtual warfare," "digital terrorism," "cybertactics," "computer warfare," "cyberattack," and "cyber-break-ins"—is used to describe what some military and political strategists describe as the "new terrorism" of our times.

Fortunately, some efforts have been made to introduce greater semantic precision. Most notably, Dorothy Denning, a professor of computer science, has put forward an unambiguous definition in numerous articles and in her testimony on the subject before the House Armed Services Committee:

> Cyberterrorism is the convergence of cyberspace and terrorism. It refers to unlawful attacks and threats of attacks against computers, networks and the information stored therein when done to intimidate or coerce a government or its people in furtherance of political or social objectives. Further, to qualify as cyberterrorism, an attack should result in violence against persons or property, or at least cause enough harm to generate fear. Attacks that lead to death or bodily injury, explosions, or severe economic loss would be examples. Serious attacks against critical infrastructures could be acts of cyberterrorism, depending on their impact. Attacks that disrupt nonessential services or that are mainly a costly nuisance would not.[13]

"Cyberterrorism," argues Green, "merges two spheres—terrorism and technology—that most lawmakers and senior administration officials don't fully understand and therefore tend to fear, making them likelier to accede to any measure, if only out of self-preservation."[14] And there is also the misunderstanding regarding the distinction between cyberterrorism and cybercrime. As Conway explains,

> Such confusion is partly caused by the lack of clear definitions of the two phenomena. Cybercrime and cyberterrorism are not coterminous. Cyberspace attacks must have a "terrorist" component in order to be labeled cyberterrorism. The attacks must instill terror as commonly understood (that is, result in death and/or large-scale destruction), and they must have a political motivation. As regards the distinction between terrorist use of information technology and terrorism involving computer technology as a weapon/target, only the latter may be defined as cyberterrorism. Terrorist "use" of computers as a facilitator of their activities, whether for propaganda, communication, or other purposes, is simply that: "use."[15]

The Appeal of Cyberterrorism for Terrorists

Cyberterrorism is an attractive option for modern terrorists for several reasons, as listed by Adam Savino:[16]

- First, it is cheaper and even easier than traditional terrorist methods. All that the terrorist needs is access to a computer server (available at public libraries, universities, etc.) or a personal computer with an online connection. Terrorists do not need to buy weapons such as guns and explosives; instead, they can spread computer viruses or damage infrastructure facilities using a laptop.
- Second, cyberterrorism provides more anonymity than the "traditional" terrorist methods. Like many Internet surfers, terrorists use online nicknames—"screen names"—or log on to a Web site as an unidentified "guest user," making it very hard for security agencies and police forces to track down their real identity.
- Third, the variety and number of targets are enormous, including the computers and computer networks of companies and banks, governments, individuals, public utilities, private

airlines, and so on. Several studies have shown that critical infrastructures, such as electric power grids and emergency services, are vulnerable to a cyberterrorist attack because the infrastructures and the computer systems that run them are highly complex, making it effectively impossible to eliminate all weaknesses.

- Fourth, cyberterrorist attack can be launched from a distance, a feature that is especially appealing to terrorists. Cyberterrorism requires less physical training, psychological investment, risk of death or capture, and travel than conventional forms of terrorism, making it easier for terrorist organizations to recruit and retain followers.

- Fifth, as the I LOVE YOU virus showed, cyberterrorist attacks have the potential to harm directly a larger number of people than traditional terrorist methods can, thereby generating greater media coverage, which is ultimately what terrorists want.

Confusing Hackers and Hacktivists with Terrorists

It is important to distinguish between cyberterrorism and "hacktivism," a term coined by scholars to describe the marriage of hacking with political activism.[17] ("Hacking" is understood here to mean activities conducted online and covertly that seek to reveal, manipulate, or otherwise exploit vulnerabilities in computer operating systems and other software. Unlike hacktivists, hackers tend *not* to have political agendas.) Hacktivists have four main weapons at their disposal: virtual blockades, e-mail attacks, hacking and computer break-ins, and computer viruses and worms.

A virtual blockade is the virtual version of a physical sit-in or blockade: political activists visit a Web site and attempt to generate so much traffic toward the site that other users cannot reach it, thereby disrupting normal operations while winning publicity—via media reports—for the protesters' cause. "Swarming" may be caused by a large number of individuals who simultaneously access a Web site, thus deliberately causing its collapse. Swarming can also amplify the effects of the hacktivists' second weapon: e-mail bombing campaigns (bombarding targets with thousands of messages at once, also known as "ping attacks"). Conway reported on an e-mail bombing campaign launched in July 1997 against the Institute for Global Communications (IGC), a San Francisco–based Internet service provider (ISP) that hosted the Web pages of *Euskal Herria* (the *Basque Country Journal*), a publication edited by supporters of the Basque separatist group ETA.[18] The attackers wanted ETA's site removed from the Internet, so they bombarded IGC's Web site with thousands of e-mails, clogging the site, and threatened to attack other organizations using IGC services. IGC pulled the *Euskal Herria* site just a few days later. The Spanish government was suspected of being behind the e-mail bombing, but the identity of the attackers remains uncertain. Whether or not the suspicion is well founded, it underlines the fact that the hacktivists' tools are widely available and can be as easily employed by governments as by small groups of political activists.

Many cyberprotesters use the third weapon in the hacktivists' arsenal: Web hacking and computer break-ins (hacking into computers to access stored information, communication facilities, financial information, and so forth). For example, Dorothy Denning's report "Is Cyber Terror Next?" refers to the Computer Emergency Response Team Coordination Center (CERT/CC), a federally funded research and development center operated by Carnegie Mellon University, which in 1997 reported 2,134 computer security cases of break-ins and hacks. The number of incidents rose to 21,756 in 2000 and to almost 35,000 during the first three quarters of 2001.[19] In 2003, CERT/CC received more than a half-million e-mail messages and more than 900 hotline calls reporting incidents or requesting information. In the same year, no fewer than 137,529 computer security incidents were reported. However, since many, perhaps most, incidents are never reported to CERT/CC or any agency or organization, these numbers are even more troubling. Moreover, Denning notes, each single incident that is reported involves, in fact, thousands of victims. This rise in cyberattacks is likely related to the growing popularity of the Internet, to an apparently growing number of vulnerable targets, and to the development of sophisticated and easy-to-use hacking tools.

The fourth category of hacktivist weaponry comprises viruses and worms, both of which are forms of malicious code that can infect computers and propagate themselves over computer networks. Their impact can be enormous. The Code Red worm, for example, infected about a million servers in July 2001 and caused $2.6 billion in damage to computer hardware, software, and networks, and the I LOVE YOU virus, unleashed in 2000, affected more than 20 million Internet users and caused billions of dollars in damage. Although neither the Code Red worm nor the I LOVE YOU virus was spread with any political goals in mind (both seem to have been the work of hackers, not hacktivists), some computer viruses and worms have been used to spread political messages and, in some cases, inflict major damage. During the NATO operation to evict Serbian forces from Kosovo, businesses, public entities, and academic institutes in NATO member-states received virus-laden e-mails from a range of Eastern European countries. The e-mail messages, which had been poorly translated into English, consisted chiefly of defenses of Serbian rights and unsubtle denunciations of NATO for its unfair aggression. But the real threat was from the viruses. This was an instance of cyberwarfare launched by Serbian hacktivists against the economic infrastructure of NATO countries.

On October 22, 2002, the *Washington Post* reported that "the heart of the Internet network sustained its largest and most sophisticated attack ever." It was the result of a DoS attack on the thirteen "root servers" that provide the primary road map for almost all Internet communications worldwide. According to security experts, the incident probably consisted of multiple attacks against a single network to stop its operation. It caused no slowdowns or outages, thanks to safeguards built into the system, but a more sustained attack could have seriously damaged the world's electronic communications. In fact, in February 2000, the sites of Amazon.com, e-Bay, Yahoo!, and a host of other powerful companies were stopped for several hours due to DoS attacks.

Hacktivism, although politically motivated, does not constitute cyberterrorism. Hacktivists do want to protest and disrupt; they do not want to kill or maim or terrorize. However, hacktivism does highlight the threat of cyberterrorism: the potential that individuals with no moral restraint may use methods similar to those developed by hackers to wreak havoc. Moreover, the line between cyberterrorism and hacktivism may sometimes blur, especially if terrorist groups are able to recruit or hire computer-savvy hacktivists or if hacktivists decide to escalate their actions by attacking the systems that operate critical elements of the national infrastructure, such as electric power networks and emergency services.

Michael A. Vatis, head of the Institute for Security Technology Studies at Dartmouth College, classifies potential attackers in four categories. (There are other groups not on Vatis's list, including criminals who engage in extortion, identity theft, credit card fraud, bank fraud, and corporate espionage; and "insiders" who engage in sabotage, fraud, and so on.)[20]

- *Terrorists:* To date, few terrorist groups have used cyberterrorism, but they have shown interest in the Internet as a weapon and as a target. According to Vatis, the trends clearly point to the possibility of terrorists using the Internet as a weapon against critical infrastructure targets.

- *Nation-states:* Several nation-states, including supporters of terrorism, such as Syria, North Korea, Iran, Sudan, and Libya, may develop cyberwarfare capabilities.

- *Terrorist sympathizers:* These are the groups Vatis finds the likeliest to engage in cyberterrorism. They are a variety of hacker groups who can launch cyberattacks to show their support for a terrorist group or its cause.

- *Thrill seekers (or "cyber-joyriders"):* These, according to Vatis, are "hackers and 'script kiddies' who simply want to gain notoriety through high profile attacks. . . . However, such individuals can still have significant disruptive impact, as evidenced by the February 2000 DoS attacks and recent destructive worms."[21]

Why are hackers seen as threatening, and why are they often associated with terrorism? First, because the hackers themselves like to exaggerate their abilities. Douglas Thomas, a professor at the University of Southern California, spent seven years studying computer hackers in an effort to understand better who they are and what motivates them. According to Thomas,

> Hacking stories make good copy, but they are very rarely accurate, tending to exaggerate threats and downplay the realities of the event. There is a big difference between hacking into NASA's central control system (which has *not* happened) and hacking into the server that hosts their web page (which has happened repeatedly). Most media reports fail to distinguish between the two (or to explain that hacking a web page is essentially the same

as spray painting a billboard, posing very little actual risk). The media, moreover, tends to exaggerate threats, particularly by reasoning from false analogies such as the following: "If a 16-year-old could do this, then what could a well-funded terrorist group do?" The reality is that there is very little that a well-funded terrorist group could do that a 16-year-old hacker couldn't. And neither of them threatens us in a way that can rightly be called "terrorism."[22]

However, even the distinction between hackers and terrorists is becoming less lucid. In February 2004, Gen. John Gordon, who also served as chair of the Homeland Security Council, spoke at the RSA Conference in San Francisco.[23] Gordon argued that terrorists and so-called cyberterrorists share some key similarities in their tactics. "The al Qaeda enemy fights from the shadows," Gordon said. "This is similar to the cyberterrorist community. Both types of attackers also can carry out their plans with limited resources and can make multiple attempts to succeed in mounting an attack."[24] According to Gordon, the real concern should be minimizing vulnerabilities, not chasing potential cyber-terrorists: "Whether someone detonates a bomb that causes bodily harm to innocent people or hacks into a web-based IT system in a way that could, for instance, take a power grid offline and result in a blackout, the result is ostensibly the same: Both are acts of terrorism. . . . The damage will be the same whether the attacker was a bored teenager, an organized criminal or a [hostile] nation or state. We need to focus on the vulnera-bilities—and not get too hung up on who the attacker will be."[25]

A Growing Sense of Vulnerability

By the late 1990s cyberterrorism appeared to be a very realistic threat, leading Barry Collin to describe several scary scenarios in his vision titled "The Future of Cyberterrorism":[26]

- A cyberterrorist will disrupt the financial system, attacking the com-puter networks of banks, the stock exchanges, and large monetary organizations. This will lead people to lose confidence in the economic system.

- A cyberterrorist will attack air traffic control systems and cause two large civilian planes to collide. Similarly, attacks can target the control computers of train and metro systems.
- A cyberterrorist will access the computers of pharmaceutical manufacturers and change the formulas of medication produced by them, making the products life-threatening.
- The cyberterrorist will access the computers of energy systems and change the pressure in gas lines and cause valve failures or failure of the electrical grid.

Mark M. Pollitt adopted Collin's scenarios of the risks of cyber-terrorism and added that the same risks apply to "computers designed for the control of processes," that is, computers that control networks of computers.[27] *Black Ice: The Invisible Threat of Cyber-Terror,* a book by *Computerworld* journalist and former intelligence officer Dan Verton, published in 2003, describes the 1997 exercise code-named "Eligible Receiver," conducted by the National Security Agency (NSA).[28] The exercise began when NSA officials briefed thirty-five "Red Team" hackers on the rules. They were instructed to attempt to hack into and disrupt U.S. national security systems. Their primary target was the U.S. Pacific Command in Hawaii. The Red Team hackers were allowed to use only hacking software that could be downloaded freely from the Internet. They were allowed to penetrate any Pentagon network but prohibited from breaking any U.S. laws. Pretending to be hackers hired by the North Korean intelligence service, they started by mapping networks and obtaining passwords gained through "brute-force cracking" (a trial-and-error method of decoding encrypted data such as passwords or encryption keys by trying all possible combinations). Often they used simpler tactics, like calling somebody on the telephone, pretending to be a technician or high-ranking official, and asking for the password. The hackers managed to gain access to dozens of critical Pentagon computer systems. Once they entered the systems, they could easily create user accounts, delete existing accounts, reformat hard drives, scramble stored data, or shut systems down. They broke the network defenses with relative ease and without being traced or identified by the authorities.

The results were chilling and stunned the organizers. The Red Team, using only hacking tools available on the Internet, could break into the

U.S. military's Pacific command-and-control system and cripple it. It also revealed much broader vulnerabilities of the military systems. The NSA officials who examined the experiment's results found that much of the private-sector infrastructure in the United States, such as the telecommunications and electric power grids, could easily be invaded and abused in the same way.

The vulnerability of the energy industry is at the heart of Verton's *Black Ice*. Verton argues that America's energy sector would be the first domino to fall in a strategic cyberterrorist attack against the United States. The book explores in frightening detail how the impact of such an attack could rival or even exceed the consequences of a more conventional, physical attack. Verton claims that during any given year, an average large utility company in the United States experiences about a million cyberintrusions. Data on cyberattacks during the six months following the 9/11 attacks, collected by Riptech, Inc., a Virginia-based company specializing in the security of online information and financial systems, showed that companies in the energy industry suffered intrusions at twice the rate of other industries, with the number of severe or critical attacks requiring immediate intervention averaging 12.5 per company.[29]

Deregulation and an increased focus on profitability has made more modern companies and utilities move their operations to the Internet for the sake of improved efficiency and reduced costs. Verton argues that the energy industry and many other sectors have become potential targets for various disruptions by creating Internet links (both physical and wireless) between their networks and the supervisory control and data acquisition (SCADA) systems. These SCADA systems manage the flow of electricity and natural gas and control various industrial systems, such as chemical processing plants, water purification and delivery systems, wastewater management facilities, and a host of manufacturing firms. A terrorist's ability to control, disrupt, or alter the command and monitoring functions performed by these systems could threaten regional and, possibly, national security.

According to Symantec, one of the world's corporate leaders in the field of cybersecurity, new vulnerabilities to a cyberattack are being discovered all the time. The company reported that the number of "software holes" (software security flaws that allow malicious hackers to exploit the system) grew by 80 percent in 2002. Still, Symantec claimed that not a single cyberterrorist attack was recorded (applying the strict definition that it originate in a country on the State Department's terror watch list). Perhaps terrorists do not yet have the know-how to launch cyberattacks or perhaps most hackers are not sympathetic to the goals of terrorist organizations. However, should the two groups join forces, the results could be devastating.

Equally alarming is the prospect of terrorists themselves designing computer software for government agencies. Remarkably, as Denning describes in "Is Cyber Terror Next?" at least one such instance is known to have occurred:

> In March 2000, Japan's Metropolitan Police Department reported that a software system they had procured to track 150 police vehicles, including unmarked cars, had been developed by the Aum Shinryko cult, the same group that gassed the Tokyo subway in 1995, killing 12 people and injuring 6,000 more. At the time of the discovery, the cult had received classified tracking data on 115 vehicles. Further, the cult had developed software for at least 80 Japanese firms and 10 government agencies. They had worked as subcontractors to other firms, making it almost impossible for the organizations to know who was developing the software. As subcontractors, the cult could have installed Trojan horses to launch or facilitate cyber terrorist attacks at a later date.[30]

Despite stepped-up security measures in the wake of 9/11, a survey of 395 IT professionals, conducted for the Business Software Alliance during June 2002, revealed that about half (49 percent) of respondents felt that a cyberattack is likely, and more than half (55 percent) said the risk of a major cyberattack on the United States has increased since 9/11.[31] The figure jumped to 59 percent among those respondents who were in charge of their companies' computer and Internet security. Seventy-two percent agreed with the statement "There is a gap between the threat of a major cyberattack and the government's ability to defend against it," and the agreement rate rose to 84 percent among those respondents who were most knowledgeable about security. Those surveyed were concerned about attacks not only on the government but on private targets as well. Almost three-quarters (74 percent) believed that national financial institutions such as big national banks would be likely targets within the next year, and around two-thirds believed that attacks were likely to be launched within the next twelve months against the computer systems that run communications networks (e.g., telephones and the Internet), transportation infrastructure (e.g., air traffic control computer systems), and utilities (e.g., water stations, dams, and power plants).

A study released in December 2003 appeared to confirm the IT professionals' skepticism about the ability of the government to defend itself against a cyberattack.[32] The study, conducted by the House Government Reform Subcommittee on Technology, examined computer security in federal agencies over the course of a year and awarded grades. Scores were based on numerous criteria, including how well an agency trained its employees in security and the extent to which it met established security procedures such as limiting access to sensitive data and purging easily guessed passwords. More than half the federal agencies surveyed received a grade of D or F. The Department of Homeland Security, which has a division devoted to monitoring cybersecurity, received the lowest overall score of the twenty-four agencies surveyed. Also earning an F was the Justice Department, whose job it is to investigate and prosecute cases of hacking and other forms of cybercrime. Thirteen agencies improved their scores slightly compared with the previous year, nudging the overall government grade from an F up to a D. Commenting on these results, Rep. Adam H. Putnam (R–Fla.), chairman of the House Government Reform Subcommittee on Technology, declared, "The threat of cyberattack is real. . . . The damage that could be inflicted both in terms of financial loss and, potentially, loss of life is considerable."

Such studies, together with the enormous media interest in the subject, have fueled popular fears about cyberterrorism. A 2003 study by the Pew Internet and American Life Project found that nearly half the one thousand Americans surveyed were concerned that terrorists could mount attacks through the networks connecting home computers and power utilities. Eleven percent of respondents were "very worried," and 38 percent were "somewhat worried" about an attack launched through computer networks. The survey was taken in early August, before the major blackout struck the Northeast and before several damaging new viruses afflicted computers throughout the country. The level of public awareness concerning cyberterrorism may be even higher today, said Lee Rainie, director of the project.[33]

Former national security adviser Anthony Lake, in his book *Six Nightmares,* writes, "Millions of computer-savvy individuals could wreak havoc against the United States."[34] Lake warns that "the genie is well outside the bottle" and that "cyberattackers could crash planes, tamper with food or medicines to poison populations, or disrupt the economy by shutting down electrical and communication systems." But Lake is not the only high-ranking official warning us of cyberterrorism: in March 2001, National Security Adviser Condoleezza Rice and Richard Clarke, who then headed the U.S. counterterrorism campaign, warned against computer attacks that could wreak havoc on vital services in the United States. "It is a paradox of our times," said Rice, "that the very technology that makes our economy so dynamic and our military forces so dominating also makes us more vulnerable."[35] But how real is the threat of cyberterrorism? If there are so many active hackers (19 million, according to Lake's estimate), why were there no real cyberterrorist attacks?

How Real Is the Threat of Cyberterrorism?

Amid all the dire warnings and alarming statistics that the subject of cyberterrorism generates, it is important to remember one simple statistic: so far, there has been no recorded instance of a terrorist cyberattack on U.S. public facilities, transportation systems, nuclear power plants, power grids, or other key components of the national infrastructure. Cyberattacks are common, but terrorists have not conducted them, and those attacks that have occurred have not sought to inflict the kind of damage that would qualify them as cyberterrorism.

Technological expertise and the use of the Internet do not constitute evidence of planning a cyberattack. Joshua Green makes this point after reviewing the data retrieved from terrorists in Afghanistan: "When U.S. troops recovered al Qaeda laptops in Afghanistan, officials were surprised to find its members more technologically adept than previously believed. They discovered structural and engineering software, electronic models of a dam, and information on computerized water systems, nuclear power plants, and U.S. and European stadiums. But nothing suggested they were planning cyberattacks, only that they were using the Internet to communicate and coordinate physical attacks."[36]

Neither al Qaeda nor any other terrorist organization appears to have tried to stage a serious cyberattack. For now, insiders or individual hackers are responsible for most attacks and intrusions, and the motives are not political. According to a 2002 report issued by IBM Global Security Analysis Lab, 90 percent of hackers are amateurs with limited technical proficiency, 9 percent are more skilled at gaining unauthorized access but do not damage the files they read, and only 1 percent are highly skilled and intent on copying files or damaging programs and systems. Many hackers, it should be noted, are trying to expose security flaws in computer systems, mainly in those produced by Microsoft. Their efforts in this direction have sometimes embarrassed corporations but have also been responsible for alerting the public and security professionals to major security flaws in software. Moreover, although there are hackers with the ability to damage systems, disrupt e-commerce, and force Web sites offline, the vast majority of hackers do not have the necessary skills and knowledge. The ones who do generally do not seek to wreak havoc. In testimony before the House Subcommittee on Government Efficiency, Financial Management and Intergovernmental Relations in 2002, Douglas Thomas, who has interviewed hundreds of hackers,[37] stated, "With the vast majority of hackers, I would say 99 percent of them, the risk [of cyberterrorism] is negligible for the simple reason that those hackers do not have the skill or ability to organize or execute an attack that would be anything more than a minor inconvenience."[38] His judgment was echoed in "Assessing the Risks of Cyberterrorism, Cyber War, and Other Cyber Threats," a 2002 report written for the Center for Strategic and International Studies by Jim Lewis, a sixteen-year veteran of the State and Commerce Departments.[39] "The idea that hackers are going to bring the nation to its knees is too far-fetched a scenario to be taken seriously," Lewis claims. "Nations are more robust than the early analysts of cyberterrorism and cyberwarfare give them credit for. Infrastructure systems [are] more flexible and responsive in restoring service than the early analysts realized, in part because they have to deal with failure on a routine basis."[40]

Many computer security experts do not believe that it is possible to use the Internet to inflict death on a large scale. Some pointed out that the resilience of computer systems to attack is the result of significant investments of time, money, and expertise. As Green describes, nuclear weapons systems are protected by "air-gapping": they are not connected to the Internet or to any open computer network and thus are inaccessible to intruders, hackers, and terrorists. For example, the Defense Department protects sensitive systems by isolating them from the Net and even from the Pentagon's internal network.

The 9/11 events and the subsequent growing awareness of cyberterrorism highlighted other potential targets for such attacks. In 2002, Senator Charles Schumer (D–N.Y.) described "the absolute havoc and devastation that would result if cyberterrorists suddenly shut down our air traffic control system, with thousands of planes in mid-flight." However, argues Green, "cybersecurity experts give some of their highest marks to the Federal Aviation Administration, which reasonably separates its administrative and air traffic control systems and strictly air-gaps the latter."[41] And yet there are other sources of concern, including subway systems, gas lines, oil pipelines, power grids, communications systems, water dams, and public services that might be attacked to inflict mass destruction. Most of these are managed and controlled by computer systems and are in the private sector and thus more vulnerable than military or government systems. To illustrate the threat of such an attack, a June 2003 story in the *Washington Post* on al Qaeda cyberterrorism gave an anecdote about a teenage hacker who allegedly broke into the SCADA system at Arizona's Theodore Roosevelt Dam in 1998 and could have, according to the article, unleashed millions of gallons of water and thus threatened the neighboring communities. However, a probe by the computer technology news site CNet.com revealed the story to be exaggerated and said that the hacker could not have risked or damaged lives or property.

To assess the potential threat of cyberterrorism, Denning suggested that two questions be asked:[42] Are there targets that are vulnerable to cyberattacks? And are there actors with both the ability and the motivation to execute such attacks? The answer to the first question is yes: critical infrastructure systems are complex and therefore bound to contain weaknesses that might be exploited, and even systems that seem "hardened" against outside manipulation could be accessed by insiders, acting alone or in concert with terrorists, to cause considerable harm.

But what of the second question? According to Green, "Few besides a company's own employees possess the specific technical know-how required to run a specialized SCADA system."[43] There is, of course, the possibility of recruiting an employee or ex-employee of a targeted company or system. In April 2002, an Australian man attempted to discharge a million gallons of raw sewage along Queensland's Sunshine Coast, using the sewage treatment plant's computer system. The police discovered that he had worked for the company that designed the plant's control software. It is possible, of course, that such disgruntled employees might be recruited by terrorist groups, but even if the terrorists did enlist inside help, the degree of damage they could cause would still be limited. As Green argues, the employees of companies that handle power grids, oil and gas utilities, and communications are well rehearsed in dealing with the fallout from hurricanes, floods, tornadoes, and other natural disasters. They are also equally adept at containing and remedying problems that stem from human causes.

Denning draws our attention to a report titled "Cyber-Terror: Prospects and Implications," published in August 1999 by the Center for the Study of Terrorism and Irregular Warfare at the Naval Postgraduate School (NPS) in Monterey, California.[44] According to Denning, the report shows that terrorists generally lack the means and human resources needed to mount attacks that involve anything more than annoying but relatively harmless hacks. The study examined five categories of terrorist groups: ethnonationalist separatist, revolutionary, religious, New Age, and far-right extremist. Of these, only the religious groups were adjudged likely to seek the capacity to inflict massive damage. Hacker groups, the study determined, are psychologically and organizationally ill suited to cyberterrorism, and any massive disruption of the information infrastructure would run counter to their self-interest.

A year later, in October 2000, the NPS group issued a second report, this one examining the decision-making process by which substate groups engaged in armed resistance develop new operational methods, including cyberterrorism. As Denning points out, this report also shows that while substate groups may find cyberterrorism attractive as a nonlethal weapon, "Terrorists have not yet integrated information technology into their strategy and tactics, and significant barriers between hackers and terrorists may prevent their integration into one group."[45]

Another illustration of the limited likelihood that terrorists will launch a highly destructive cyberattack comes from a simulation sponsored by the U.S. Naval War College.[46] The college contracted with a research group to simulate a massive cyberattack on the nation's information infrastructure. Government hackers and security analysts met in July 2002 in Newport, R.I., and conducted a joint war game dubbed Digital Pearl Harbor. The results were far from devastating: the hackers failed to crash the Internet, although they did cause sporadic damage. According to an August 2002 CNet.com report on the exercise, terrorists hoping to launch such an attack "would require a syndicate with significant resources, including $200 million, country-level intelligence and five years of preparation time."

In May 2004, cyberterrorism expert Andy Cutts of Dartmouth College's Institute for Security Technology Studies reported a nationwide cyberterrorism simulation named Operation Livewire,[47] undertaken to test the preparedness of the United States in the event of a major cyberattack. It focused on an East Coast state and city, a West Coast state and city, and several corporations from the energy, banking, telecommunications, and trading sectors.

Cutts highlighted "the possibility of a sustained, campaign-level attack on the United States' computing networks, such as banking, law enforcement, energy and emergency response networks, by an unknown adversary. Because of the anonymous nature of cyberterrorism, such an attack could come from virtually any source, including an enemy state or a small terrorist group. . . . There have been examples of cyber attacks that have gone on for years, and the National Security Agency still does not know who is perpetrating them. There are hundreds of thousands of computers in this country that are compromised."[48] Cutts finds that through simulations like Operation Livewire, valuable lessons can be learned on how various agencies should respond to cyberattacks and what their own specific vulnerabilities are.

In May 2005 the CIA conducted a simulation of a sophisticated wave of cyberattacks on the United States, dubbed "Silent Horizon." The three-day war game was designed to test the capabilities of government and private agencies and counterterrorism units to respond to the threat of a sophisticated cyberattack. The scenario, set five years into the future, presented an attack by an imaginary coalition of anti-American terrorists and anti-globalization hackers. The simulation included devastating attacks with an impact that was compared with the 9/11 attacks. According to an Associated Press report, "The CIA's little-known Information Operations Center, which evaluates threats to U.S. computer systems from foreign governments, criminal organizations and hackers, was running the war game. About 75 people, mostly from the CIA, along with other current and former U.S. officials, gathered in conference rooms and pretended to react to signs of mock computer attacks."[49] Although the results of "Silent Horizon" were not reported, the significance of the simulation is in its premise that contravenes declarations by U.S. officials that such devastating impact of a cyberattack is not likely.

Cyberterrorism Today and Tomorrow

Following the 9/11 attacks, a group of computer scientists sent an alarming letter to President Bush about the danger of cyberterrorism, calling for the creation of a major Cyber-Warfare Defense Project, modeled on the Manhattan Project. However, despite the fears and the numerous warnings, the June 2005 editorial of the *New York Times* argued that,

> disturbingly little has been done. The Government Account-
> ability Office did a rigorous review of the Department of Home-
> land Security's progress on every aspect of computer security,
> and its findings are not reassuring. It found that the department
> has not yet developed assessments of the threat of a cyberattack
> or of how vulnerable major computer systems are to such an
> attack, nor has it created plans for recovering key Internet func-
> tions in case of an attack. The report also expressed concern that
> many of the department's senior cybersecurity officials have left
> in the past year. Representative Zoe Lofgren, the California
> Democrat who was among those who requested the G.A.O.
> report, said last week that it proved that "a national plan to
> secure our cybernetworks is virtually nonexistent."[50]

As Denning concludes, "At least for now, hijacked vehicles, truck bombs, and biological weapons seem to pose a greater threat than cyber terrorism. However, just as the events of September 11 caught us by surprise, so could a major cyber assault. We cannot afford to shrug off the threat."[51] There is growing evidence that modern terrorists are seriously considering adding cyberterrorism to their arsenal. "While bin Laden may have his finger on the trigger, his grandchildren may have their fingers on the computer mouse," remarked Frank Cilluffo of the Office of Homeland Security in a statement that has been widely cited. Verton, for example, argues that "al Qaeda [has] shown itself to have an incessant appetite for modern technology" and provides numerous citations from bin Laden and other al Qaeda leaders that show their recognition of this new cyberweapon.[52] After the 9/11 attacks, bin Laden stated to an editor of an Arab newspaper that "hundreds of Muslim scientists were with him who would use their knowledge . . . ranging from computers to electronics against the infidels."[53] And indeed, U.S. troops searching the caves in Afghanistan found plans by al Qaeda to attack computer systems after sending al Qaeda recruits to train in high-tech systems. One of these recruits was L'Houssaine Kherchtou, a thirty-six-year-old Moroccan who joined al Qaeda in 1991 and was sent to learn high-tech methods of surveillance from Abu Mohamed al-Ameriki ("the American").[54] Kherchtou joined other trainees in using electronic databases to learn about potential targets such as bridges and major sports stadiums. After his basic training, he joined al Qaeda's electronic workshop at Hyatabad in Peshawar, Pakistan, the center of al Qaeda's research and development for forging of electronic documents, message encoding and decoding, encryption techniques, and methods of breaking encryption. Several hacker groups have affiliated themselves with al Qaeda or with the global jihad, including al Qaeda Alliance Online, which appeared after 9/11 and consisted of three Pakistani hacker groups, and, more recently, OBL Crew, Islamic Hackers, and Afghan Hackers.[55]

Future terrorists may indeed find more possibilities for cyberterrorism than do the terrorists of today. Furthermore, the next generation of terrorists are now growing up in a digital world, one in which hacking tools are sure to become more powerful, simpler to use, and easier to access. "Cyber terrorism," says Denning, "could also become more attractive as the real and virtual worlds become more closely coupled, with automobiles, appliances, and other devices attached to the Internet. Unless these systems are carefully secured, conducting an operation that physically harms someone may be as easy as penetrating a Web site is today."[56] The notion of "coupled" attacks, or use of "magnifiers" (combining conventional strikes and cyberattacks), is the most alarming: for instance, a terrorist group might simultaneously explode a bomb at a train station and launch a cyberattack on the communications infrastructure, thus compounding the destructive impact of the event.

Ironically, success in the war on terror is likely to make terrorists turn increasingly to unconventional weapons such as cyberterrorism. The challenge before us is to assess what needs to be done to address this ambiguous but potential threat of cyberterrorism, but to do so without inflating its real significance and manipulating the fear it inspires. The threat of cyberterrorism may be exaggerated and manipulated, but we dare not deny or ignore it.

The use of the Internet by terrorists as described in the preceding three chapters has led several societies, and in particular the United States, to apply counterterrorism measures on the Net. In the next chapter we will examine these responses.

6

Fighting Back
Responses to Terrorism on the Internet, and Their Cost

> *Those who would give up essential liberties for a measure of security deserve neither liberty nor security.*
> —Benjamin Franklin

FIGHTING TERRORISM RAISES THE ISSUE of countermeasures and their cost. As terrorism experts John Arquilla and David Ronfeldt argue, "Terrorist tactics focus attention on the importance of information and communications for the functioning of democratic institutions; debates about how terrorist threats undermine democratic practices may revolve around freedom of information issues."[1] Since the advent of the Internet, the CIA, National Security Agency, FBI, and security services all over the world have seen it as both a danger and a useful instrument. Official statements have warned us of the ability of modern terrorism to use the Internet for global communication with relative anonymity. Recently many security services and agencies have been focusing on monitoring the Net, tracking down the terrorists using it, and learning from their Internet messages by means of monitoring networks based in as many as sixty countries. There have been numerous attempts, some secret and some not, to apply various systems and defense mechanisms against terrorists on the Internet. We will review some of these efforts and then examine their cost in terms of civil liberties.

Post 9/11 Counterterrorism Measures on the Net

Less than a week after the 9/11 attacks, several legislative steps were introduced to minimize the risk of additional terrorist attacks. Forty-five days later, President Bush signed the USA PATRIOT Act, a legislative step that increased the surveillance and monitoring capabilities of law enforcement agencies. The Electronic Privacy Information Center (EPIC), a civil liberties group based in Washington, D.C., criticizes the act, saying, "Though the Act makes significant amendments to over 15 important statutes, it was introduced with great haste and passed with little debate, and without a House, Senate or conference report. As a result, it lacks background and legislative history that often retrospectively provides necessary statutory interpretation."[2] The act was in fact a legislative step intended to strengthen the nation's defense against terrorism, including in its provisions the problematic monitoring of private communications and access to personal information. The act also included a so-called sunset provision, according to which certain "sections of the act automatically expire after a certain period of time, unless they are explicitly renewed by Congress." Some of the sunset provisions concern electronic surveillance and the FBI's use of an Internet-monitoring system called Carnivore.

New antiterror measures were suggested in other Western societies as well: in October 2001 Canada's justice minister presented a bill that proposed new police powers to monitor the Internet and private telephones: "Taking a cue from American anti-terror proposals, federal justice lawyers have drafted new provisions that would give police broader wiretap powers for criminal 'terrorist investigations' similar to those the Canadian Security Intelligence Service (CSIS) now has for security intelligence gathering."[3] The bill would have amended the Canadian Criminal Code, the Official Secrets Act, the Canada Evidence Act, and the National Defense Act. While legal concerns and procedures delayed passage of the Canadian bill, Canadian authorities remained anxious to extend their powers. Canadian police chiefs made clear in July 2004 that they "want the laws changed to make it easier for officers to access internet and cell phone communications."[4] Edgar MacLeod, president of the Canadian Association of Police Chiefs, stated, "Those who decide to prey on society—whether they are terrorists, those who move child pornography across borders within our country and across to other countries—use technology that police are unable to lawfully access."[5] France, too, reacted to the shock of 9/11 by adopting tougher antiterrorism measures that gave police the right to eavesdrop on private phone calls and e-mail. It also allowed investigative judges to require telephone or Internet companies to save wiretapped conversations and Internet data for up to a year. Similar measures were applied in Germany, the United Kingdom, and other European countries. This led Reporters Without Borders, an international media rights group, to criticize "not only authoritarian states such as China that tightly police Internet use, but also Western governments including the United States, Britain, France, Germany, Spain, Italy and Denmark and the European Parliament for using the fight against terrorism to increase surveillance on the Internet."[6]

The U.S. provisions suggested and applied after 9/11 have serious implications regarding civil liberties, including those affected by the interception of information transmitted over the Internet. EPIC argues:

> The [USA PATRIOT] Act increased the ability of law enforcement agencies to authorize installation of pen registers and trap and trace devices to record all computer routing, addressing and signaling information (a pen register collects the outgoing phone numbers placed from a specific telephone line; a trap and trace device captures the incoming numbers placed to a specific phone line). . . . By expanding the nature of the information that can be captured, the Act clearly extended pen register capacities to the Internet, covering electronic mail, Web surfing, and all other forms of electronic communications. However, the authorization is only for the traffic associated with the named subject of investigation.[7]

It is still difficult to assess the full impact of the act's most controversial measures, but civil libertarians and civil rights activists have been particularly worried about the act's green light to the government to eavesdrop on the Web browsers of innocent people. But as George Washington University law professor Orin Kerr argues, this is simply a misunderstanding of the act's provisions.[8] Kerr describes the USA PATRIOT Act's effect on Internet surveillance law as "the Big Brother that isn't."[9] According to Kerr, before the act no statute clearly limited the ability of the government, or even of a private party, to obtain basic information about electronic communications (such as private e-mails). But he notes that the act "made the privacy protections for the Internet as strong as those for phone calls and stronger than for mail," and that "the common wisdom on the USA Patriot Act is wrong. Far from being a significant expansion of law enforcement powers online, the Patriot Act actually changed Internet surveillance law in only minor ways and added several key privacy protections." Kerr focuses on three specific provisions of the act: "the provision applying the pen register law to the Internet, the provisions relating to Carnivore, and the new computer trespasser exception to the Wiretap Act." Kerr shows how "the Internet surveillance provisions of the Patriot Act updated the law in ways that both law enforcement and civil libertarians should appreciate." The act's Internet provisions, he concludes, "updated the surveillance laws without substantially shifting the balance between privacy and security."[10]

In 2003 a revised version of the USA PATRIOT Act was prepared. This version, titled the "Domestic Security Enhancement Act of 2003" and labeled informally as "PATRIOT II," expanded surveillance power, increased government access to private data, and broadened the definition of terrorist activities. "We're still reeling from the original USA Patriot Act's impact on civil liberties and now the government wants more," said Cindy Cohn, the legal director of the Electronic Frontier Foundation (EFF). "Where is the evidence that the law passed less than two years ago is insufficient? When will Congress draw the line and say 'this much of our civil liberties you've taken under the guise of terrorism—you may have no more'?"[11] The EFF attempted to document "the chilling effect that responses to the terrorist attacks of September 11, 2001, have had on information availability on the Internet as well as some sense of the effect on people trying to provide this information."[12] This is demonstrated by EFF's list of information available at its Web site, including Web sites shut down by the U.S. government, Web sites shut down by other governments, Web sites shut down or partially removed by the Web sites' owners, and U.S. government Web sites that have shut down or removed information.

Major criticism of PATRIOT II came also from the American Civil Liberties Union (ACLU). The ACLU argued, "The new 'anti-terrorism' legislation goes further than the USA PATRIOT Act in eroding checks and balances on presidential power and contains a number of measures that are of questionable effectiveness, but are sure to infringe on civil liberties."[13] Timothy H. Edgar, an ACLU legislative counsel, claims that "the new Ashcroft proposal threatens to fundamentally alter the Constitutional protections that allow us to be both safe and free. If it becomes law, it will encourage police spying on political and religious activities, allow the government to wiretap without going to court and dramatically expand the death penalty under an overbroad definition of terrorism."[14]

In January 2004, a federal judge struck down part of the USA PATRIOT Act: "In Los Angeles, the judge, Audrey B. Collins of Federal District Court, said . . . that a provision in the law banning certain types of support for terrorist groups was so vague that it risked running afoul of the First Amendment."[15] The case involved prosecuting people in Lackawanna, New York; Portland, Oregon; Detroit, Michigan, and elsewhere who were accused of providing funds, training, Internet services, and other forms of support to terrorist groups. This was based on a provision in the act that in fact broadened the former antiterrorism laws to prohibit any person from providing "expert advice or assistance" to known terrorist groups. The decision was hailed by civil liberties organizations, who saw it as an important victory in their war on certain federal antiterrorism initiatives.

There have been numerous other attempts to monitor the Internet, however: According to a report in the *Washington Post* in January 2003, "The Bush administration is quietly assembling an Internet-wide monitoring center to detect and respond to attacks on vital information systems and key e-commerce sites. The center, which has been in development for the past 15 months, is a key piece of the White House's national cybersecurity strategy and represents a major leap in the federal government's effort to achieve real-time tracking of the Internet's health."[16] Furthermore, as John Schwarz reported in the *New York Times* in December 2002:

> The Bush administration is planning to propose requiring Internet service providers to help build a centralized system to enable broad monitoring of the Internet and, potentially, surveillance of its users. The proposal is part of a final version of a report, "The National Strategy to Secure Cyberspace," set for release early next year, according to several people who have been

briefed on the report. It is a component of the effort to increase
national security after the Sept. 11 attacks. Such a proposal,
which would be subject to Congressional and regulatory
approval, would be a technical challenge because the Internet
has thousands of independent service providers, from garage
operations to giant corporations like America Online, AT&T,
Microsoft and Worldcom."[17]

Internet service providers expressed their concerns that the suggested
system could be used to track the activities of all individuals who use the
Net. Comparing the proposed monitoring system with Carnivore, the
Internet wiretap system used by the FBI, one official with a major data
services company said, "Am I analogizing this to Carnivore? Absolutely.
But in fact, it's 10 times worse. Carnivore was working on much smaller
feeds and could not scale. This is looking at the whole Internet."[18]
Stewart Baker, a lawyer representing large U.S. Internet providers, said,
"Internet service providers are concerned about the privacy implications
of this as well as liability, since providing access to live feeds of network
activity could be interpreted as a wiretap . . . used on phones without a
judicial order."[19]

According to a national survey conducted by the Pew Internet and
American Life Project, "The American public is sharply and evenly
divided on the question of whether the government should be able to
monitor people's e-mail and online activities. The opinion breakdown
on the question is 47% of Americans believe the government should not
have the right to monitor people's Internet use and 45% say the government should have that right. A majority of Internet users oppose government monitoring of people's e-mail and Web activities."[20]

The Singaporean Model

In any discussion of Internet security and legal measures to protect it,
several East Asian countries, and especially Singapore, can provide an
instructive example. According to James Gomez, in his article "Careful:
Someone Is Watching You Surf," "Governments in Asia have become
increasingly interested in cyber-surveillance, both to monitor and to
intimidate Internet users. In Asia, the politics of Internet security have
taken on a new urgency in the aftermath of September 11. For example,

legislation has been passed in almost every country in the region that expands the ability of state intelligence agencies to monitor the Internet. When combined with other regulatory pressures on the Internet coming from the private sector, the contours of control become tighter."[21]

The "war on terror" led by the United States has provided many Asian governments with a good excuse for cracking down on opposition groups, separatists, and dissidents who use the Net. Gomez points to the Thai example: "The cyber-information–surveillance relationship is well demonstrated by the Thai National Information Technology Committee, which announced intentions to restrict 'inappropriate' Internet content by retaining log files and caller IDs for three months, monitoring Internet cafes, as well as other measures."[22] Another example comes from India: in June 2000 the Indian Parliament passed a law that allows the government to capture private communications that seem to be potential threats to national security. The Indian government also passed provisions that target cybercafés and allow the Indian police to intercept Internet communication and even to require encryption keys or, if denied, subject users to up to seven years in jail.

China is widely regarded as the most repressive regime on Internet policy, and yet online activism has become more evident even as controls have been tightened. Alan Boyd's article "The Business of Stifling the Internet" provides some details on the measures used by the Chinese government: "China, with a reputed 30,000 full-time Internet surveillance operatives for the country's 45 million web surfers, now has access to the same cutting-edge technology that content providers were using to skirt its censorship regime. The Amnesty International report named Cisco Systems, Microsoft, Nortel Networks, Websense, and Sun Microsystems as multinationals that had supplied Beijing with Internet equipment without imposing any conditions on its use."[23] As Gomez reports,

> In January 2002, China's Ministry of Information Industry announced new regulations that required Internet service providers operating in "sensitive and strategic sectors" such as news sites and bulletin board services to record details about users, including viewing times, addresses, phone numbers and account numbers. ISPs are also required to install software that would record every message sent and received by their users. If an ISP finds a message that it thinks violates the law, the ISP must send

a copy of the message to three government agencies—the Ministry of Information Industry, the Ministry of Public Security and the Bureau for the Protection of State Secrets—then delete the message.[24]

In January 2004, Amnesty International listed the names of fifty-four Chinese nationals who had been detained or sentenced since November 2002 for expressing their opinions online or downloading information from the Internet. This was in addition to an unknown number of detained Chinese who were accused of disseminating information over the Net about the spread of severe acute respiratory syndrome (SARS). The model for China, as well as for other East Asian countries such as Myanmar, Laos, and Vietnam, was Singapore, whose Internet control system is arguably the most effective in Asia. Gomez argues that since the Singaporean government controls the three Internet service providers operating in Singapore, "the authorities were able to set up a computerized proxy server in the 1990s that screens all websites for content viewed as 'objectionable' or a potential threat to national security."[25]

Garry Rodan, in his article "The Internet and Political Control in Singapore,"[26] describes how the Singaporean model was learned and applied by its neighbors:

In September 1996, the Association of Southeast Asian Nations (ASEAN) committee on culture and information met in Singapore and agreed to collaborate on finding ways to control activities on the Internet. Although the agreement did not include the adoption of a common regulatory framework, only the representative of the Philippines rejected the idea of political control. Even before this, several Vietnamese delegations had visited Singapore to learn about Internet policing practices, and China sent senior information official Zeng Jianhui to the city-state for the same purpose. In both Vietnam and China, the intention is to steer electronic information flows through officially controlled channels to enhance monitoring and censorship. After a brief period of blocking access to 137 sites in September 1996, Chinese officials followed the Singapore example of more selective restriction and a greater reliance on the threat posed by the possibility of monitoring. In China the technique for this is more blunt, with subscribers to the Internet having to register with local security bureaus, enabling officials to ascertain who is visiting which web sites. In Indonesia there had been a comparatively tolerant and unregulated climate for the Internet, but this changed following the Jakarta riots of July 1996. Authorities banned a mailing list and arrested and interrogated a local university lecturer for messages sent to Holland about the riots. The Indonesian Armed Forces also subsequently established its own web page to counter critical perspectives on the regime. In Malaysia, where there is an ambitious program to attract the world's leading multimedia companies, Minister of Information Mohamed Rahmat has proposed that Internet users be licensed for "better control on the materials that appear in the Net."[27]

Singapore's Internet control laws were meant to deal with pornography and e-commerce but can now be adapted to terrorism-related threats or political communication. Singapore's strict laws to protect the country's computer systems from cyberattacks allow the monitoring of all computer activity and even the use of "preemptive" actions. Singapore has been tightening security since the 2002 Bali bomb attacks in neighboring Indonesia. In Japan, the interception of communication by the authorities (including e-mail) became legally possible with the May 2002 regulation of the monitoring of traffic on the Internet. In Malaysia, Web sites are monitored for "rumors" or "negative content." The Thai government shut down the Web site of the Muslim separatist group Pattani United Liberal Organization on October 26, 2002.

Since 9/11 many Asian governments are more eager to share information both on the methods of Internet surveillance and on their results: "In June 2002, Singapore proposed that Asian and European law enforcement agencies share intelligence in the name of combating terrorism and organized crime. The current US administration has indicated it is also in favor of information sharing and is currently designing the technology to do just that. This is a concerning possibility as it means that people can potentially be subject to all sorts of national laws besides their own."[28]

Monitoring the Internet

In April 2004, an e-mail message intercepted by National Security Agency (NSA) investigators led to a massive investigation conducted by intelligence officials of several countries. This investigation ended with the arrest of nine men in the United Kingdom and one in Ontario, Canada, who were later charged with facilitating a terrorist act and being part of a terrorist group.[29] This was the first time that the American regular monitoring of e-mail traffic led to an arrest. Behind the monitoring and the arrest was the "Puzzle Palace"—the NSA system at Fort Meade, Maryland. This is the nickname for the world's most powerful and sophisticated electronic eavesdropping and antiterrorism system. U.S. monitoring systems are positioned to monitor mostly U.S. Internet traffic, because many international gateways are located in the United States; once that electronic traffic reaches an American computer or server, it is routinely monitored by NSA spies. The Puzzle Palace operators rely on a sophisticated system of supercomputers to monitor and investigate millions of online and telephone messages every day.

The monitoring of the Internet by eavesdropping on e-mail and phone calls was supposed to help prevent crime and fight terrorism. Terrorists and criminals can be tracked better than before because their online moves, such as using a credit card, sending an e-mail message, booking a flight, or paying a toll, leave an electronic trail.[30] As Markoff and Schwartz report,

> In the Pentagon research effort to detect terrorism by electronically monitoring the civilian population, the most remarkable detail may be this: Most of the pieces of the system are already in place. Because of the inroads the Internet and other digital network technologies have made into everyday life over the last decade, it is increasingly possible to amass Big Brother-like surveillance powers through Little Brother means. The basic components include everyday digital technologies like e-mail, online shopping and travel booking, A.T.M. systems, cellphone networks, electronic toll-collection systems and credit-card payment terminals. In essence, the Pentagon's main job would be to spin strands of software technology that would weave these sources of data into a vast electronic dragnet.[31]

This development has an ironic dimension: as described in chapter 1, it was the Pentagon in the 1960s that first came up with the technology that led directly to the modern Internet. Now the same agency is relying on sophisticated technology to monitor abuse of the Internet, the same network it pioneered. This is the national surveillance system called Total Information Awareness, which was suggested by John M. Poindexter, the national security adviser under President Ronald Reagan. It is meant to search and identify the suspicious messages of potential terrorists from the everyday electronic traffic of millions of Internet users. The very notion of "total information awareness" has been criticized by civil libertarians, who "question its legal or constitutional grounds to conduct such electronic searches, and by others who called it an outlandishly futuristic and ultimately unworkable scheme on technical grounds."[32]

In March 2004, the FBI and the U.S. Justice Department demanded that technology companies be required to allow law enforcement agencies to install wiretaps on Internet communication traffic. This would increase the scope of the Communications Assistance for Law Enforcement Act, a 1994 law requiring telecommunications manufacturers to build into their products tools that U.S. investigators, after obtaining a court order, can use to eavesdrop on conversations. Fearful that federal agents cannot install wiretaps against criminals who have access to the most up-to-date communications technologies, lawyers for the Justice Department, FBI, and DEA argued that their proposals "require immediate attention and resolution" by the Federal Communications Commission. They called wiretaps "an invaluable and necessary tool for federal, state, and local law enforcement in their fight against criminals, terrorists, and spies."[33] "The ability of federal, state, and local law enforcement to carry out critical electronic surveillance is being compromised today," the government's lawyers wrote in legal papers filed with the FCC. "Communications among surveillance targets are being lost. . . . These problems are real, not hypothetical."[34]

Sniffers on the Net

Capturing traffic over the Net is called "sniffing," with the "sniffer" being the software that searches the traffic and grabs those items it is programmed to find. Intrusion detection systems (IDSs) use sniffers to match transmitted data, including e-mail messages, against a set of rules. Law enforcement agencies that need to monitor e-mail during an investigation may use a sniffer designed to capture extremely specific traffic. How does a sniffer operate? Computers are constantly communicating with other computers, using mostly a local area network (LAN). The network uses switches (a switch is a device that filters and directs packets sent on the Net) to block or not block users from getting the messages. If the network is not "switched," then the traffic destined for a computer in the network is broadcast to every computer. The sniffer program tells a computer to monitor the traffic headed to other computers. Then the sniffer peels away the layers of encapsulation and decodes the relevant information stored in the packet sent, including the identity of the source computer, that of the targeted computer, and every piece of information exchanged between the two computers. Following the 9/11 attacks, the FBI unveiled the (already in use) sniffer named Carnivore. The FBI explains the origin of the code name: "Carnivore *chews* all the data on the network, but it only actually *eats* the information authorized by a court order." Recently Carnivore was renamed DCS1000 to prevent it from sounding too much like a privacy-consuming predator.

In December 2004 it was reported that the CIA "had contributed money for a counterterrorism project that promised, among other things, an automated surveillance system to monitor conversations on Internet chat rooms."[35] The system was developed by two computer scientists at Rensselaer Polytechnic Institute in Troy, New York, and was supported by a special program of the National Science Foundation (NSF) called Approaches to Combat Terrorism. The CIA's targeting of chat rooms is based on the findings (see chapter 3) that modern terrorists communicate through public chat channels, where the volume of exchanged messages makes it difficult to know who is talking to whom. The new system would monitor both content and timing of messages to help isolate and identify conversations.

Carnivore and Its Threats

According to the FBI, Carnivore is much like the common Internet monitoring tools and commercial "sniffers" used daily by many Internet companies, Internet service providers (ISPs), and monitoring agencies. Basically, Carnivore operates like a telephone wiretap applied to the Internet. It examines each of the exchanged packets and records those that relate to suspicious issues. Carnivore's primary purpose is to intercept large volumes of e-mail and other forms of online communication passing through the Net. Jack Karp, in his article "Chewing on Carnivore," describes its functions: "Carnivore can be configured to perform several tasks: it can record all the e-mail messages sent to and from a specific e-mail account; it can record all of the network traffic to and from a specific IP address; it can record all of the e-mail headers sent to and from a specific e-mail account; it can record all of the servers, webpages or FTP files visited by a particular IP address; or it can track everyone who accesses a particular webpage or FTP file."[36]

Carnivore remains passive at all times; it does not change contents or messages and prevents no message from getting to its destination. This sophisticated sniffer theoretically can scan millions of e-mails per second, processing as much as six gigabytes (6,000 megabytes) of data every hour.[37] For Carnivore to gain access to Internet traffic, it must be plugged directly into the network at a central location. Since most Internet traffic in the United States flows through large ISPs, the FBI installs the Carnivore boxes inside the ISPs' data centers.

When the FBI's use of Carnivore was confirmed publicly, many concerns and criticisms were expressed by legislators, politicians, and activists who wanted to examine this new measure and its implications. Attorney General Janet Reno announced while in office that Carnivore would be considered by a Justice Department review panel and that the panel's recommendations would be made public. However, no such report was ever published, even after Reno left office. The main concern is that Carnivore gives the FBI access to the Internet traffic of *all* users of a given ISP, not just those identified by a court. This raises concerns about privacy issues. However, according to Pew Internet and American Life Project polls conducted in 2002, most Americans have not heard about Carnivore:

> While a majority of Americans approve of e-mail interception to fight crime, only 21% of all Americans have heard about Carnivore, the FBI's digital surveillance tool. Not surprisingly, Internet users, who are generally more likely to follow the news than non-users, are more likely to have heard about Carnivore. Twenty-six percent of Internet users have heard about it, compared to 15% of non-users. Online veterans (those with three or more years of online experience) are more likely to have heard about it than the newest users (those with six months' experience or less)—36% compared to 16%.
>
> Americans who have heard about Carnivore are split down the middle about whether it is good or bad. Forty-five percent of

people who have heard of it say Carnivore is good because it will
allow the FBI a new way of tracking down criminals. Another
45% say Carnivore is bad because it could be used to read
e-mails to and from ordinary citizens. Four percent of these
Carnivore-savvy Americans say "both" and 6% answer, "I don't
know."

While Internet users are more likely to have heard of Carnivore, online experience does not seem to play a role in forming
an opinion about it. Internet users and non-users express similar
views on both sides. Online veterans hold the same views on
Carnivore as newcomers.[38]

Most of the discussion about Carnivore has focused on the Fourth
Amendment. Some argue that by its nature, Carnivore violates the
Fourth Amendment protection against unreasonable search and seizure,
while others argue that a software tool by itself cannot violate the Con-
stitution if it is used properly and with proper authorizations. Moreover,
the reason the FBI developed Carnivore is that the sniffers then available
did not filter out what was needed—they pretty much swept up everything. However, according to the anonymous online report "Stop Carnivore Now," in addition to the threat to the Fourth Amendment, Carnivore poses three other dangers: the backdoor problem, the rogue agent
problem, and the mishap problem.

The Backdoor problem: In order to function, Carnivore must be
allowed full access to the data pipeline. When installed, Carnivore therefore provides a very high level of access to the data
pipeline that it monitors. In order to achieve this access, Carnivore must, by design, bypass all of the ISP's security measures,
which would otherwise block such efforts by an outside entity to
spy on the ISP's users. This opens up a backdoor into the network, and ISPs are powerless to protect it. There is no question
that there are hackers and computer experts who can break into
"secure" computer networks, and Carnivore provides hackers,
and those that fund them, with a new and very fruitful target. If
someone with untoward motives were to gain control of a Carnivore installation, they would have full, unrestricted access to
all of the data coming through that particular pipeline. This
means they could do anything from spying on people and
accessing their computers to shutting down websites and company servers, and so on. They could access identity information,
bank information, credit card information, etc. And all of this

presumably occurs without being detected by the ISP's security systems. However, some argue that if hackers get into a server, they can (and often do) install their own sniffers, so they do not need to bother with the FBI's Carnivore.

The Rogue Agent problem: What can a rogue agent do with access to Carnivore? Basically, anything he or she wants to. If Carnivore is scanning a server that hosts a bank, the rogue agent can access bank files. The rogue agent can intercept and even alter e-mails or websites, perform damaging acts, commit corporate espionage, and so on. Instead of having to steal papers, the rogue agent powered by Carnivore simply loads the info onto a disk, or even e-mails it to his or her cohorts, and then covers up his or her tracks. This argument is criticized, too: Carnivore cannot be used to access bank files. It only picks up network traffic. Carnivore also doesn't have the capability to alter the data stream or to alter websites. It just filters and collects packets.

The Mishap problem: As noted above, Carnivore is installed at the very central part of a network, and all the data to and from that location flows through it. If something goes wrong in a Carnivore installation, it could interfere with a substantial portion of the Internet. Indeed, Carnivore has been at the root of at least one network mishap already (in 1999 the FBI forced Earthlink to install Carnivore on one of their networks and caused that portion of their network serious problems). There may be more instances of Carnivore disrupting service in other installations, but no information has been released about any other case in which Carnivore has been used. Carnivore takes ultimate control out of the hands of Internet Providers, and puts it in the hands of those whose primary motivation is not providing secure Internet connectivity, but rather surveillance and investigation.[39]

Magic Lantern

Encryption is software that locks computerized information to keep it private; only those with an "electronic key" can decode the information. Finding a way to crack encryption has typically baffled law enforcement agencies. According to legal expert Matthew Parker Voors, "If the government discovered a suspicious e-mail that was encrypted, and wanted to read it, it had two options: it could obtain the private key from the sender, or it could attempt to break the code through a brute-force attack. The first option, requiring that a terrorist supply the private key, is not plausible, because this would alert the terrorists to the investigation. The second option, cracking the code by a brute-force attack, is possible, but the process involves a massive amount of computer power and a correspondingly large number of staff hours."[40] Neither option is attractive, so a third option evolved: the FBI has confirmed the introduction of its latest Internet-eavesdropping system, code-named "Magic Lantern." Magic Lantern is a program that, once installed on a suspect's computer, records every keystroke typed. These gathered keystrokes are then analyzed by the FBI to find passwords, and using these "harvested" passwords, the FBI can access the suspect's e-mail messages and documents and even the computers contacted by the suspect. Thus, Magic Lantern allows the FBI to record a suspect's keystrokes and learn his private encryption key. And yet the FBI is not "stealing" the key but records it only after a process of authorization and when the individual involved is a suspect in terrorist activity. Therefore, FBI-developed tools such as Magic Lantern, some argue, are designed to protect civil liberties more than they are usually protected by commercial surveillance tools.

Magic Lantern differs substantially from Carnivore in design and, as civil libertarians will argue, in its intrusion on personal privacy. While Carnivore is installed "between" the suspect's computer and the Internet, typically at the suspect's Internet service provider, Magic Lantern is installed directly on the suspect's computer. The FBI has already employed Magic Lantern and used it for the conviction of mobster Nicodemo Scarfo. By recording Scarfo's keystrokes, the FBI was able to find his encryption keys and decode files that were later used in his prosecution.[41]

Civil liberty groups argue that the use of Magic Lantern raises important legal issues, such as the need for a wiretap order from a U.S. judge: "It's an open question whether the covert installation of something on a computer without a physical entry requires a search warrant," said David Sobel, a lawyer with EPIC.[42] Sobel does not reject outright the use of Magic Lantern but raises several cautions: "This is breaking new ground for law enforcement, to be planting viruses on target computers. It raises a new set of issues that neither Congress nor the courts have ever dealt with." Stealing encryption keys is a sensitive issue, as Sullivan points out:

"[It] could be touchy ground for federal investigators, who have always fretted openly about encryption's ability to help criminals and terrorists hide their work. During the Clinton administration, the FBI found itself on the losing side of a lengthy public debate about the federal government's ability to circumvent encryption tools. The most recently rejected involved so-called key escrow—all encryption keys would have been stored by the government for emergency recall."[43]

Other experts, including Voors, see Magic Lantern as capable of curing many of the ills that trouble law enforcement: Magic Lantern can turn monitoring encrypted e-mail and other Internet traffic into a selective process. Also, the Fourth Amendment concerns about the Carnivore system are reduced, since Magic Lantern targets only specific computers or e-mails, thus eliminating the need to cast too wide a net. Voors concludes:

> These factors, when coupled with a form of judicial oversight, will provide law enforcement with the tools they need to investigate suspects while adhering to constitutional guarantees. . . . Not only does Magic Lantern allow lax encryption regulation, but it also targets only those individuals who the government has probable cause to suspect of engaging in terrorist activities. It ensures privacy and protection for businesses while giving terrorists a false sense of security. Further, Magic Lantern should be governed by existing constitutional protections; thus, there would not be a need for additional regulations. Magic Lantern solves the problem of encryption regulation as it takes away the need to regulate encryption altogether.[44]

"Virtual Warriors": Private Initiatives

Fighting terrorism on the Net is not purely a governmental domain; there are numerous forms of private initiatives as well. One of them is the brainchild of Professor Abraham Kandel, executive director of the National Institute for Systems Test and Productivity in the United States, a federally funded research institute operated by the University of South Florida and sponsored by the Space and Naval Warfare Systems Command. Although most of the institute's work is secret, it is reported to be developing tools to monitor information about terrorist activity on the Internet.[45] The programs that Kandel's team is working on are sniffers that constantly check online traffic to find those e-mails that could lead them to terrorists. "Our programs analyze sentences such as 'I sent you ten yams and five lemons' and have to decide whether the sender of the message is a greengrocer or a terrorist who is informing someone about a shipment of explosives," Kandel explained to Yuval Dror, author of an April 2004 article titled "Cyberspace Warriors," which appeared in *Haaretz*.[46] "We want to know everything. We want to know who's using the Internet and how they are using it. 'Who's who in the zoo' is the best description I can offer of our motivation: we want to know where everyone is located, in which cage. If he changes his color, like a chameleon, and disappears, we still want to locate him using our method of operation. We want to identify transfers of money, knowledge or instructions of terrorist bodies." Kandel was unwilling to reveal whether his system integrates with Carnivore: "Carnivore is not a program but a concept. It's possible that our tools can be integrated into Carnivore, but that's not my decision, and in any event those who use our programs don't report to me about where and how they use them."

Kandel uses a combination of mathematics and computers known as "computational intelligence." It encompasses developments and theories in fields such as "fuzzy logic," sensor networks, genetic algorithms, data mining, and others. Using these methods, the computers apply a "learning" system. Instead of employing thousands of people to go over every item and evaluate it, the computer does the necessary filtering by emulating people's evaluations and decision-making style. The result is that only the pieces of information that the computer deems especially important are selected for human examination. Moreover, the computers are programmed to learn from each new decision they make, thus becoming "smarter."

"The real battle is moving from the conventional fields to cyberspace," Kandel explains. "Ten divisions of tanks and five air squadrons wouldn't have helped stop September 11. Accordingly, the tools that are used to fight the new warfare also have to be different. We are an organization of five initials; we get our information from organizations of three initials," he says, referring both to USF (University of Southern Florida) and intelligence organizations of three initials: the CIA, FBI, and NSA. "The systems we have developed don't search aimlessly through databases and Internet communications. They are fed with diverse pieces of information. If you don't know what to look for, everything seems to be the same color and there's no way to select between the legal and the illegal. But if you know where to start, it becomes simpler."

Kandel is aware of the privacy concern, but he points out, "Our job is to find the needle in the haystack before it's too late." When asked about the problem of balance—do we have to fight terrorism at any price?—he replies, "No, not at any price, but it seems to me that the price we are paying is a proper one. Do you have any doubt that every one of the families of those who were killed in the terrible attack would be ready to have their e-mail scanned, to have it monitored, if that would have prevented the attack?"

Since September 11, terrorism-on-the-Web experts have been in high demand by counterterrorism agencies, private companies, and security services. But as *Los Angeles Times* journalist Richard Schmitt points out, "There are experts, and there are 'experts.' Some who have been in the terrorism field a long time say that although the number of new entrants has increased, the quality of the debate has declined—and often borders on sensationalism."[47] "You have *Foreign Affairs* meeting the *National Enquirer*," says Brian Jenkins, a senior researcher at RAND Corporation who has been studying terrorism for more than thirty years and remembers when the number of people seriously studying the topic was "a tiny little mafia."[48] Questions are also being raised about the credentials and motives of some of the experts.

Rita Katz, a leading investigator of jihadi and Islamist Web sites who heads the SITE Institute, is an Iraqi-born Jew whose father was executed by the Saddam Hussein regime. She has worked with federal investigators in terrorism cases and is cited in Richard A. Clarke's book *Against All Enemies* as helping to provide information to the U.S. government on the al Qaeda network. However, Katz has been criticized for her work, and she argues that she has been the victim of a smear campaign: "As they were never able to challenge the accuracy of my research, and as they were upset by the ramifications of it in terms of arrests, indictments, and raids, a few Muslim activist organizations have on occasion tried to portray me as a Muslim-basher," she said in a statement. "I have no quarrel with Islam or Muslims, and I only target terrorists and their supporters."[49] Katz does contract work for U.S. governmental departments and is frequently quoted in the media both within the United

States and elsewhere, suggesting that many regard her work as reliable and accurate.

Evan Kohlmann, a law student at Georgetown University, got an internship with the Investigative Project, a counterterrorism think tank directed by Steven Emerson. Emerson, a former investigative journalist, is a terrorism researcher whose 1994 documentary *Terrorists among Us: Jihad in America* revealed militant Islamic groups operating within the United States. Kohlmann studied, undercover, terrorist groups in Europe and wrote articles for scholarly journals. One article published in the spring of 2000, describing the growth of Internet sites commissioned by Islamic militants, concluded, "Unless decisive action is taken soon, this building fanaticism will certainly manifest itself beyond mere online propaganda into an outburst of uncontrolled violence."[50]

Since the September 11 attacks Kohlmann has combined his studies with his consulting business, served as a witness in two federal terrorism prosecutions, and briefed government officials. Much of his work has involved online swapping of intelligence such as terrorist training manuals and the location of Web sites used by alleged terrorist groups—a process he likens to "trading baseball cards." He stores what he retrieves in a huge electronic archive that can be mined for future use. For example, Kohlmann assisted U.S. officials in a trial in Virginia in February 2004 in which individuals were charged with aiding the Pakistan-based LeT, designated by the State Department as a terrorist group. The evidence against them included e-mail exchanges that referred to several Web sites that were no longer online. Kohlmann was able to track down these sites in his computer archive and reported that they contained anti-American propaganda as well as a graphic presentation of the New York skyline in flames—two years before the September 11 attacks.

The American Anti-Terrorism Coalition (ATC) was founded on April 30, 2003, by a Web master known by the nickname Stalfos.[51] According to Stalfos, "[The ATC's] goal is to unite as many anti-terrorists against terrorism as possible, and within a month, the ATC became the most famous anti-terrorism webring on the Internet . . . which has so far over a thousand members." In April 2004, ATC released a database of terrorist Web sites and groups (with over three hundred entries), focusing mainly on extreme Islamic groups. The ATC Web site states, "The purpose of this list is to expose all the terrorist and pro-terrorist websites and e-Groups that exist," and it also provides the details of the ISPs so that protests can be forwarded to those hosting companies.

Removing Information from the Net

The government has responded to the threat of terrorist data mining by removing "sensitive" information from the Internet. As a study published in 2003 by the Pew Internet and American Life Project concludes,

> One of the most important and potentially long-term impacts of the 9/11 events and their aftermath is how they compelled government officials and ordinary Americans to consider what kinds of information should be made available online. As a rule, and in many cases by the dictates of law, much of the information that government collects about American manufacturers, utilities, and transportation firms is made public. But after 9/11, the creators of various government Web sites chose to remove sensitive information that could potentially be useful to terrorists. This included information such as emergency response plans for chemical plants, GIS data, detailed maps and descriptions of nuclear facilities, reports on chemical transportation security, and information on water supplies.[52]

OMB (Office of Management and Budget) Watch, a nonprofit organization that promotes government accountability, published a report in 2002 that listed more than a dozen U.S. government agencies and three state Web sites that had moved to prevent public access to information previously available without restriction.[53] The report noted:

- The Agency for Toxic Substances and Disease Registry removed a report on security at chemical plants, and the Army Corps of Engineers site that contained information about a military command center near Washington was placed behind a firewall so that a username and password are now required for access.
- The Department of Energy's National Transportation of Radioactive Materials site has been replaced with the note, "This site temporarily unavailable."
- Most Geographic Information Services at the Bureau of Transportation Statistics were made unavailable.

- The Department of Transportation (DOT) limited access to the National Pipeline Mapping System of the Office of Pipeline Safety, which lays out the network of high-pressure natural gas pipelines throughout the nation, and to the site of the Geographic Information Services section of the DOT's Bureau of Transportation Services. Access to these highly detailed maps of roads and utilities is now limited to federal, state, and local government officials.

- The Environmental Protection Agency has pulled from its site risk management plans, which contain detailed information about the dangers of chemical accidents—such as toxic plume maps and emergency response plans after a refinery explosion.

- The Federal Aviation Administration has pulled data from a site listing enforcement violations such as weaknesses in airport security.

- The Federal Energy Regulatory Commission has removed documents that detail specifications for energy facilities from its Web site.

- The International Nuclear Safety Center has removed its reactor maps and left the following message: "If you requested access to the maps of nuclear power reactor locations, these maps have been taken offline temporarily pending the outcome of a policy review by the U.S. Department of Energy and Argonne National Laboratory."

- The Los Alamos National Laboratory has removed a number of reports from its laboratory publications page.

- NASA's John Glenn Research Center noted, "Public access to many of our web sites is temporarily limited. We apologize for any inconvenience."

- The Nuclear Regulatory Commission took down its Web site.

- The U.S. Geological Survey has removed a number of pages from its registered online water-resources reports database.

- The Internal Revenue Service removed a page that contained information for IRS employees displaced as a result of 9/11.

- The National Archives and Records Administration discontinued access to some archival materials.

- The National Imagery and Mapping Agency stopped the sale of large-scale digital maps as well as the downloading of maps from its archives.

- The U.S. Geological Survey removed multiple reports on water resources.

- The State of Florida prevented access to information on crop dusters and certain driver's license information.

- The State of New Jersey removed chemical storage information.

- The State of Pennsylvania withheld certain environmental information.[54]

In addition, the *Washington Post* reported on October 4, 2001, that "the Centers for Disease Control and Prevention, housed under the Department of Health and Human Services, removed a report on chemical terrorism from their Web site."[55]

On October 12, 2001, Attorney General John Ashcroft "urged federal departments and agencies to 'carefully consider' the disclosure of sensitive information under the Freedom of Information Act (FOIA) and assured them that any decisions to withhold records would be defended by the Department of Justice. On March 19, 2002, a memo issued by White House Chief of Staff Andrew Card called for an immediate re-evaluation of any classified, reclassified, declassified or 'sensitive but unclassified' material whose disclosure could prove to be harmful."[56] These calls resulted in the removal of material and, in some cases, in the shutting down of entire Web sites. The Pew survey from June 26 to July 26, 2002, found little awareness among Americans of these acts, but also strong support for removal of information:

> Just 25% of the public (28% of Internet users) were aware that government agencies had pulled information from Web sites. And only 5% of Internet users said they had noticed that information they expected to be on a government Web site was missing. Nonetheless, Americans have definite views about what government agencies should and should not do with sensitive information on their Web sites: . . . 67% of Americans believe the government should remove information from its Web sites that might potentially help terrorists, even if the public has a right to know that information. Similarly, two-thirds of Americans believe businesses and utilities should not put information that might help terrorists on their Web sites.[57]

Despite wide support for the removal of Web sites containing sensitive information, "many Americans believe that taking government information off the Internet will not make a difference in battling terrorists: 47 percent say that the act of withholding or removing information from government sites will not make a difference in deterring terrorists; 41 percent say that taking information off government websites will hinder terrorists; and some 12 percent of Americans are uncertain whether those acts will help or not."[58] The Pew interviewers also asked those who favored the continued posting of sensitive information on certain Web sites "whether their views would change if the government argued that this information could help terrorists."[59] Their responses indicated a widespread readiness to bar the information from the Internet:

- 60 percent of those who originally believed the government should post information about chemical plants and the chemicals they produce said that material should be removed from the Internet if the government said it could help terrorists.

- 55 percent of those who originally believed the government should post information about nuclear plants said that material should be removed from the Internet if the government said it could help terrorists.

- 54 percent of those who originally believed the government should post information about the pollution caused by individual factories said that material should be removed from the Internet if the government said it could help terrorists.[60]

In chapter 4 we saw that the Internet is a useful source of information for terrorists, but is the removal of Web sites and whole libraries of information from Web sites an effective step in combating terrorism? Not really, judging from a RAND Corporation study published in 2004.[61] The RAND study turned up no publicly accessible federal geospatial information considered critical to terrorists' needs. The report, titled *Mapping the Risks: Assessing the Homeland Security Implications of Publicly Available Geospatial Information,* states, "Although publicly available geospatial information on federal Web sites and in federal databases could potentially help terrorists select and locate a target, attackers are likely to need more detailed and current information—better acquired from direct observation or other sources." These other sources include textbooks, nongovernmental Web sites, trade journals, and street maps.

RAND noted that "[p]ublic access to this vast quantity of federal geospatial information has many benefits for the nation. For example, the information is used to assist law enforcement agencies, advance scientific knowledge, inform people about environmental risks, help communities prepare and respond to natural disasters and other emergencies, create more accurate maps, assist economic development efforts, and help a wide array of government agencies do their jobs more effectively."[62]

Assaults on Web Sites

While some information is being removed from Web sites, other sites may serve as the battleground for a virtual war in cyberspace, and such battles are already on. Web sites are being attacked, hacked, and destroyed. One of the apparently easiest ways to challenge terrorists on the Net is to attack their sites. Such actions are not new. In October 2000, the Hezbollah Web site contained a surprise: any hit on the Hezbollah home page was greeted with the Israeli flag, some text in Hebrew, and a short recording of "Hatikva," the Israeli national anthem. Israeli hackers had launched their Internet assault on Hezbollah. In the same week, Arab hackers struck back: "In a sustained, coordinated counterattack, Web sites of the Israeli army, Foreign Ministry, prime minister and parliament, among others, have been staggered by a barrage of hundreds of thousands—possibly millions—of hostile electronic signals. 'We checked it and for what we found, this is the first full-scale war in cyberspace,' said Gilad Rabinovich, CEO of NetVision, Israel's largest Internet provider. 'It's costing a lot of money and human resources. . . . Instead of being billable, our technical experts are busy protecting the Web sites.'"[63]

In 2001, an Israeli hackers' group named "m0sad" (not to be confused with Mossad, the Israeli intelligence agency) defaced the Internet home page of the ISP Destination, a company that serves al-Manar television, the official Web site of Hezbollah. Visitors to the defaced Web site found a black screen with the title: "site closed by m0sad." Then the hackers posted a question: "How come that the [P]alestinians that claims that they want to be like Europians [sic] are executing people in public without a fair justice like in Pakistan, Iran, Iraq?" In August 2001 Israeli hackers shut down the site of the official Palestinian news agency, Wafa, and replaced an unofficial Hamas site with a link to a pornography site.

Despite these Israeli hack attacks, Palestinian hackers are fighting back fiercely: According to Robyn Weisman, "There have been around 40 pro-Israeli assaults against Web sites sympathetic to the Palestinian cause, versus over 200 assaults against Israeli Web sites by Palestinian hackers."[64]

Since the beginning of the second Intifada in October 2000, Israeli and Palestinian hackers have been exchanging virtual blows in cyberspace, spamming some sites with junk mail to cause overload and knock the site off the Web, and manipulating code to deface others. Although no blood is spilled, the war is dangerous despite its virtual nature. In an interview for the *Jerusalem Post,* the author pointed out, "Internet violence, or virtual violence on the Internet and in cyberspace, is a scary option because you never know where it will end. I see it as a very risky battle when virtual blows are exchanged on the Internet in the form of harming one another's sites. The whole idea of the Internet is that it is free, that nobody controls it, and everybody can say what he wants."[65]

The 9/11 attacks triggered a vicious cycle of hacker wars. Western hackers and hacking groups called for retaliation for the terrorist attacks on the World Trade Center and Pentagon. They specified as targets Pakistani and Afghani Web sites. On September 12 the official Web site of the government of Pakistan was defaced, and so were the Web sites of the Afghan News Network and Afghan Politics, Taleban.com, and other sites. Spam was also used as a weapon in attacks on the Web sites of those supporting Islamic fundamentalism and terrorism. On September 16, 2001, the Dispatchers, a group that promised to target the terrorists behind 9/11 and to attack Palestinian and Afghan Web sites, defaced the Web site of the Iranian Ministry of the Interior. Another group, the Young Intelligent Hackers Against Terror (YIHAT), a prominent pro-U.S. hacking group founded by the German hacker Kim Schmitz, set out to gather information on terrorists and give this information to U.S. authorities. Although YIHAT condemned Web defacements, numerous defacements have been committed in YIHAT's name. In retaliation for these pro-U.S. hack attacks, on September 14 a hacker known as Fluffi Bunni defaced thousands of Web sites. The message he posted in the defaced sites read, "Fluffi Bunni Goes Jihad." Another revenge attack was launched by a Pakistani hacker group, GForce Pakistan, known for defacements of Israeli, Indian, and U.S. government Web sites. On October 17, 2001, GForce Pakistan hacked the National

Oceanic and Atmospheric Administration's Web server, and a few days later, the Web site of the U.S. Department of Defense was defaced by GForce hackers.

One of the most active players in the war launched against terrorist Web sites is Aaron Weisburd, who operates Internet Haganah (internet-haganah.co.il/haganah/). On its Web site, Internet Haganah describes itself as "a volunteer effort to research, report on, and stop the use of the Internet as a communications and propaganda tool by Islamist terrorist groups, their supporters and apologists." Weisburd and his colleagues try to find and identify terrorist sites and inform their ISPs so that the ISPs will remove the sites from the Net (the "name-and-shame" strategy). Most ISPs quickly remove the site when they learn that it belongs to a terrorist organization or has content that violates the terms of service. In July 2004 a Muslim group called Kataeb Mujahedeen sent Weisburd a letter threatening him with decapitation unless he closed down his Web site. As of mid-2004 Internet Haganah has helped to get more than 450 "terrorist-supporter sites" shut down. These include sites of organizations such as al Qaeda, al-Muhajiroun, Hamas, Palestinian Islamic Jihad, Popular Resistance Committee, and many others. Listed below are three of Weisburd's successes:

- *Maac.ws* and *qawim.org*—Weisburd described these Arabic-language sites as "linked to al Qaeda." Internet Haganah notified the sites' host, Amana Technology in Canada, which took them down.

- *Alerhat.com*—Another Arabic-language site, it featured an Arabic-language forum that was frequently visited by supporters of al Qaeda, along with pages dedicated to instructions on how to stage cyber-attacks against Internet Haganah Web sites. The Arabic name of the site was nothing if not forthright: "The Islamic Terrorist Forum."

- *Alneda*—This was the primary site of al Qaeda, located by Weisburd, which (like many others) frequently goes down but keeps popping back up with different names.[66]

Sometimes the counterattack takes the form of a network shutdown. In November 2001, the Bush administration charged the Somalia Internet Company (SIC), Somalia's only Internet company, and a major Somali telecom business, with being financially linked to Osama bin

Laden. SIC's operations were closed as a consequence. "Along with deny-
ing all Internet access to Somalis, the closures have severely restricted the
country's international telephone lines and shut down vitally needed
money transfer facilities. In addition, all Internet cafes were shut down,
and international phone lines run by two other companies were failing
to cope with the extra pressure of calls."[67]

In July 2002, the Israeli Defense Forces (IDF) captured Palnet, the
leading Palestinian Internet service provider, and shut down the ISP's
operations. The move reduced Internet access for most of the users in
the West Bank and Gaza. This was part of a larger effort by the Israeli
military to limit Palestinians' use of the Internet and other media. The
Israelis argued that they did this to fight terrorism and the use of the Net
by Palestinian terrorists. The IDF presented evidence of the ways in
which terrorists are using the Internet to plan and instruct. For example,
the IDF posted on its own Web site material allegedly downloaded from
the Hamas site. This material included debates among Hamas members
on whether arsenic, rat poison, or cyanide would be most effective in
killing Americans.

On December 15, 2004, the FBI raided the Web site of the Islamic
Bloc (al-Kotla al-Islamiyyah) on the Internet and closed it down. The
Islamic Bloc, reportedly linked to Hamas, promised to repost its Web
site within two days. Four days later this author found the "reemerging"
site by using a link posted on a pro-Hamas chat room.

Banning Terrorist Web Sites: The Kahane-Kach Case

In October 2003, the United States included on its terrorism blacklist,
for the first time, Internet Web sites. These were four Web sites run by
supporters of Rabbi Meir Kahane, founder of the Kach movement, and
designated thereafter as being operated by "foreign terrorist organizations (FTO)."[68] The four Web sites were www.Kahane.org, www.Kahane
.net, www.Kahanetzadak.com, and www.newkach.org. The Kach movement promotes "the restoration of the biblical state of Israel," and its
members have been involved in attacks against Arabs. Baruch Goldstein
was one of the main reasons for the Kach movement's reputation: Goldstein killed twenty-nine Arabs in a February 1994 shooting spree in
Hebron's Tomb of the Patriarchs. He was affiliated with Kach and was

praised by the movement. Kahane himself was killed in 1990 by a member of an al Qaeda–aligned terrorist group. Kahane's son, Binyamin, and Binyamin's wife were killed in a Palestinian attack in the West Bank in 2000. Neither the Kach movement nor its splinter groups have been formally charged in Israel or the United States.

The State Department designation bans donations to the Kach Web sites. Three of the sites offer books and provide information on where contributions can be sent. Israel declared the Kahane movement a terrorist group in 1994, and the Kach and Kahane Lives organizations were declared terror organizations and placed on the State Department blacklist in 1995, with their supporting Web sites being added eight years later.

The significance of the State Department's terrorist designation was not immediately clear for the organization's Internet presence and certainly not very effective. Despite the fact that the two banned organizations (Kach and Kahane Lives) ceased their activities in the United States, numerous other groups emerged.[69] These new groups were, according to the State Department, nothing more than new names for Kach and Kahane Lives. Their names included the Kfar Tapuah Fund, Jewish Legion, the Way of the Torah, the Yeshiva of the Jewish Idea, and Dikuy Bogdim (Hebrew for "Repression of Traitors"). These new groups and Web sites were all added to the State Department's blacklist.

Some of the Web sites on the new State Department list did cease their activities. Some, such as newkach.org, decided to delete all content related to Kach. However, kahane.org continues to operate and even posted a response to the U.S. decision to define it as a terror organization: "This recent designation will definitely go down in history as one of the most irrational and obscene decisions ever carried out by the U.S. government." Other Web sites, such as the Jewish Legion's Web site, were modified to direct all visitors to another site called Gedud Haivri. But the new site, not on the list of banned sites, is almost identical to that of the original Jewish Legion site. Thus, it appears that the State Department's attempt to bar Kach and Kahane Lives from the Internet is doomed to fail.

The multiple means by which terrorists are using, misusing, and abusing the Internet today, and the potential for greater abuse in the future, has instigated these various attempts to fight back at the terrorists, from ISPs exercising oversight to vigilantism to government regulation. Each counterpunch taken at the "bad guys" inevitably strikes at the civil liberties, rights, and freedoms of the "good guys." Do we punish the entire global community of Internet users in order to cull a few bad apples, all in the name of security? Or do we, in the name of liberty, leave terrorists free to operate unfettered in cyberspace, and risk letting their actions spoil the wealth of good information and constructive exchanges made possible by the Internet? Each option contains a part of the solution, but most reasonable people would agree that neither option is ideal. The final chapter will review various suggestions that have been put forward in this debate. The chapter will also propose its own strategy for striking a balance between security and liberty.

7

Balancing Security and Civil Liberties

Terrorists hope to strike hard enough so that alarmed governments in democracies adopt anti- and counterterrorist laws and regulations that curb highly esteemed civil liberties and thereby weaken the very fabric of liberal democratic societies.

—Brigitte Nacos, "The Terrorist Calculus behind 9/11"

Security versus Liberty

FREEDOM OF SPEECH, FREE FLOW OF INFORMATION, and the Internet are seen by many as very closely related. Democracies and liberal societies rely on open communication, and the Internet appears to be the best medium to provide the fundamental components of open communication. Vinton G. Cerf, one of the Internet's distinguished pioneers and widely known as one of the "fathers of the Internet," commented in his 2003 report "The Internet under Surveillance":

> The Internet is one of the most powerful agents of freedom. It exposes truth to those who wish to see and hear it. It is no wonder that some governments and organizations fear the Internet and its ability to make the truth known. The phrase "freedom of speech" is often used to characterize a key element of democratic societies: open communication and especially open government. But freedom of speech is less than half of the equation. It is also vital that citizens have the freedom to hear and see. It is the latter area in which many governments have intervened in an attempt

to prevent citizens from gaining access to information that their governments wish to withhold from them.[1]

Despite the Internet's advantages for open and free communication, it is far from being an absolutely free medium. Many governments try to limit the Internet's freedom, and often it is done for worthy reasons, such as fighting child pornography and the sexual traffic in women and children. But we have been warned repeatedly that any censorship may turn into a slippery slope and should thus be regarded with caution, even in the worst cases of Internet content abuse. For example, governments can hide political censorship behind a moral facade. To quote again from Cerf, "Citizens must do their best to guard against government censorship for political purposes. . . . In this 21st century information age, Internauts have significant responsibilities. They must guard against abusive censorship and counteract misinformation. They must take responsibility for thoughtful use of the Internet and the World Wide Web and all of the information services and appliances yet to come. Free flow of information has a price and responsible Internauts will shoulder the burden of paying it."[2]

The measures used and being considered after the 9/11 attacks could change the balance between privacy and security. According to Stewart Baker, however, the measures are not a threat to this balance. In a personal interview with the author, Baker explains:

> I wonder if it's the kind of problem that we can just solve with regulations, because it is still difficult to enforce rules on the Internet . . . and if we had the cooperation of every government that would be necessary to deal with terror in the Internet, we wouldn't have a terrorist problem, so I'm not sure there's a regulatory answer. Right now I do think that we need to do a better job of protecting public networks and have a better sense of what safety features have been built into our networks, because they are vulnerable. But I think attacking it turns out to be harder than originally expected.
>
> The private industry that is best at dealing with cyberattacks today is the financial industry. Now, why is that? Because they're constantly under attack. Why are they constantly under attack? Because you can make money by attacking them. So, in an odd way, things that create financial incentive to use those hacker techniques also encourage countermeasures.

> I do think that we are gradually building up the public responses and the public infrastructure to deal with it. Most of the threats of using the Internet happen because of the perceived anonymity, but anonymity is going to get harder and harder to achieve, thanks in part to the recording industry of America, which has been going around establishing that they can find out by subpoenaing the records of the ISPs [Internet service providers], the identities of people who share files. . . . However, if you're looking for an ISP on the Internet, you're not going to have a problem finding an ISP. So if there was a strategy of keeping al Qaeda off the Internet, I can't believe it would work, because you could not shut them down in all the world's ISPs.[3]

Since September 11, many governments have sought to address concerns that terrorists are using the Net to communicate, plan attacks, distribute instructions, transfer funds, and promote their ideas. As discussed in chapter 6, these concerns led to several countermeasures that in turn prompted fears among activists and organizations committed to the defense of civil liberties. Groups such as the Electronic Privacy Information Center and Privacy International worry that under the guise of fighting terror it will be easier to erode users' privacy and freedom of speech. In 2002, the organization Reporters Without Borders (or Reporters Sans Frontières) argued, "Several Western democracies are using the fight against terrorism to increase surveillance on the Internet." The organization criticized not only authoritarian states such as China that tightly police Internet use, but also Western democracies: "many countries have adopted laws, measures and actions that are poised to put the Internet under the tutelage of security services."[4] Referring to the United States, the United Kingdom, France, Germany, Spain, Italy, Denmark, and the European Parliament, Reporters Without Borders claimed: "Several Western democracies have become 'predators of digital freedoms,' using the fight against terrorism to increase surveillance on the Internet. . . . A year after the tragic events in New York and Washington, the Internet can be included on the list of 'collateral damage.'. . . Cyber liberty has been undermined and fundamental digital freedoms have been amputated."[5]

Reporters Without Borders listed dozens of measures adopted or proposed by governments to control the Net, including the following:

- A Canadian antiterrorist law that "clearly undermines the confidentiality of exchanges of electronic mail"
- "Magic Lantern" technology being developed by the FBI that will allow investigators to secretly install powerful eavesdropping software to record every keystroke made on a person's computer
- A French law requiring Internet providers to keep records of e-mail exchanges for one year and to make it easier for authorities to decode messages protected by encryption software[6]

The Internet itself has never been free of government censorship. According to Reporters Without Borders, forty-five governments restrict their citizens' access to the Internet, usually by forcing them to use only a state-operated ISP, which may filter out offensive messages, content, or sites. In many countries, cyberdissidents are under attack.[7] For example, in November 2003, a leading Chinese democracy activist, He Depu, joined the ranks of jailed cyberdissidents after being sentenced to eight years in prison for posting his political views on the Net. He Depu was one of the founders of the China Democratic Party and was also the first of six democracy advocates sentenced by the Hu Jintao government. Under Hu, China has become the world leader in jailing political dissidents who use the Internet to express their views. On December 1, 2003, the *Washington Post* reported, "China released three Internet essayists who were detained a year before for criticizing the government, including Liu Di, a college student in Beijing whose arrest on subversion charges had attracted international attention."[8] Liu Di, twenty-three, was a psychology student at Beijing Normal University and was known online by the pen name "Stainless Steel Mouse." The same day, Jiang Lijun, a fourth writer charged in the case, was convicted of subversion and sentenced to four years in prison. However, it is important to note that government censorship of the Internet in countries such as China is not taking away privacy and free-speech rights—the citizens of these countries never had them. These are just the same old policies being adapted to a new medium, the Internet.

Karen Kleiss, in the *Toronto Star,* says, "Many authoritarian governments around the world, from Tunisia to Vietnam to Malaysia, are cracking down hard on the Internet in an attempt to control or limit the flow of alternative political information."[9] In their book *Open Networks,*

Closed Regimes, Shanthi Kalathil and Taylor C. Boas report the findings of their study on Internet use in eight authoritarian and semiauthoritarian countries: China, Cuba, Singapore, Vietnam, Burma, the United Arab Emirates, Saudi Arabia, and Egypt.[10] They discovered that "authoritarian governments, far from fearing the information age, have chosen to direct Internet development in ways that bolster the state. At the same time, many regimes are struggling to cope with the potent challenges posed by new technologies. Authoritarian regimes recognize the benefits of the Internet to economic growth, but at the same time feel threatened by the unprecedented degree of freedom of speech."[11] "We've seen a real growth in the last five years, growth that mirrors the growth of the Internet," says Minky Worden, electronic media director for Human Rights Watch. "So, just as in the old days the government might shut down a newspaper, now they shut down a Web site."[12] Although no one knows just how many cyberdissidents are in jail, at least forty-eight are widely publicized cases.

In July 2003, the United States government passed the Global Internet Freedom Act (GIFA), allocating about $50 billion to fight state-sponsored Internet censorship: "Oppressive regimes habitually monitor activity on the Internet," argued Rep. Christopher Cox (R–Calif.), who was a key author of the bill. "In this way, technology has become a new tool of the police state. The GIFA will give millions of people around the globe the power to outwit repressive regimes that would silence them."[13]

However, we must remember that the U.S. government and U.S. corporations are developing the monitoring technologies that oppressive states use to control Internet access. The Chinese government, for example, is buying and using Western-made technologies and software to jam Internet access for a population of more than 1 billion people. So we see the inherent contradiction when the United States is also involved in providing liberalizing technologies, including the development of software that allows people to surf the Web anonymously and bypass censor filters such as those used in China.

Another example of contradictory policy comes from Saudi Arabia. As Stephen Schwartz noted in his article "The Islamic Terrorism Club," "The same Riyadh regime that continually promises to curb incitement by its state-supported Wahhabi clerics and media—the same regime that successfully blocks websites airing enlightened attitudes toward women,

Islam, pluralism, freedom, and democracy—leaves unimpeded inflammatory websites that recruit for violent Jihad."[14] A study titled "Documentation of Internet Filtering in Saudi Arabia," by Jonathan Zittrain and Benjamin Edelman from the Harvard Law School, found that "the Saudis were blocking Web sites run by the Anne Frank House and Amnesty International, as well as sites relating to Shia Islam, Christianity, the Baha'i faith, and tolerance and interfaith dialogue in general."[15] The summary of the report states:

> Saudi-installed filtering systems prevented access to certain requested Web pages; the authors tracked 2,038 blocked pages. Such pages contained information about religion, health, education, reference, humor, and entertainment. The authors conclude (1) that the Saudi government maintains an active interest in filtering non-sexually explicit Web content for users within the Kingdom; (2) that substantial amounts of non-sexually explicit Web content is in fact effectively inaccessible to most Saudi Arabians; and (3) that much of this content consists of sites that are popular elsewhere in the world.[16]

Missing the Opportunity:
The Internet as a Nonviolent Arena

The Internet has the potential to serve as one of the ideal tools for the nonviolent management of conflicts. Dorothy Denning states:

> Several case studies show that when the Internet is used in normal, non-disruptive ways, it can be an effective tool for activism, especially when it is combined with other media, including broadcast and print media and face-to-face meetings with policy makers. As a technology for empowerment, the Net benefits individuals and small groups with few resources as well as organizations that are large or well-funded. It facilitates activities such as educating the public and media, raising money, forming coalitions across geographical boundaries, distributing petitions and action alerts, and planning and coordinating events on a regional or international level. It allows activists in politically repressive states to evade government censors and monitors.[17]

In other words, we should not let the discourse on terrorism and counterterrorism on the Net overshadow the bright side of the Internet's use for nonviolent debates and conflicts. There is no doubt that this new medium, the Internet, offers a useful channel for nonviolent political action. The Internet offers advocacy groups and individuals a stage from which to present information, arguments, and calls for action. Says Denning, "They can send it through e-mail and post it to newsgroups. They can create their own electronic publications or contribute articles and essays to other publications. They can put up webpages with documents, images, audio and video clips, and other types of information. The websites can serve as a gathering place and source of information for supporters, potential supporters, and onlookers."[18] One of the reasons why the Internet became popular among activists is its low cost and ease of access compared with conventional mass media. Practically anyone can afford to be a communicator in cyberspace, and it is the cheapest and easiest medium to access or operate. Moreover, its reach is global: a message posted on the Net can reach millions of people within hours. Also, activists are not subjected to any censorship or editorial practices and can present their versions, claims, and arguments as they wish. Denning describes five modes of using the Internet for peaceful conduct of political activism: collection, publication, dialogue, coordination of action, and direct lobbying of decision makers.

- *Collection:* "Activists may be able to locate legislative documents, official policy statements, analyses and discussions about issues, and other items related to their mission. They may be able to find names and contact information for key decision makers inside the government or governments they ultimately hope to influence. They may be able to identify other groups and individuals with similar interests and gather contact information for potential supporters and collaborators."

- *Publication:* "The Internet offers several channels whereby advocacy groups and individuals can publish information to further policy objectives. They can send it through e-mail and post it to newsgroups. They can create their own electronic publications or contribute articles and essays to those of others. They can put up webpages with documents, images, audio and video clips, and other types of information. Such webpages provide a source of information to anyone

who is interested, and also serve as a virtual gathering place for supporters, potential supporters, and onlookers."

- *Dialogue:* "The Internet offers several venues for dialogue and debate
on policy issues. These include e-mail, newsgroups, Web forums and
chatrooms. Discussions can be confined to closed groups, for example
through e-mail, as well as being open to the public. Some media sites
offer Web surfers the opportunity to comment on the latest stories
and current issues and events. Government officials and field experts
may be brought in to serve as catalysts for discussion, debate issues or
answer questions."

- *Coordination of action:* "Advocacy groups can use the Internet to
coordinate action among members and with other organizations and
individuals. Action plans can be distributed by e-mail or posted on
websites. The Internet lets people all over the world coordinate action
without regard to constraints of geography or time. They can form
partnerships and coalitions or operate independently."

- *Lobbying decision makers:* "Activists can use the Internet to lobby decision makers. One of the methods suggested by the Kosovo Task Force
for contacting the White House, for example, was e-mail. Similarly, a
Canadian website with the headline, 'Stop the NATO Bombing of
Yugoslavia Now!' urged Canadians and others interested in stopping
the war to send e-mails and/or faxes to Canadian Prime Minister Jean
Chrétien and all members of the Canadian Parliament. A sample letter was included. The letter concluded with an appeal to stop aggression against Yugoslavia and seek a peaceful means to resolve the
Kosovo problem."[19]

The case of the Zapatistas in Mexico provides a good example of the
positive potential of the Internet. In 1994, the Zapatista National Liberation Movement and Army (EZLN) launched a violent campaign of
harassment and low-intensity military operations against the government of Mexico. Consequently, the Zapatistas appeared on the U.S.
State Department's list of terrorist organizations in the late 1990s. However, this movement changed its character and activities and adopted
a nonviolent agenda. Tania O'Neil uses the case of the Zapatistas as
an example of "a new and revolutionary model for organization in the
current global age"—the movement used the Internet to "counter the

characterization of its organization put forward by the Mexican government, to link itself to international supporters, and to attempt to stimulate global resistance to neoliberalism and globalization."[20] The Zapatista movement has used the Internet since it began in 1994. According to several assessments, the Zapatistas represent "one of the most successful examples of the use of computer communications by grassroots social movements."[21] This designation results from its use of the Internet to organize, communicate, and counter Mexican government propaganda through an electronic community that works as an information distribution network. The network is based in Mexico and is made up of more than one hundred autonomous groups that lie outside the movement but are sympathetic to the Zapatista cause. Subcomandante Marcos, leader of the Zapatistas, is reportedly able to use his laptop to issue orders, distribute communiqués, and communicate directly with foreign media. The Zapatistas use the Internet to conduct disinformation campaigns and computer network attacks, which have led its style of protest to be called "digital Zapatismo." Ronfeldt and Arquilla refer to the new Zapatista insurrection as a "social netwar," in which the activists turn to the Internet and use it efficiently to disseminate information, attract support and sympathy, and transform their role in the conflict—"a traditional guerrilla insurgency changed into an information-age social netwar."[22]

O'Neil sees the Zapatista movement as successfully using the Internet to further its cause, but she believes it "likely will either sputter along as a Mexican government irritant or be assimilated within Mexican political discourse,"[23] as it has not gained momentum lately and its theoretical foundation has weakened. It is unlikely to gain momentum, because it has become increasingly mainstream, and once it achieves the legislation it wants, it could lose its raison d'être. Also, it has primarily used the Internet to communicate with the international community, but the medium is an ineffective method for communicating with its own constituents in Mexico, who largely do not have Internet access.

Another example comes from Afghanistan. The Revolutionary Association of the Women of Afghanistan (RAWA) was instituted to support and potentially empower oppressed groups, despite its being considered a terrorist organization by some states. RAWA was established in 1977 in Kabul, Afghanistan, by a group of Afghan women fighting for human rights and social justice. The founders were led by Meena, who in 1987 was assassinated by Afghan agents of the KGB.[24] Before the Moscow-directed revolution of April 1978 in Afghanistan, RAWA was involved only in the struggle for women's rights and democracy. But after the coup, and as a reaction to the Soviet occupation of Afghanistan in 1979, RAWA became more active in direct militant resistance. During that time 11 million women were held under house arrest and denied the most basic human needs and rights, including freedom of movement, health care, education, justice, and speech. Following the advent of the Taliban in 1994, RAWA both intensified its resistance and modified the manner in which it resisted. The women discovered a powerful new tool in the Internet, which enabled them to gain international attention and to make the world aware of their oppression and abuse. This movement continues to gain public and political recognition, with the potential to achieve powerful results. However, RAWA emphasizes that although it needs and wants Western assistance, it is not the job of the West to speak on its behalf. The organization states that these women have been silenced long enough, and now is their time to have a voice, to become participants in their own destiny rather than merely abused observers. The Internet gives them this voice.

It is evident that the Internet can serve as a vital emancipatory mechanism for persecuted groups, at both local and transnational levels. Nonviolent activism can and in fact does benefit from the advantages of the Internet. At the same time, terrorist organizations are usurping the Internet for its many capabilities while maintaining their "real-life" violent tactics. It appears that the Internet does not encourage violent actors to conduct nonviolent dialogues and communication. Rather, violent groups and individuals merely add the Internet to their arsenal of more conventional weapons. Except for the Zapatistas and RAWA, there are no cases of terrorist groups that have rejected their violent tactics after establishing an Internet presence. Sadly, the Internet has become just another instrument for extremist and racist groups to radiate hate and violence while interacting with one another and with sympathizers.

Missing an Opportunity: Virtual Diplomacy

Richard Solomon, the director of the United States Institute of Peace (USIP), and Sheryl Brown, the director of USIP's Virtual Diplomacy Initiative, presented their vision of using the Net for diplomatic and peaceful resolution of conflicts to the Conference on Crisis Management and Information Technology in Helsinki, Finland, on September 12, 2003. In their presentation they argued:

> No constellation of technologies has been more powerful in reshaping the post–Cold War international system than those of the information revolution. Over the past two decades, nation-states and subnational groups, international businesses and multinational organizations have struggled to incorporate the dramatic possibilities for their work of satellite communications, the Internet, inexpensive telephone and cell phone services, fax machines, and global computer networks. The innovations have occurred largely without central direction or a clear game plan, and the effects of the ongoing revolution in the way we communicate on international affairs will continue. We are only beginning to see purposeful efforts to channel all the power in these technologies in support of good governance or effective and expedient management of international conflicts and crises.[25]

The new communication technologies and especially the Internet offer new channels for foreign-affairs agencies to reach vast publics and to maintain constant contact with their counterparts in other countries. The development of communication technologies has also produced many invaluable channels for humanitarian and human rights initiatives. Yet international agencies have tended to resist such technological changes. USIP's 1996 conference "Managing Communications: Lessons from Interventions in Africa" examined the potential contributions of new communication technologies and information-sharing practices in and among humanitarian and peacekeeping organizations in Somalia, Rwanda, and Liberia. The conference determined two levels of communications improvements that were most needed: (1) loosening an organizational hierarchy that limited the free flow of information; and, if this information control could be loosened, (2) expanding and enhancing the technological infrastructure, which tends to be limited or subject to disruption in war-torn areas and can thereby have the added negative effect of lessening the face-to-face communications so important to alleviating tensions. From that conference and subsequent studies, we have learned that seven elements of communication must be in place and functioning during a crisis:

1. communication within organizations
2. communication between organizations (bilaterally)
3. communication among organizations (multilaterally, as in a networked community)
4. communication with local leaders
5. communication with and between decision makers
6. communication with the media
7. communication among the parties to the conflict.[26]

Computer-mediated communication can serve as an ideal channel for all these forms of communication, especially with regard to conflict management and resolution. A good example—and, sadly, one of very few—is the USIP initiative on peace in Liberia. In October 2003, fighting factions in that nation's fourteen-year civil war chose Gyude Bryant as interim leader of the National Transitional Government of Liberia. In February 2004, USIP hosted a special Virtual Town Hall Meeting featuring Bryant. During the online interactive session, Bryant engaged the Liberian diaspora in an Internet-based discussion on the prospects for peace in their war-weary homeland and what the expatriates could do to support such efforts.

Another virtual approach to training for peace is the use of computer simulations to create peace support operations. Donna Bolz, in her report "Information Technology and Peace Support Operations," highlights the potential of computer-assisted simulations:

> Designed to train leaders in decision making for such operations, these applications allow actors to observe the impact of decisions and refine or modify practices without actually affecting a community moving toward resettlement or a local police force reorganizing in an operation's postconflict phases, for example. The introduction of analytical tools developed specifically for peace support operations came on line slowly. Despite early recognition of the role computer-assisted simulations could play in planning and executing peace support operations, trainers continued to rely on existing war analysis tools to fill this need.[27]

The potential for virtual diplomacy has yet to be fully tapped. Solomon and Brown conclude that this lag can be attributed partly to how the field has emerged to date: "The innovations [of the information revolution] have occurred largely without central direction or a clear game plan, and the effects of the ongoing revolution in the way we communicate on international affairs will continue. We are only beginning to see purposeful efforts to channel all the power in these technologies in support of good governance or effective and expedient management of international conflicts and crises."[28] In their *iMP: The Magazine on Information Impacts* article "Imagining Technology," Jonathan Spalter and Kevin Moran suggest, "To address these challenges of multiple non-state actors and rapid communications and to remain as relevant and effective as possible in this new environment, the United States and its foreign affairs apparatus must adapt its diplomatic strategy and develop a new 'digital' diplomacy. This digital diplomacy must be increasingly networked and technology-driven, and it must be able to react with speed, flexibility, reach, and efficiency."[29]

The Counterweight of Counterterrorism Measures

Every few years, says Lindsey Wade, we observe a "new" wave of social panic.[30] These waves include AIDS or SARS, racial clashes, environmental disasters, homeless minorities, anthrax, nuclear waste, and organized crime. Although these dangers are very real, they may be exaggerated and even manipulated. Technological advances have created fresh spheres in which increasing criminality and new threats can appear. The escalating popularity of the Internet is allegedly posing a new and difficult threat to societies, predominantly because of the invisibility of both offender and victim. Despite the cybercommunity's considerable success in policing itself unofficially, the actions of a minority of abusers are prompting more authoritative policing of cyberspace.

The need to protect the public from the threats of modern terrorism opens the door to the use of surveillance. Investigation and surveillance processes cause immense concern in contemporary society because they create and maintain social distinctions as certain groups are subjected to repressive measures for purposes of social control. David Lyon, sociologist and author of *Surveillance Society,* acknowledges that while such practices are portrayed as protective of order and security, we should be asking whose purposes they serve.[31] And how do we know that these ostensible purposes are served? Lyon emphasizes that surveillance is a tool that reinforces social and economic divisions, channels choices, and directs desires; it constrains, controls, and proves seriously problematic in issues of privacy.

Why should law-abiding citizens care about counterterrorism measures on the Internet? According to the report titled "The Tools of Freedom and Security," we do have reasons to be worried:

> Computer databases store the most intimate details of our daily lives, including medical records, banking and investment transactions, credit reports, employment records, credit card purchases, photographs, fingerprints, and so on. Surveillance cameras are ubiquitous at ATMs, airports, and other public places. The courts and lawmakers have, over the years, sought to protect this private information from unnecessary disclosure and to enact strict guidelines on the interception and gathering of such information by government agencies. At press time debate was still under way in Congress on House and Senate actions to expand the powers of law-enforcement and intelligence agencies to conduct electronic surveillance and searches. . . . One concern is that new powers granted to law enforcement in time of war not be abused when the threats abate.[32]

Some people argue that, paradoxically, we must give up some freedoms in order to enjoy the ones we cherish the most. Amitai Etzioni, author of *The Limits of Privacy,* argues in his essay "Seeking Middle Ground on Privacy vs. Security" that it is wrong to define counterterrorism surveillance tools such as Carnivore, Magic Lantern, and others as good or evil: "As with all technologies, the proper question is how it will be used. For instance, if evidence about a suspected terrorist is presented to a court of law, Magic Lantern should be allowed to decode the suspect's messages. But if it is installed at the discretion of every cop on the beat, the rights of many innocent people could be violated."[33] Proper guidelines are key, and if these are not established, then such measures will usurp a large part of our liberties. Surveying the public, argues Etzioni, may well be unavoidable in the post-9/11 world, but he also warns that "retaining information about innocent conduct by innocent people poses a massive threat to privacy."[34]

Questions of how and why counterterrorism measures affect licit Internet use have been presented by a number of published books lamenting the state of individual privacy and liberty, especially after September 11.[35] These books focus on changes to laws and regulations made by the Bush administration in the name of fighting terrorism. The first concern, according to the authors, is that the changes do little if anything to improve security, while harming civil liberties. The second concern relates to the very essence of what we mean today by privacy and reflects a more general worry about the "retreat of privacy" resulting from the use of many high-tech surveillance tools. While pre-9/11 legislation aimed at protecting people's privacy from invasion has been shelved, new antiterrorism laws give the authorities broad new powers to wiretap, monitor, and otherwise eavesdrop on Internet activity. Legislation to combat global and domestic terrorism has been gradually restricting democratic freedoms over the past decades. The policies proposed and passed since 9/11 are significantly accelerating the loss of civil liberties; moreover, this is being achieved with almost no public resistance, because it is portrayed as a normal, almost rhetorical process in the "war on terror." The legislative proposals and practices of the United States and the United Kingdom demand evaluation of laws and programs in terms of possible effectiveness and the implications they possess for civil rights, privacy, and security.

These developments could wind up having profound implications for democracies and their values, exacting a heavy price on civil liberties and increasing the destructive effects of terrorism in the Internet. In the war with modern terrorism, timely information is more valuable than guns or missiles in saving lives. "The issue is how to gather that information efficiently without adopting the draconian methods of those extreme ideologies we are fighting. The first step in reconciling the need for security with the principles of our democracy is to understand the various technological approaches being proposed to fight terrorism, and how they might affect us as citizens."[36]

Voices of Concern

Many in the Western world and especially in the United States worry about the potential abuse of civil liberties in the name of fighting terrorrism. Most privacy advocates say it is not the technology that should worry us, but the lack of judicial oversight in its use. For example, Jennifer Granick, director of the Stanford Law School's Center for Internet and Society, does not object to the FBI's use of Internet-monitoring tools, though she is concerned about their potential misuse.[37] "Advances in technology may require new law enforcement techniques," Granick notes. "These tools, if properly used within the system of checks and balances, may work, and then we can embrace them." But, Granick says, "the same privacy protections that apply everywhere else should also apply in the digital world."[38] Let us review some of these voices of concern and their calls for some important modifications to surveillance as it is now being conducted on the Net.

The American Civil Liberties Union (ACLU) warns that two developments are putting the Unites States "at risk of turning into a full-fledged surveillance society": (1) the sudden increase in surveillance technologies, and (2) the weakening of legal restraints that protect privacy. In a series of reports and publications, the ACLU offers four recommendations for securing personal privacy:[39]

1. *Change the terms of the debate:* Every new surveillance technology that emerges must be understood and publicly debated, but each one must also be viewed as a part of the rising "surveillance society" that is developing and encroaching on our privacy. If Americans do not see the big picture, they are not likely to become alarmed, since each technological development and each incremental loss of privacy may seem small, and they will not likely understand the true aggregate loss of privacy that they face.

2. *Pass comprehensive privacy laws:* Americans are shielded from government surveillance by wide-ranging protections, such as wiretapping laws, but these laws are being weakened. Furthermore, surveillance is increasingly carried out by the private sector (often for the government), and laws protecting citizens from private surveillance are weak. According to the ACLU, "In contrast to the rest of the developed world, the U.S. has no strong, comprehensive law protecting privacy—only a patchwork of largely inadequate protections. . . . With the glaring exception of the United States, every advanced industrialized nation in the world has enacted overarching privacy laws that

protect citizens against private-sector abuses."[40] U.S. law, in contrast, protects the privacy only of children under the age of thirteen. As Jay Stanley and Barry Steinhardt from the ACLU point out, "We need to develop a baseline of simple and clear privacy protections that crosses all sectors of our lives and give it the force of law. Only then can Americans act with a confident knowledge of when they can and cannot be monitored."[41]

3. *Develop new laws for new technologies:* "In the past, new technologies that threatened our privacy, such as telephone wiretapping, were assimilated over time into our society. The legal system had time to adapt and reinterpret existing laws, the political system had time to consider and enact new laws or regulations, and the culture had time to absorb the implications of the new technology for daily life."[42] Today, however, new surveillance technologies are developing so rapidly that our laws have not been adapted to protect us from them, and the rush to pass antiterrorism legislation without careful consideration and debate has exacerbated this problem. We must develop or adapt laws and legal principles to control and restrain the use of new technologies to prevent them from invading our privacy.

4. *Revive the Fourth Amendment:* The Fourth Amendment was created to protect Americans from the use of "general warrants" to conduct broad searches, which the British used against rebelling colonists, and it is our main constitutional protection shielding us from government invasion of our privacy. However, in recent years, initiatives such as the "war on drugs" have weakened our right to privacy by relaxing the conditions under which law enforcement can conduct searches without a warrant; in addition, historically, U.S. courts react slowly to adapt our laws to emerging technologies. The Fourth Amendment must be revived and expanded so that "reasonable expectation of privacy cannot be defined by the power that technology affords the government to spy on us."[43]

Another source of recommendations is the Center for Democracy and Technology (CDT). Mere days after September 11, the CDT released a statement warning that responding to the attacks and to future threats would challenge our resolve to uphold the American principles of freedom, openness, and diversity.[44] In the statement, the CDT emphasized that "surrendering freedom will not purchase security," "democratic values are strengths, not weaknesses," and "open communications networks are a positive force in the fight against violence and intolerance." It also stated, "There is clearly much that can be done to continue improving the government's technological sophistication to fight terrorism. But it would be wrong to overreact. The wiretap laws already give law enforcement and intelligence agencies wide latitude. Indeed, it has been recognized for some time that the laws need to be updated in light of technological changes to provide more protection for privacy, not less."[45] The CDT sees the Internet as "the people's voice" and argues that as such it should remain both open and innovative; it warns that "building government surveillance features into communications networks can reduce security and create new risks of vulnerability," and that there is nothing "to be gained by limiting freedom of expression. Pushing dissenting voices off the Internet does not increase security."[46]

Like the ACLU, the CDT is urging the public to pressure Congress to amend the USA PATRIOT Act: "The PATRIOT Act didn't just encourage information sharing so intelligence agencies could 'connect the dots' to prevent the next attack. The Act gave the Executive Branch broad discretionary powers that are not needed in the fight against terrorism and serve only to infringe on Americans' fundamental liberties."[47] The CDT has called for "reasonable limitations" to be applied to some of the most broad-based surveillance powers that the act granted the government, so that the FBI is subject to judicial and congressional oversight. The organization details what it sees as the biggest problems with the USA PATRIOT Act and puts forth its own "roadmap for restoring the balance." In 2003 the CDT also published a joint report with the Center for American Progress and the Center for National Security Studies, titled "Strengthening America by Defending Our Liberties: An Agenda for Reform." The report makes many recommendations concerning the Internet and the USA PATRIOT Act.

In November 2003 Human Rights First, an organization aiming to "create a secure and humane world by advancing justice, human dignity and respect for the rule of law," suggested several measures to protect privacy:

1. Congress should amend the Homeland Security Act to give the agency's Privacy and Civil Rights Officers full access to information, enforcement authority, and resources.

2. Congress should amend the Homeland Security Act to establish a designated official within the Inspector General's office to receive complaints regarding specific violations of civil rights.

3. Congress should amend Article 215 of the USA PATRIOT Act to restore safeguards against abuse of the seizure of business records, and in particular the records of libraries, bookstores, and educational institutions where seizure poses a particular risk of endangering freedom of expression.

4. Congress should require regular reports of federal authorities' use of special powers to seize personal records, disaggregating data so that those measures involving the records of libraries, bookstores, and schools are clear.

5. Congress should hold hearings on the use of data mining of personal information within the United States, by both public and private agencies, and its implication on the right of privacy and on the data protection norms required to safeguard against abuse.

6. Congress should prohibit the Department of Defense from pursuing its Total Information Awareness (TIA) data mining program.

7. Congress should enact legislation requiring any governmental or government contractor's use of data mining techniques to be in accord with public guidelines based on the highest data protection and privacy standards, which are developed on the basis of broad consultations.

8. Congress should hold detailed hearings on any proposals by the Executive Branch to increase its powers under the Foreign Intelligence Surveillance Act (FISA).

9. Congress should amend Section 218 of the USA PATRIOT Act, giving the FBI authority to use its FISA powers only when foreign intelligence gathering is the "primary purpose" of the warrant application under FISA.[48]

The Electronic Frontier Foundation (EFF) describes itself as "a nonprofit group of passionate people—lawyers, volunteers, and visionaries—working to protect your digital rights."[49] They track technical and civil liberties issues and mobilize legal responses to restraints on Internet and electronic usage. Regarding the USA PATRIOT Act, the EFF urges the following:

1. That law enforcement and the intelligence agencies use these new powers carefully and limit their use to bona fide investigations into acts of terrorism.

2. That the courts appropriately punish those who misuse these new laws and that Congress reexamine its decision to grant such broad, unchecked powers.

3. That if these laws are misused to harm the rights of ordinary Americans involved in low-level crimes unrelated to terrorism, the courts refuse to allow evidence collected through implementing these broad powers to be used in prosecuting them.

4. That the many vague, undefined terms in PATRIOT Act be defined in a manner that protects the civil liberties and privacy of Americans.

5. That ISPs and others served with "roving" wiretaps and other Orders that do not specify them as recipients require the Attorney General to certify that the order properly applies to them.

6. That Congress require the law enforcement and intelligence agencies who operate under provisions of PATRIOT Act that are set to expire in December, 2005, to provide it with comprehensive reports about the use of these new powers, so as to enable Congress to reasonably determine whether these provisions should be renewed.[50]

The Electronic Privacy Information Center (EPIC), established in 1994 to focus public attention on emerging civil liberty issues and to protect privacy, the First Amendment, and constitutional values, uses new Internet capabilities, such as e-mail alerts and online newsletters, to raise awareness about civil liberties in the information age.[51] EPIC also weighs in on Internet surveillance issues. In its 2001 "Letter to Congress on Proposed Anti-Terrorism Legislation," the organization urged Congress to consider the following:

1. Any expansion of existing authorities should be based upon a clear and convincing demonstration of need. Congress should assess the likely effectiveness of any proposed new powers in combating the threats posed by terrorist activity.

2. Any new authorities deemed necessary should be narrowly drawn to protect the privacy and constitutional rights of the millions of law-abiding citizens who use the Internet and other communications media on a daily basis.

3. The longstanding distinction between domestic law enforcement and foreign intelligence collection should be preserved to the greatest extent possible consistent with the need to detect and prevent terrorist activity.

4. Specifically, we recommend that the FISA standard for surveillance authority not permit the gathering of evidence for routine criminal investigations. . . . Any measures deemed necessary to address the current circumstances should be confined to cases involving suspected terrorist activity. [52]

Policy Recommendations: Seeking the "Golden Path"

If an elastic band is overstretched, notes Wade, it will eventually snap back with a sharp sting to the hand that forced it.[53] Similarly, intensifying repression of civil liberties and exploitation of privacy are far more sinister in the long run than the threat of terrorism, international or domestic. We should recognize that terrorism has been around for hundreds of years and is not likely to go away. Modern societies, it appears, will have to learn to live with some terrorism, which leads to the issue of trade-offs. A Harris poll conducted in October 2001 found that 63 percent of Americans favored monitoring of Internet discussions and chat rooms, and 54 percent favored monitoring cell phones and e-mail.[54] In 2003 Kip Viscusi and Richard Zeckhauser conducted a study to examine "people's willingness to sacrifice civil liberties in an effort to reduce terrorism risks, and also to explore aspects of individuals' terrorism risk perceptions that govern the character of their responses."[55] They tried to outline the basics of the civil-liberties–versus–terrorism-risk trade-off. Since the desired balance between these conflicting concerns depends in large part on individual attitudes, the researchers surveyed a sample of Americans for their willingness to trade safety for civil rights.

To measure the willingness for trade-offs, Viscusi and Zeckhauser examined "(a) civil liberty issues pertaining to the targeting of passengers for screening at airports based on their demographic characteristics, most often salient characteristics such as ethnic background and country of origin; and (b) surveillance of private mail, e-mail, and phone communications. In particular, the respondents considered the following question: Would you support policies that make it easier for legal authorities to read mail, e-mail, or tap phones without a person's knowledge so long as it was related to preventing terrorism?"[56] The study found a willingness among respondents to sacrifice some civil liberties for increased security—a finding that tallies with a widespread belief that, as articulated by Louis Kaplow and Steven Shavell, "many legal rights and liberties are not absolutes."[57] The report concludes by stating,

> Civil liberties and the prevention of terrorism are two attributes for which society often makes extreme symbolic commitments toward the highest level. Many would argue that civil liberties are guaranteed rights, rights that cannot be compromised. In much the same way, advocates of risk control often claim that so long as any individual is at risk of being killed involuntarily, the risk must be reduced to ensure that we are in fact truly safe. Taken to the logical limit, this leads to the zero-risk mentality that pervades many legislative mandates of U.S. government risk and environmental regulation agencies, and is reflected in public risk attitudes as well.[58]

These findings show that the public believes that, in practice, civil liberties should not necessarily be expressed to their fullest extent. In other words, Americans are willing to trade a degree of civil liberty for other valued benefits, such as the prevention of terrorism. The optimal level of civil liberties varies according to circumstances. For example, we would not normally tolerate having every car driving along a roadway stopped and inspected, but we would be more understanding if a serial killer were on the loose. Thus, a more realistic way to protect the Internet, to prevent its abuse by terrorists while at the same time protecting civil liberties, is to look for the "golden path"—that is, the best compromise. The twelfth-century Jewish philosopher Rambam termed the "golden path" the "Right Path," a balance between two diametrically opposed extremes. Finding such a path means that we will have to accept both some vulnerabilities of the Internet to terrorism and some constraints on civil liberties, but the underlying principle should be to minimize both sorts of ills by finding effective trade-offs. A number of approaches seem particularly well suited to helping us achieve this balance between security and liberty within today's cyber-reality:

- Modifying legislation (including the USA PATRIOT Act)
- Self-policing
- Applying the social responsibility model
- Fostering international collaboration
- Establishing a proactive presence on the Net
- Promoting peaceful uses of the Internet

Modifying Legislation

In the short time that the Internet has been publicly available (since the early 1990s) and the even shorter time that it has been widely used (since the late 1990s), it has, for better or for worse, revolutionized multiple aspects of lives in all corners of the world: commerce, communications, education, entertainment, and politics. Couple the Internet's ubiquitous and extensive influence with the unprecedented rate of development in Internet technology, and there is little doubt that the medium is going to continue evolving and affecting all the world's populations. Never before have policymakers or the general public had to deal with such an evolution in their midst. Any laws, policies, or technologies intended to influence the development of the Internet must be unusually forward-looking and sensitive to the dynamic, rapidly changing nature of the Internet. The legal system as it functions today is not adept at addressing terrorism on the Internet. While the Internet changes, laws in the United States remain in place until challenged in a court. The flexibility and adaptability of laws pale in comparison to the flexibility of Internet technologies to adapt to new scenarios. Therefore, laws and policies addressing Internet uses and abuses must be crafted carefully and judiciously.

The USA PATRIOT Act and other legislative acts were designed and approved in the aftermath of the shocking events of 9/11. Now, years later, we can reexamine these measures, learn lessons from our efforts, and attempt to refine the laws and their implementation. One needed modification is to transform these laws into a "public pact" between society and the administration and security agencies. We are willing to submit ourselves to security procedures of the TSA (Transportation Security Administration) in U.S. airports because the procedures are based on agreed-upon trade-offs (our privacy and time in return for a reduced risk of being victimized while flying). Moreover, we know who the officials allowed to perform the search are, we know the search routines, and we know the limits of the procedures. Similar public understanding and acceptance should be applied to counterterrorism measures on the Net. We will let the authorized officials search us and order us to take off shoes, coats, or belts, but we do it based on an agreed-upon "pact" that generally excludes further measures. We know that the American public supports monitoring of the Internet, including private e-mail traffic, but as in the case of TSA measures, this acceptance relies on known procedures, known agents, and agreed-upon limits. If "sniffer" technology is to be used, we need to know who is using it and how it is regulated, and that it is limited to antiterrorism uses only. We also need to know what kind of information is stored and who has access to such information. As with airline travel, a pact is needed to regulate the authorities' access to our private online communications.

Moreover, in addition to surveillance and monitoring Internet traffic there is also the issue of the information gathered and stored. Zittrain has suggested that while monitoring the Internet is acceptable, the government should not be allowed to store Internet traffic: "Our desire to form a cocoon against terrorists is understandable . . . [but] Even with safeguards, allowing the government to store Internet traffic is an awful idea."[59] Why? According to Zittrain,

> First, because supply creates demand. As soon as comprehensive databases of the public's communications or activities exist, the pressures to use them for purposes beyond those for which they were chartered will be inexorable. We might, for instance, create a database of all available e-mail traffic that would be searched for conspirators in a major terrorist act. But such a lode will surely be sought by defense attorneys—which means private parties coming to learn what's inside. . . . What was intended as an emergency tool for limited cases will, by its own breadth of coverage and success at limited purposes, become commonplace for any behavior deemed harmful.[60]

The security and investigative authorities may be willing to ignore certain warrant requirements when it means collecting valuable intelligence—even if it may mean that the information collected is not usable as evidence in court. And the existence of such a sophisticated system, argues Zittrain, may serve "as an irresistible invitation for purposes beyond those authorized: To make snooping routine, rather than a reaction to a reasonable suspicion of particular wrongdoers, is the sine qua non of a police state. It means spying on people otherwise presumed innocent, since it means spying on everyone."[61]

Any renewal of the USA PATRIOT Act and relevant laws should apply several modifications recommended by civil rights organizations (see the "Voices of Concern" section above), especially those modifications that guarantee that law enforcement and intelligence agencies use these new powers carefully and only when investigating acts of terrorism. A badly needed modification concerns definitions. In particular, EFF cites "the lack of definitions of 'content' that cannot be retrieved without a warrant, and of the term 'without authority' in the definition of a computer trespasser. Packets of data that comprise e-mail messages may contain both content and non-content information (such as routing information). The Act allows law enforcement officials access to non-content information, but not to content."[62] Precise definitions could thus play an important role in distinguishing where the balance lies between protected and unprotected information—and in guarding Americans' civil liberties and privacy. Since some of the modifications may include tougher measures, any change of the existing laws should show a clear and compelling need.

Self-Policing

Because Internet access relies on ISPs, ISPs' self-policing may be a key to limiting terrorists' use of the Net. Most of the terrorist Web sites, forums, and chat rooms are posted on sites provided in Western, democratic, liberal countries. The Madrid bombing of March 11, 2004, for instance, was suggested and then detailed on a Web site hosted on a U.S. server and sponsored by U.S. companies. In another example, American Northeast Intelligence Network discovered Global Islamic Media (GIM),[63] one of al Qaeda's important mouthpieces on the Internet, on the Web site of Yahoo! Groups.[64]

Al Qaeda's GIM online group had more than 7,400 members in 2004, and al Qaeda used this group to communicate with members and supporters throughout the world.[65] Postings, which use an IP address in Ottawa, Canada, include the major online publications of al Qaeda, such as *Sawt al-Jihad* and *Al Battar*. Additionally, messages taking credit for terrorist attacks are often posted on this Web site. Laura Mansfield, a terrorism analyst, notes, "Whenever a new statement of importance to the jihadis is released, such as one from Osama Bin Laden, Ayman al-Zawahiri, or Abu Musad al Zarqawi, an announcement usually occurs on this forum. Statements by lesser clerics and morale boosting messages, as well as press releases, are posted here on a regular basis as well. The group is so well established that Al Qaeda has informed its followers to disregard any information released on the internet that is not confirmed through Global Islamic Media on Yahoogroups.com."[66]

GIM, however, is just one of many group sites on Yahoo! that are used by terrorist groups. For example, al Qassam Brigades, the military wing of Hamas, operates its own Yahoo! group called "Qassem." This Web site presents the goals of the group and openly supports the use of violence. Terrorists enjoy other free Internet services as well: they use the free Web-based e-mail services provided by Yahoo! and by Hotmail (owned by Microsoft). According to Mansfield,

> One of our analysts received an email from Abu Mus'ad al Zarqawi, who used his Hotmail account to communicate. A quick check of the IP address showed that Zarqawi was dialing in to the internet through an IP address assigned to the Telephone Company of the Islamic Republic of Iran. Most of the terrorists have email addresses on either Hotmail.com or Yahoo.com, and are quite open about posting these email addresses publicly. They even answer these emails, apparently without any concern over being intercepted. A quick check of the IP addresses shows that these terrorists log in from all over the world. Many log in directly from the Middle East, most often Saudi Arabia, the United Arab Emirates, the Palestinian territories, Iran, and Egypt. A surprising number log in from Germany, the U.K., the Netherlands, Canada, and even the United States. While some of these may be proxy servers, many of them in fact reflect dial-up accounts and internet cafes in the various countries.[67]

In 2004 MEMRI released two reports titled "Islamist Websites and Their Hosts."[68] In the first report, MEMRI listed twenty-five "terror-affiliated or official Web sites active as of July 16, 2004":

> Based on the information shown, 76 percent of the Web sites are hosted in the United States, while only two sites, or 8 percent, are from the Middle East. The American hosted sites include the website of Palestinian Islamic Jihad, Army of Ansar Al-Sunnah; known supporters of Al-Qaeda, several pro Al-Qaeda sites including one that publishes Al-Qaeda's *Al-Battar Training Camp* magazine, the official website of Hamas, a pro-Hezbollah weekly magazine, Al-Aqsa Martyrs Brigades, the military wing of Arafat's Fatah organization, Hezbollah TV station Al-Manar, website of Palestinian Islamic Jihad Secretary General Dr. Abdallah Ramadhan Shalah, and Al-Quds Brigades, military wing of Palestinian Islamic Jihad. While the site for Izz Al-din Al-Qassam, military wing of Hamas, is hosted in Kelowna, Canada.[69]

Usually U.S.-based Internet service providers host suspect Web sites without even knowing it. According to Mark Hosenball's report in *Newsweek*, "[In mid-2002] the operators of an obscure Internet service provider in a Northeastern U.S. city were astonished to learn from business contacts that their computers were hosting Jehad.net, which officials regard as a semiofficial Qaeda site. Jehad.net carried a message from bin Laden's official spokesman, as well as copies of two purported jihadi training manuals: *The Mujahideen Explosives Handbook* and *The Mujahideen Poisons Handbook.* Sources say that the U.S. Internet company had subcontracted part of its capacity to another firm, which in turn may have subcontracted to others."[70]

A May 2004 report published online by Internet Haganah lists twenty-one sites representing Hezbollah that promote martyrdom and terrorist activities.[71] Of these twenty-one sites, nineteen receive services from two U.S. companies: Alabanza of Baltimore, Maryland, and ServePath of San Francisco. A total of twelve companies are involved in keeping Hezbollah online:

> ServePath, USA, nine sites
> Alabanza, USA, eight sites
> FastsHosts, UK, two sites
> VeriSign, USA, two sites

Everyone's Internet, USA, two sites

1-800hosting, USA, two sites

RackForce, Canada, two sites

ITXSarl/DataPipe, USA, two sites

CIHost, USA, one site

Soroush, Iran, one site

Cyberia, Lebanon, one site

Inco, Lebanon, one site

Any fruitful way of limiting the use of the Net by terrorists must rely on access providers' awareness and willingness to regulate the Internet. This should apply to any abuse of the Internet, from child pornography to terrorism. Some ISPs offer guidelines regarding prohibited Internet content and usage, terms for service cancellation, and even user responsibilities. ISPs may prohibit posting legally seditious or offensive content. For example, Yahoo!'s rules prohibit any content that is "unlawful, harmful, threatening, abusive, harassing, torturous, defamatory, vulgar, obscene, libelous, invasive of another's privacy, hateful, or racially, ethnically or otherwise objectionable."[72] One American ISP, DataPipe, specifically prohibits users from transmitting, distributing, or storing material "that is obscene, threatening, abusive or hateful, including the advocating of terrorism and/or the killing of any individual or group."[73] E-mails that intend to harass or annoy recipients are also prohibited.

ISPs, however, take no responsibility for the content they are hosting. Yahoo! states that it "is concerned about the safety and privacy of all its users, particularly children"; it then states that all posted materials, "whether publicly posted or privately transmitted, are the sole responsibility of the person from which such Content originated. This means that you, and not Yahoo!, are entirely responsible for all Content that you upload, post, email, transmit or otherwise make available via the Service."[74] Content may or may not be prescreened; ISPs have "the right (but not the obligation) in their sole discretion to pre-screen, refuse, or move any Content that is available via the Service."[75] ISPs retain the right to terminate service under any circumstances and without prior notice, especially if content violates the Terms of Service agreement or if law enforcement or other government agencies request the removal. Some ISPs reserve the right to remove information that is untrue, inaccurate, not current or incomplete, or reasonably suspected of being untrue, inaccurate, not current, or incomplete. However, if such content is not removed by the ISP, neither it nor its partners assume any liability.[76]

While ISPs claim very little responsibility for monitoring content, some encourage user responsibility for monitoring content. One newsgroup guideline puts the onus on the users for "becoming familiar with any written charter or FAQ governing use of such newsgroups and complying therewith."[77] Another guideline goes so far as to say, "Internet users . . . are responsible for monitoring use of the Internet by others."[78] In exchange, the ISP promises to respond to any user complaints of prohibited activities. In such cases, ISP rules are in place that define prohibited content, retain the right to remove such content, and establish a means to report such content to the ISP. The question is, to what extent are ISPs enforcing their own rules? Given the extensive presence of terrorists on the Internet, should ISPs be accepting some responsibility for the content they host? On the one hand, we would like to see them fighting abuse of the Net, but on the other hand, we certainly must not let ISPs determine the boundaries of the freedom of speech and enforce censorship on political discourse. Thus, what we need is a lively public discussion on this issue, a public debate that will result in agreed-upon principles to be applied by the ISPs.

Applying the Social Responsibility Model

The mass media, including computer-mediated communication, do not operate in a vacuum. Many researchers have studied the relationship between mass media and the social and political environments in which they operate. The first attempt to describe the relationships between mass media and the political society was introduced in 1963 in *Four Theories of the Press,* by Frederick Siebert, Theodore Peterson, and Wilbur Schramm.[79] They proposed four normative theories or models to describe the various forms of this relationship. These four models—authoritarian, libertarian, Communist, and social responsibility—are recognized by most media researchers as the best classification to describe how different media systems operate in the world.

The authoritarian model relies on direct governmental control of the mass media. This model is more common in predemocratic societies, where the media are not allowed to print or broadcast anything that could undermine the established authority or criticize the existing political system. The libertarian model rests on the "free market" philosophy, wherein all individuals should be free to publish whatever they want. This model traces back to John Milton, the seventeenth-century poet who believed that human beings inevitably choose the best ideas and values: "Let all with something to say be free to express themselves. The true and sound will survive. The false and unsound will be vanquished. Government should keep out of the battle and not weigh the odds in favor of one side or the other." Milton's principles of the "self-righting process" and the "open marketplace of ideas" were popularized by Thomas Paine and influenced Thomas Jefferson, who argued that "any government which cannot stand up to published criticism deserves to fall."[80]

The best-known and most influential philosopher of the right to free press is John Stuart Mill, whose seminal work *On Liberty* declares:

> If all mankind minus one were of one opinion, and only one person was of the contrary opinion, mankind would be no more justified in silencing that one person than he, if he had the power, would be justified in silencing mankind. The peculiar evil of silencing the expression of an opinion is that it robs the human race, posterity as well as the existing generation. If the opinion is right, they are deprived of the opportunity to exchange error for truth; if wrong, they lose what is almost as great a benefit—the clearer perception and livelier impression of truth, produced by its collision with error.[81]

It is hard to find fully libertarian media systems: even the American system is only close to this model and not fully compatible with it. The Communist model is traced back to the 1917 Russian Revolution and is based on the postulates of Karl Marx and Friedrich Engels. The media, according to this model, are not intended to be privately owned and should serve the interests of the working class. Thus, the mass media are expected to be self-regulatory according to Marxist-Leninist principles. The best present-day example of the Communist media model is China, whose Communist government controls television, radio, newspapers, and the Internet.

A revision of the libertarian model resulted in the social responsibility model. When the American Commission on Freedom of the Press realized that the market had failed to fulfill the promise of high-quality free press and free media access, it suggested a model in which the media have certain obligations to society. These obligations are "informativeness, truth, accuracy, objectivity, and balance." Thus, the goal of the social responsibility model is that media will be pluralized and responsible, reflect the diversity of society, and offer access to various points of view. Mass-media scholars Jack McLeod and Jay Blumler argue that these models were intended to be *normative,* that is, that "they do not attempt to stipulate how social systems *do* operate, but rather with specification of how they *should* or *could* work according to some preexisting set of criteria."[82] The models are thus expected not to provide perfect descriptions of the various political systems but rather to lead to a better understanding of the mass media's functions in different social systems.

In considering the social responsibility model's applicability to our concern with media and terrorism, we must emphasize that this model requires the media to consider the social and political implications of their products and to be responsible for self-regulation. Siebert, Peterson, and Schramm also note that "freedom of expression under the social responsibility theory is not an absolute right, as under pure libertarian theory. . . . One's right to free expression must be balanced against the private rights of others and against vital social interests."[83] Following this model, many different journalistic codes of ethics have been suggested, most tailored to a specific organization, medium, or media system. Among them is the ethical code presented by the Associated Press Managing Editors (APME), titled "Proposal for a Newsroom Ethics Policy."[84] The APME code states that several core values should guide journalism: responsibility ("The newspaper should be fair, accurate, honest, responsible, independent and decent. Truth is its guiding principle"); accuracy ("The newspaper should guard against inaccuracies, carelessness, bias or distortion through emphasis, omission or technological manipulation"); integrity ("The newspaper should strive for impartial treatment of issues and dispassionate handling of controversial subjects. It should provide a forum for the exchange of comment and criticism, especially when such comment is opposed to its editorial positions"); and independence ("The newspaper and its staff should be free of obligations to news sources and newsmakers").

How can these principles be applied to the Internet? When we examine the Internet as an emerging mass medium, these models are relevant to some extent. "By design, the Internet is chaotic," argues Robert Stevenson. "It has no center and functions with virtually no oversight. An argument can be made that with the Internet, national sovereignty as we know it is threatened. Since control of communication, especially press freedom, is traditionally an element of national sovereignty, the growth of the Internet presents new challenges to all national governments."[85]

And yet, now that Internet-based journalism has emerged, it requires some of the codes applied to the conventional media. Moreover, ISPs and Web site owners and operators will be expected to consider the same ethical issues and responsibility concerns since they represent the owners, publishers, and operators of the new medium. However, these expectations will not be realistic in authoritarian societies. As discussed in the previous chapter, a small number of governments do try to limit access to the Internet. Singapore was one of the leaders in developing techniques to control the Internet, while at the same time the Singapore government created a large Internet presence and promoted a program to bring the country online. In 2001, according to the Committee to Protect Journalists (CPJ), organizations promoting free expression and democracy were forced to register as political organizations, which denied them foreign funding.[86] Organizations not affiliated with the ruling party, PAP, were prohibited from posting information online.

Other nondemocratic societies are equally censorious, even if some of them have tried to avoid seeming heavy-handed:

> In Saudi Arabia, a request to access a banned URL at one point returned a page that explained why the page was not accessible, and the government even cooperated with a Harvard University study to test [the scheme's] effectiveness. For a period in 2002, the Chinese government blocked use of the Google search engine; an attempt to use it or to access a banned page resulted in a 20-minute time-out that presumably cooled the enthusiasm for seeking out information the government thought was dangerous or inappropriate.[87]

Even in democratic societies the Internet is not entirely free: in Germany, for example, Hitler's autobiography, *Mein Kampf,* was banned on the German Web site of Amazon.com. Posting of Nazi propaganda is forbidden in Germany, but with Web sites originating in other countries, control of access from within Germany is effectively impossible. As Stevenson notes, "All Western governments—including the libertarian United States—prohibit child pornography, but they face the same problem: when the material emanates from outside your borders, how can you enforce national laws without adopting the methods of China or Saudi Arabia? Even if some global agreement were approved—and the record of enforcement of international treaties is not encouraging—it is unlikely that Internet-based child pornography would disappear."[88]

The social responsibility model appears to complement the Internet in liberal societies, expecting the operators and producers, providers, and Web administrators to apply their own guidelines and restrictions. But Internet users, too, should implement a degree of social responsibility. This need is apparent when we consider the current limited ability of governments to police the Internet in light of potential future technological development and Internet growth. Society cannot expect all known and potential abuses of the Internet to be policed by the Internet administrators, government, or other agencies. The Internet is becoming ubiquitous and infiltrating ever more aspects of more and more people's lives: communicating, gathering information, shopping, banking, and paying bills. This greater dependence on the Net will necessitate some "Internet etiquette" or social responsibility. Already savvy users of e-mail are careful to use the "blind carbon copy" function when sending a group e-mail so as not to distribute unwittingly people's e-mail addresses to others. On a larger scale, people can report a violent or obscene Web site to the ISP. Parents and teachers can become involved in children's Internet activities and establish healthy Internet-use guidelines and principles.

Fostering International Collaboration

The war on terrorism is not a local war or an American war. It is a human, global, transnational war against unjustified use of violence, despicable and illegal conduct of conflict, and mass victimization of innocent civilians. To combat terrorism and to minimize its threat and potential, there must be international cooperation. This need applies also to the new arena of the Internet. Any attempt to limit the accessibility and usability of the Internet by terrorists must be internationally based. The global nature of modern terrorism and the even more global nature of its use of the Internet require an international front to fight terrorists' abuse of the Internet. Without such collaboration, terrorists will simply move their sites from one country to another, seeking those hosts that will not interfere with their Internet activities. The American effort to fight Internet terrorism is being carefully watched and even replicated or implemented by other societies. Yet if the struggle is limited to the United States, the war is lost. As we see in this study, terrorist organizations find virtual shelter in various countries in Europe, the Far East, the Middle East, Russia, and Africa.

The abuse of the Internet is taking the violent forms of "parasites" and takeovers. For example, in March 2003 an organization associated with al Qaeda hijacked a Web site of an Alaskan fishing town. The innocent text on this site was replaced with calls for attacks on U.S. and Israeli targets because of the war in Iraq. The site urged Muslims to strike back against the United States for the war in Iraq, provided links to gruesome photos of what were described as civilian war casualties, and even provided specific tactics for launching a campaign against U.S. forces. The Center for Islamic Studies and Research (CISR), whose messages were posted on the Alaskan Web site, had seen its own site shut down, reportedly by U.S. authorities, before the war in Iraq. Josh Devon, an analyst with the SITE Institute in Washington, D.C., has called CISR a "mouthpiece of al Qaeda," adding, "The site has been traveling from one unsuspecting server to another to spread its message. This is one of al Qaeda's most important Web sites. It regularly issues the al Qaeda leadership's latest communiqués, exhorts individuals to violence, and disseminates other vitriolic propaganda."[89] Devon explains, "The government has tried several times to shut down the Web site, but with limited success."

Increasingly, U.S. security officials worry that extremists may take over the ownership of U.S. computer companies. As *Newsweek* reported, in December 2002 "FBI agents arrested in Dallas the operators of Infocom, an Internet service firm allegedly financed by a leader of the militant Palestinian group Hamas."[90] In mid-December of the same year, "U.S. Customs officials searched the office of a Quincy, Mass., software firm called Ptech that had been financed by Yassin Qadi, a Saudi businessman whose assets were frozen by the Bush administration after 9/11. The company had software contracts with several U.S. government agencies, including the FBI, Federal Aviation Administration, Navy and Energy Department. A senior Defense official said about this case, 'We do polygraphs and security background checks on our contractors, but in the borderless world of the Web, culprits could be anywhere.'"[91]

Defending the Internet on an international front is not merely a practical issue: the abuse of the Internet must be declared a multifaceted global threat. Moreover, this international front to defend the Internet must also protect the very nature of the medium and its future. There are several forms that this international front might take, ranging from cooperation among nations to an international organization supported by many nations. The Internet adheres to the weakest-link principle, argues Stevenson: "If it's possible in any country, that becomes the standard around the world. In most cases, we applaud because it puts the authoritarian government on the defensive and makes censorship difficult. But sometimes, the weakest link becomes a global standard to the detriment of free expression as we define it."[92] Stevenson goes on to describe several cases of transnational limits on Internet content:

> In 1998, the head of the German subsidiary of the Internet provider CompuServe was convicted in a Bavarian court for failure to block child pornography and computer games with swastikas that had been distributed in user groups. The conviction was later overturned. Two years later, a French judge ordered Yahoo to remove Nazi paraphernalia from its auction website after a complaint was brought by groups devoted to fighting anti-Semitism and racism. The judge ordered Yahoo, which is based in the United States, to prohibit French access to the material. Inciting racism is a crime in France, and selling Nazi material, the judge said, offended "the collective memory of the country." Yahoo later got a ruling from a U.S. court that French law had no jurisdiction over its activities in the United States, including posting of materials that are illegal in France. Still, Yahoo and other Internet-based companies became more sensitive to laws in other countries where they had an important presence and pulled materials that could be offensive—and potentially the basis of litigation—in other countries.[93]

These few cases, however, underscore the difference between the United States and most other Western democracies in dealing with the Internet. For example, regarding the question of whether ISPs that host discussion groups and massive Web sites are responsible for those sites' content, the American answer is usually no, while in other countries the answer is typically yes. Says Stevenson, "In the United States, the answer is clearly in favor of free expression, even in issues involving child pornography or national security. In most other countries, it is usually the privacy and good name of individuals and the stability and order of the nation that take priority."[94]

Given today's political environment, there is, of course, little or no chance for a global agreement, since political cleavages will prevent a wall-to-wall global front and leave several countries outside such a coalition. However, the more states that join this front and collaborate, the smaller the opportunities for terrorists will be. Today most of the terrorists' sites are using Western servers, Western networks, and Western ISPs. Thus, Western societies should lead the international effort to fight terrorism on the Net by seeking measures that will significantly limit terrorists' access to this medium and hamper their abuse of its liberal character.

In 2000 the United States proposed creating an international cyber–police force to fight cybercrimes. Such a system would need to be worldwide in both coverage and participation, thereby enabling police to conduct rapid investigations over global communication networks.[95] The European Union reacted unfavorably, citing privacy implications as well as national differences in the definition of cybercrimes. Nevertheless, some forms of international cooperation are required to combat transnational terrorism and cyberterrorism.

The need for international cooperation was laid out in "A Proposal for an International Convention on Cyber Crime and Terrorism," a project initiated by the Hoover Institution, the Consortium for Research on Information Security and Policy (CRISP), the Center for International Security and Cooperation (CISAC), and Stanford University:

- Cyber crime is transnational, and requires a transnational response.
- Cyber criminals exploit weaknesses in the laws and enforcement practices of States, exposing all other States to dangers

that are beyond their capacity unilaterally or bilaterally to respond.

- The speed and technical complexity of cyber activities requires prearranged, agreed procedures for cooperation in investigating and responding to threats and attacks.
- A multilateral convention will ensure that all States Parties:
  - □ adopt laws making dangerous cyber activities criminal;
  - □ enforce those laws or extradite criminals for prosecution by other States;
  - □ cooperate in investigating criminal activities and in providing usable evidence for prosecutions; and
  - □ participate in formulating and agree to adopt and implement standards and practices that enhance safety and security.[96]

A draft of a proposal written by the International Convention to Enhance Protection from Cyber Crime and Terrorism combined protective and reactive measures with provisions for protecting privacy and other civil liberties.[97] The draft called upon States Parties to establish cyberoffenses as crimes under domestic law but "[t]hereafter, investigations, extraditions, prosecutions, mutual legal assistance, and judicial proceedings are to be carried out in accordance with the laws of the States Parties. Intrusive international law enforcement procedures may be allowed, but only in accordance with domestic legal standards and mutual legal assistance treaties."[98] The proposed convention explicitly stated:

> It should not be construed to require an infringement of the privacy or other human rights of any person as defined by the laws of the requested state. In some cases, especially those involving international exchanges of sensitive information and monitoring of networks by law enforcement, special procedural safeguards for privacy may also be necessary. Domestic and international exchanges among technology and law enforcement experts, of data on past and suspected computer crimes, anomalies in computer operation, network vulnerabilities, modes of penetration, alerts, and warnings all fall into this category.[99]

Establishing a Proactive Presence on the Net

In April 2004, the British domestic secret service, known as MI5, launched a Web site (www.mi5.gov.uk) providing detailed antiterrorism advice to the public.[100] It warned the British public that al Qaeda was active in the country and declared a heightened state of alert. "The threat from international terrorism remains real and serious. Osama bin Laden has in several statements publicly named Britain and British interests as a target, and encouraged attacks to be carried out against them," its warning stated. Some of its posted suggestions detailed how to "carry out risk assessments, look at mail-handling procedures, and check that staff are who they say they are." Visitors to the Web site can e-mail or telephone security agencies if they have information relating to terrorism, as well as apply for a job with the service.[101] The site also provides information about MI5, its methods of gathering intelligence, and its oversight mechanisms. For example, writing on the site, MI5 director general Eliza Manningham-Buller noted, "For the most part details of our operations must and should remain secret. But stopping terrorists is only one part of our collective defenses against terrorism." She added, "Another part of our work is to use the knowledge we have about these organizations to provide sensible and practical advice on how best to protect yourself against these threats. Traditionally this advice was confined mainly to government, but the threat of global terrorism makes it important for us to extend this advice to a wider range of people."

As the MI5 Web site illustrates, the advantages of the Internet should not serve only terrorists but also those who confront them, not only in terms of monitoring and learning about terrorists but also in launching antiterrorism campaigns. For example, educational campaigns that encourage nonviolent forms of debate and teach conflict resolution techniques can provide a viable counterweight to terrorist campaigns. Web sites that expose the terrorists' lies and challenge their morally disengaged rhetoric can provide potential recruits with a logical analysis of a group's purported grievances and activities. Bearing in mind that terrorism is a war over minds and souls and that it often targets young people and children, Web sites can be particularly valuable in countering the insidious claims and arguments of terrorist organizations. A wide range of groups and organizations, from concerned citizens to NGOs and social organizations, can launch such alternative sites and provide well-reasoned nonviolent voices.

Promoting Peaceful Uses of the Internet

Attempts to minimize the abuse of the Internet by terrorists should not divert all the attention from the actors and motives that create terror. As Cory Smith, legislative counsel for Human Rights First, notes, "guns don't kill people, people kill people. There's always going to be people that use technology for bad uses. You see this with fuel oil and fertilizer combination for bombs; farmers use these all the time in their day-to-day activities. You can't control certain elements or what [they] are going to use these elements for."[102] The Internet has become a weapon, too, but it is people who activate it, use it, and aim it at others. Thus, proactive initiatives should not be confined to the medium only but should also include addressing ideological, political, and religious motivations that promote terrorism. Here the Internet can be used as an educational instrument, as a bridging tool, and as a channel for antiviolence messages. Smith argues, "I think if we encourage (a) greater access to the Internet, and then (b) open access, unfettered access for people to communicate and have freedom of expression and freedom of association, my feelings are that we would greatly mitigate [terrorism], because this would be proactive instead of reactive, by opening up these societies for them and providing another avenue." Moreover, Smith notes,

> At the end of the day, are we going to allow the terrorists to win by changing our fundamental democracy? . . . I think the worst thing would be to allow them the victory by changing what we are. . . . After all the problems and issues, we have to be very careful about that. And it also has a bad effect down the line . . . like there's slippage, and we feel like we have to hold the line, that the bar's been lowered now for a lot of countries because they do look to the United States as an example of human rights, civil rights, democracy, and so I think that's a real problem.

Communication technology can benefit society, culture, science, and the quality of life in general. However, it can also serve up aggression, violence, pornography, crime, hate, racism, and extremism. The new communication technologies and especially the Internet carry a paradigm shift: they empower individuals over states or societies. They do so by allowing free access to information, to mass media, to communities, and to alternative sources. Indeed, governments and states do employ these technologies for their own purposes, but the power shift is more away from central, monolithic, and hierarchical structures and more toward individuals and groups. The Internet's beauty as a mass medium is in its liberal, free, and unregulated nature. These advantages, as we have seen, are also being abused by modern terrorists. Is this one of the unavoidable prices of free, democratic media? Perhaps, but there is a proactive "golden path" that will minimize the abuse of the Internet by both terrorism and counterterrorism.

In conclusion, avoiding any search for compromises and best trade-offs may have disastrous consequences, for terrorist use of the Internet will only grow and become more sophisticated and more manipulative. This may in turn lead to harsher counterterrorism measures enforced by terror-stricken governments and security agencies. A vicious cycle of terrorism-counterterrorism is being played out on the Internet. As Timothy Lynch of the Cato Institute warns,

> Government officials typically respond to terrorist attacks by proposing and enacting "antiterrorism" legislation. To assuage the wide-spread anxiety of the populace, policymakers make the dubious claim that they can prevent terrorism by curtailing the privacy and civil liberties of the people. Because everyone wants to be safe and secure, such legislation is usually very popular and passes the legislative process relatively smoothly during times of trouble. . . . This cycle of terrorist attack followed by government curtailment of civil liberties must be broken—or our democracy will eventually lose the key attribute that has made it great: freedom.[103]

Appendix
Terrorist Organizations on the Internet

Definition

Although no single definition of "terrorism" holds universal acceptance, we will, for the purposes of this study, use the definition as applied by the U.S. State Department and contained in Title 22 of the United States Code, Section 2656f(d):

- The term "terrorism" means premeditated, politically motivated violence perpetrated against noncombatant targets by subnational groups or clandestine agents, usually intended to influence an audience.
- The term "international terrorism" means terrorism involving citizens or the territory of more than one country.
- The term "terrorist group" means any group practicing, or that has significant subgroups that practice, international terrorism.

The U.S. government has used this definition of terrorism since 1983 for all statistical and analytical purposes. Because the present study was conducted from 1998 to 2005, there have been several "designations" and "redesignations," and thus our database contains all the groups designated at least once in this period.

The following list comprises the thirty-six terrorist groups as of October 1997 that were designated by the secretary of state as foreign terrorist organizations (FTOs).[1] The designation carries legal consequences:

- It is unlawful to provide funds or other material support to a designated FTO.
- Representatives and certain members of a designated FTO can be denied visas or excluded from the United States.
- U.S. financial institutions must block funds of designated FTOs and their agents and must report the blockage to the U.S. Department of the Treasury.[2]

Designated Foreign Terrorist Organizations (1997–98)

1. Abu Nidal Organization (ANO)
2. Abu Sayyaf Group (ASG)
3. Armed Islamic Group (GIA)
4. Aum Shinrikyo (Aum)
5. Democratic Front for the Liberation of Palestine–Hawatmeh Faction (DFLP)
6. Euzkadi Ta Askatasuna (ETA)
7. Gama'a al-Islamiyya (Islamic Group, IG)
8. Hamas (Islamic Resistance Movement)
9. Harakat ul-Ansar (HUA)
10. Hezbollah (Party of God)
11. Japanese Red Army (JRA)
12. al-Jihad
13. Kach
14. Kahane Chai
15. Khmer Rouge
16. Kurdistan Workers' Party (PKK)
17. Liberation Tigers of Tamil Eelam (LTTE)
18. Manuel Rodriguez Patriotic Front Dissidents (FPMR/D)
19. Mujahedin-e Khalq Organization (MEK, MKO)

20. National Liberation Army (ELN)
21. Palestine Liberation Front–Abu Abbas Faction (PLF)
22. Palestinian Islamic Jihad–Shaqaqi Faction (PIJ)
23. Popular Front for the Liberation of Palestine (PFLP)
24. Popular Front for the Liberation of Palestine–General Command (PFLP-GC)
25. Revolutionary Armed Forces of Colombia (FARC)
26. Revolutionary Organization 17 November (17 November)
27. Revolutionary People's Liberation Party/Front (DHKP/C)
28. Revolutionary People's Struggle (ELA)
29. Shining Path (Sendero Luminoso, SL)
30. Tupac Amaru Revolutionary Movement (MRTA)

Designated Foreign Terrorist Organizations (2003–04)

1. Abu Nidal Organization (ANO)
2. Abu Sayyaf Group (ASG)
3. Ansar al-Islam
4. al-Aqsa Martyrs Brigades
5. Armed Islamic Group (GIA)
6. Asbat al-Ansar
7. Aum Shinrikyo (AUM)
8. Basque Fatherland and Liberty (ETA)
9. Communist Party of the Philippines/New People's Army (CPP/NPA)
10. Gama'a al-Islamiyya (Islamic Group)
11. Hamas (Islamic Resistance Movement)
12. Harakat ul-Mujahidin (HUM)
13. Hezballoh (Party of God)
14. Islamic Movement of Uzbekistan (IMU)
15. Jaish-e-Mohammed (JEM) (Army of Mohammed)
16. Jemaah Islamiya Organization (JI)
17. al-Jihad (Egyptian Islamic Jihad)
18. Kahane Chai (Kach)

19. Kurdistan Workers' Party (PKK), aka Kurdistan Freedom and Democracy Congress (KADEK)
20. Lashkar e-Tayba (LeT) (Army of the Righteous)
21. Lashkar i Jhangvi
22. Liberation Tigers of Tamil Eelam (LTTE)
23. Mujahedin-e Khalq Organization (MEK)
24. National Liberation Army (ELN)
25. Palestine Liberation Front (PLF)
26. Palestinian Islamic Jihad (PIJ)
27. Popular Front for the Liberation of Palestine (PFLP)
28. Popular Front for the Liberation of Palestine (PFLP)–General Command (PFLP-GC)
29. al Qaeda
30. Real IRA (RIRA)
31. Revolutionary Armed Forces of Colombia (FARC)
32. Revolutionary Nuclei (formerly ELA)
33. Revolutionary Organization 17 November
34. Revolutionary People's Liberation Army/Front (DHKP/C)
35. Salafist Group for Call and Combat (GSPC)
36. Shining Path (Sendero Luminoso, SL)
37. United Self-Defense Forces of Colombia (AUC)

Other Terrorist Groups

al-Badhr Mujahedin
Alex Boncayao Brigade (ABB)
al-Ittihad al-Islami (AIAI)
Allied Democratic Forces (ADF)
Ansar al-Islam (Iraq)
Anti-Imperialist Territorial Nuclei (NTA)
Army for the Liberation of Rwanda (ALIR)
Cambodian Freedom Fighters (CFF)
Communist Party of Nepal (Maoist)/United People's Front

Continuity Irish Republican Army (CIRA)

Eastern Turkestan Islamic Movement

First of October Antifascist Resistance Group (GRAPO)

Harakat ul-Jihad-i-Islami (HUJI)

Harakat ul-Jihad-i-Islami–Bangladesh (HUJI-B)

Hizb-i Islami Gulbuddin

Hizb ul-Mujahedin

Irish Republican Army (IRA)

Islamic Army of Aden (IAA)

Islamic International Peacekeeping Brigade

Jamiat ul-Mujahedin

Japanese Red Army (JRA)

Kumpulan Mujahidin Malaysia (KMM)

Libyan Islamic Fighting Group

Lord's Resistance Army (LRA)

Loyalist Volunteer Force (LVF)

Moroccan Islamic Combatant Group (GICM)

New Red Brigades/Communist Combatant Party (BR/PCC)

People Against Gangsterism and Drugs (PAGAD)

Red Hand Defenders (RHD)

Revolutionary Proletarian Initiative Nuclei (NIPR)

Revolutionary United Front (RUF)

Riyadus-Salikhin (Reconnaissance and Sabotage Battalion of Chechen Martyrs)

Sipah-i-Sahaba

Special Purpose Islamic Regiment

Tunisian Combatant Group (TCG)

Tupac Amaru Revolutionary Movement (MRTA)

Turkish Hezbollah

Ulster Defense Association/Ulster Freedom Fighters (UDA/UFF)

Notes

Introduction

1. Matthew Parker Voors, "Encryption Regulation in the Wake of September 11, 2001: Must We Protect National Security at the Expense of the Economy?" *Federal Communications Law Journal* 55, no. 2 (2003): 331–352. Voors cites articles from the *Guardian* (London), *U.S. News and World Report,* and *Washington Post.*

2. These include the Privacy Foundation; Terrorism Research Center; RAND Corporation; Center for National Security Studies (CNSS); Center for Strategic and International Studies (CSIS); large Internet service providers such as America Online and EarthLink; government agencies and officials; and civil liberties organizations such as the Electronic Privacy Information Center (EPIC), American Civil Liberties Union (ACLU), Center for Democracy and Technology (CDT), Electronic Frontier Foundation (EFF), People For Internet Responsibility (PFIR), Human Rights First, and others.

3. Yariv Tsfati and Gabriel Weimann, "Terror on the Internet" [in Hebrew], *Politika* 4 (1999): 45–64; and Yariv Tsfati and Gabriel Weimann, "WWW.Terrorism.com: Terror on the Internet," *Studies in Conflict and Terrorism* 25, no. 5 (2002): 317–332.

4. Oli R. Holsti, "Content Analysis," in *The Handbook of Social Psychology,* ed. Lindzey Gardner and Elliot Aronson (Reading, Mass.: Addison-Wesley, 1968).

5. U.S. State Department, "Patterns of Global Terrorism," Appendix B (1996), http://www.milnet.com/milnet/state/terrgrp.htm; U.S. State Department, "Patterns of

Global Terrorism" (2000), http://www.mipt.org/Patterns-of-Global-Terrorism.asp; and
U.S. State Department, "Patterns of Global Terrorism" (2002), http://www.mipt.org/
Patterns-of-Global-Terrorism.asp. The definition of "terror" was elaborated by Alex P.
Schmid and Albert J. Jongman in *Political Terrorism* (Amsterdam: North-Holland Pub-
lishing, 1988). See also Gabriel Weimann and Conrad Winn, *The Theater of Terror*
(New York: Longman, 1994).

   6. Weimann and Winn, *Theater of Terror.*

   7. Tsfati and Weimann, "WWW.Terrorism.com: Terror on the Internet," 325.

   8. Brian Krebs, "Feds Building Internet Monitoring Center," Washingtonpost
.com, January 31, 2003, http://www.washingtonpost.com/ac2/wp-dyn/A3409-2003Jan
30?language=printer.

   9. Ibid.

1. New Terrorism, New Media

   1. Under the Antiterrorism and Effective Death Penalty Act (AEDPA) of 1996.

   2. Gabriel Weimann, *WWW.Terror.Net: How Modern Terrorism Uses the Internet,*
Special Report (Washington, D.C.: United States Institute of Peace, 2004); and Gabriel
Weimann, "Terrorists and Their Tools: Using the Internet," *Yale Global Online,* http://
yaleglobal.yale.edu/display.article?id=3768.

   3. The best description of the Internet's history, written by those who oversaw its
development—including Barry M. Leiner, Vinton G. Cerf, David D. Clark, Robert E.
Kahn, Leonard Kleinrock, and Larry G. Roberts, among others—is Barry M. Leiner et
al., "A Brief History of the Internet," http://www.isoc.org/internet/history/.

   4. Ibid.

   5. Ibid.

   6. Ibid.

   7. Ibid.

   8. From the report "World Internet Users and Population Stats," February 3,
2005, http://www.internetworldstats.com/stats.htm.

   9. Ibid.

   10. John D. H. Downing, "Computers for Political Change: PeaceNet and Public
Data Access," *Journal of Communication* 39, no. 3 (1989): 154–162; Michael Jaffe,
"Interactive Mass Media and Political Participation" (paper presented at the annual
conference of the Midwest Association for Public Opinion Research [MAPOR], 1994),
http://research.haifa.ac.il/~jmjaffe/poli_cmc.html.

11. Wayman Mullins, *A Sourcebook on Domestic and International Terrorism,* 2nd ed. (Springfield, Ill.: Charles Thomas Publisher, 1997), 11.

12. Weimann and Winn, *Theater of Terror,* 20.

13. Joseba Zulaika and William A. Douglass, *Terror and Taboo: The Follies, Fables, and Faces of Terrorism* (New York: Routledge, 1996), 96.

14. Mullins, *Sourcebook on Domestic and International Terrorism,* 9.

15. Ian M. H. Smart, "The Power of Terror," in *Contemporary Terrorism: Selected Readings,* ed. J. D. Elliot and L. K. Gibson (Gaithersburg, Md.: IACP, 1978).

16. At http://www.terrorismanswers.org/terrorism/introduction.html.

17. Council on Foreign Relations, "Terrorism: An Introduction." At http://www.terrorismanswers.com/terrorism/introduction.html. Cited April 12, 2003.

18. Alex P. Schmid and Albert J. Jongman, *Political Terrorism* (Amsterdam: North-Holland Publishing; New Brunswick, N.J.: Transaction Books, 1988), 5.

19. Boaz Ganor, "Defining Terrorism: Is One Man's Terrorist Another Man's Freedom Fighter?" (online report, International Policy Institute for Counter-Terrorism [ICT], September 24, 1998), http://www.ict.org.il/articles/define.htm.

20. Xavier Raufer, "Al Qaeda: A Different Diagnosis," *Studies in Conflict and Terrorism* 26 (2003): 391–398.

21. Shabtai Shavit, "Contending with International Terrorism," *Journal of International Security Affairs* 6 (2004): 65–66.

22. Michele Zanini and Sean J. A. Edwards, "The Networking of Terrorism in the Information Age," in *Networks and Netwars: The Future of Terror, Crime, and Militancy,* ed. John Arquilla and David Ronfeldt (Santa Monica, Calif.: RAND Corporation, 2001), 30.

23. CLC Media Policy Program, "Cyberpolitics," http://www.bettercampaigns.org/issuebriefs/display.php?BriefID=11.

24. Rob Kitchin, *Cyberspace: The World in Wires* (Chichester, U.K.: John Wiley and Sons, 1998).

25. Robert A. Saunders, "Nationality: Cyber-Russian," *Russia in Global Affairs* 4, (October–December 2004), http://eng.globalaffairs.ru/printver/716.html.

26. CLC Media Policy Program, "Cyberpolitics."

27. Kevin A. Hill, *Cyberpolitics* (New York: Rowman and Littlefield, 1998).

28. Saunders, "Nationality: Cyber-Russian."

29. Yale H. Ferguson and Richard W. Mansbach, *Remapping Global Politics: History's Revenge and Future Shock* (Cambridge: Cambridge University Press, 2005).

30. Robert A. Saunders, "A Web of Postnational Identities: National Minorities, Identity Politics and Cyberspace" (paper presented at Voronezh State University's international symposium "Typology and Classification of Culture Post," Voronezh, Russian Republic, October 28–30, 2003), 2.

31. Ronald J. Deibert, *Parchment, Printing, and Hypermedia: Communication in World Order Transformation* (New York: Columbia University Press, 1997).

32. Saunders, "Web of Postnational Identities," 3.

33. Tsfati and Weimann, "Terror on the Internet"; and Tsfati and Weimann, "WWW.Terrorism.com."

34. Weimann and Winn, *Theater of Terror.*

35. Bruce Hoffman, "Al Qaeda, Trends in Terrorism, and Future Potentialities: An Assessment," *Studies in Conflict and Terrorism* 26 (2003): 427–440.

36. John Arquilla and David F. Ronfeldt, "Networks, Netwars, and the Fight for the Future," *First Monday, October 25, 2003* (2001); John Arquilla and David Ronfeldt, "The Advent of Netwar (Revisited)," in *Networks and Netwars,* ed. Arquilla and Ronfeldt (Santa Monica, Calif.: RAND Corporation, 2001), 1–25; and John Arquilla, David Ronfeldt, and Michele Zanini, "Networks, Netwar, and Information-Age Terrorism," in *Countering the New Terrorism,* ed. Ian O. Lesser et al. (Santa Monica, Calif.: RAND Corporation, 2001).

37. Timothy L. Thomas, "Al Qaeda and the Internet: The Danger of 'Cyberplanning,' " *Parameters* (Spring 2003): 112–123.

38. Attorney General John Ashcroft, in his announcement of a grand jury's indictment of Ahmed Omar Saeed Sheikh, a British citizen, for acts of terrorism against two United States citizens (March 14, 2002): "Using the Internet to communicate, Saeed assumed a false identity to lure Daniel Pearl to a meeting in Karachi with a fictitious source. It was from this meeting that Pearl was abducted."

39. Yoni Fighel, "Falling into the Al-Qaida Trap Again" (online report, ICT, March 9, 2003), http://www.ict.org.il/articles/articledet.cfm?articleid=466.

40. See http://groups.yahoo.com/group/globalislamicmedia/message/173.

41. The Middle East Media Research Institute (MEMRI), "Islamist Website Issues Warning of Imminent Attacks: Calls on Muslims to Leave DC, NY and LA" (online special dispatch, November 4, 2003), http://memri.de/uebersetzungen_analysen/themen/islamistische_ideologie/isl_Anschlagswarnung_04_11_03.pdf.

42. Translation and excerpts provided by MEMRI, ibid.

43. Fighel, "Falling into the Al-Qaida Trap Again."

44. Cited in "Information Security News: Militants Wire Web with Links to Jihad," *InfoSec News,* July 11, 2002, http://seclists.org/isn/2002/Jul/0050.html.

45. Rita Katz and Josh Devon, "WWW.Jihad.com," *National Review Online,* July 14, 2003, http://nationalreview.com/comment/comment-katz-devon071403.asp.

46. Ibid.

47. Ibid.

48. Ibid.

49. Marc Rogers, "The Psychology of Cyber-Terrorism," in *Terrorists, Victims, and Society,* ed. Andrew Silke (Chichester, U.K.: John Wiley and Sons, 2003), 77–92.

50. National Commission on Terrorist Attacks, *The 9/11 Commission Report: Final Report of the National Commission on Terrorist Attacks upon the United States* (New York: W. W. Norton, 2004), i.

51. Ibid., x.

52. Ibid., 88.

53. Ibid.

2. The War over Minds: The Psychology of Terrorism

1. American Psychological Association, "Coping with Terrorism" (2001), http://helping.apa.org/daily/terrorism.html.

2. Clark McCauley, "The Psychology of Terrorism" (online essay, Social Science Research Council, 2000), http://www.ssrc.org/sept11/essays/mccauley.htm.

3. Boaz Ganor, "Terror as a Strategy of Psychological Warfare" (online report, ICT, 2000), http://www.ict.org.il/articles/articledet.cfm?articleid=443.

4. McCauley, "Psychology of Terrorism."

5. C. E. Stout, ed., *The Psychology of Terrorism* (Westport, Conn.: Praeger, 2002).

6. Clark McCauley, "Psychological Issues in Understanding Terrorism and the Response to Terrorism," in *The Psychology of Terrorism,* ed. Stout, 3.

7. Martha Crenshaw, "The Psychology of Terrorism: An Agenda for the 21st Century," *Political Psychology* 21 (2002): 405–420.

8. Hari Heath, "The War on Terrorism: Psychological Warfare? Again?" *Idaho Observer,* 2001, http://proliberty.com/observer/20011001.htm.

9. See Christopher Simpson, *The Science of Coercion* (Oxford: Oxford University Press, 1996).

10. Jerrold Post, "Psychological Operations: A Critical Weapon in Countering Terrorism" (paper presented at the International Conference on Counter-Terrorism in Democracies: Political and Psychological Perspectives, University of Haifa, Haifa, Israel, January 2003).

11. Boaz Ganor, "Terrorism as a Strategy of Psychological Warfare," in *The Trauma of Terrorism,* ed. Y. Danieli, D. Brom, and J. Sills (New York: Haworth, 2004), 33–43.

12. Ibid., 1.

13. Alex P. Schmid, *Political Terrorism* (New Brunswick, N.J.: Transaction, 1983).

14. Cited by Christopher Dobson and Ronald Paine, *The Carlos Complex: A Pattern of Violence* (London: Hodder and Stoughton, 1977), 15.

15. See Hans-Bernd Brosius and Gabriel Weimann, "The Contagiousness of Mass-Mediated Terrorism," *European Journal of Communication* 6 (1991): 63–75; Brian M. Jenkins, *International Terrorism: A New Kind of Warfare* (Santa Monica, Calif.: RAND Corporation, 1974); Gabriel Weimann, "The Theater of Terror: The Effects of Press Coverage," *Journal of Communication* 33 (1983): 38–45; Gabriel Weimann, "Media Events: The Case of International Terrorism," *Journal of Broadcasting and Electronic Media* 31, no. 1 (1987): 21–39; Gabriel Weimann, "Mass-Mediated Theater of Terror: Must the Show Go On?" in *The News Media and Terrorism,* ed. P. Bruck (Ottawa: Carleton University Press, 1988), 1–22; Gabriel Weimann, "Redefinition of Image: The Impact of Mass-Mediated Terrorism," *International Journal of Public Opinion Research* 2, no. 1 (1990): 16–29; Gabriel Weimann and Hans-Bernd Brosius, "The Newsworthiness of International Terrorism," *Communication Research* 18, no. 3 (1991): 333–354; and Weimann and Winn, *Theater of Terror.*

16. Philip A. Karber, "Urban Terrorism: Baseline Data and Conceptual Framework," *Social Science Quarterly* 52 (1971): 529.

17. Ralph E. Dowling, "Terrorism and the Media: A Rhetorical Genre," *Journal of Communication* 35 (1986): 14.

18. Weimann and Winn, *Theater of Terror.*

19. Brigitte Nacos, "The Terrorist Calculus behind 9-11: A Model for Future Terrorism?" *Studies in Conflict and Terrorism* 26 (2003): 1–16.

20. From the translations of a videotape, presumably made in mid-November 2001 in Afghanistan, http://www.washingtonpost.com/wp-srv/nation/specials.

21. Nacos, "Terrorist Calculus."

22. Ibid.

23. Hamza Hendawi, "Terror Manual Advises on Targets," http://story.news.yahoo.com/news?tmpl=story&u+/ap/20…/afghan_spreading_terror_.

24. Nacos, "Terrorist Calculus," 5.

25. Ibid., 9.

26. Ibid., 7.

27. Ibid., 10.

28. Felicity Barringer, "New Tactic of Terrorists Is to Attack the Media," *New York Times,* October 15, 2001, C1.

29. Ibid.

30. Gabriel Weimann, "The Theater of Terror: The Challenge for Democracy" [in Hebrew], in *Basic Issues in Israeli Democracy,* ed. R. Cohen-Almagor (Tel Aviv: Sifriyat Poalim, 1999).

31. Bruce Hoffman, "Al Qaeda, Trends in Terrorism, and Future Potentialities: An Assessment," *Studies in Conflict and Terrorism* 26 (2003): 429.

32. Translated by SITE Institute, http://www.siteinstitute.org/exposing.asp?id=203.

33. Cited in "Eleventh Issue of *Sawt-al-Jihad* Released" by SITE Institute, February 24, 2004, http://freerepublic.com/focus/f-news/1084923/posts.

34. Hoffman, "Al Qaeda."

35. Paul Eedle, "Terrorism.com," *Guardian,* July 17, 2002, 10, http://www.guardian.co.uk/print/0,3858,4462872-103680,00.html.

36. Hoffman, "Al Qaeda," 435.

37. Posted on the Internet at http://1.anwar-islam.com/v/11/6.rm. Translated by MEMRI, http://www.memri.info/bin/articles.cgi?Page=countries&Area=saudiarabia&ID=SA1103.

38. Cited in the MEMRI report, ibid.

39. Yoram Schweitzer, "Terrorism and Propaganda" (online research report, ICT, October 10, 2000), http://www.ict.org.il/spotlight/comment.cfm?id=688.

40. Ibid.

41. Ibid.

42. Hoffman, "Al Qaeda," 434–435.

3. Communicative Uses of the Internet for Terrorism

1. Vinay Lal, "Terror and Its Networks: Disappearing Trails in Cyberspace," http://www.nautilus.org/archives/virtual-diasporas/paper/Lal.html.

2. Thomas, "Al Qaeda and the Internet," 112–123.

3. Mark Wrighte, "The Real Mexican Terrorists: A Group Profile of the Popular Revolutionary Army (EPR)," *Studies in Conflict and Terrorism* 25: 207–225. According to Wrighte, "With the exception of their violent uprising in 1994, the EZLN has focused more on political dialogue, whereas the Marxist inspired EPR has primarily relied on terrorism to highlight social inequities in the state of Guerrero. The EZLN is older and larger, but unlike the EPR, it has refrained from conducting terrorist attacks since its initial uprising. However, in most of the 1990s this group was included in the State Department's list of terrorist groups."

4. On the historical roots of radical Islam's war against the West, see Daniel Benjamin and Steven Simon, *The Age of Sacred Terror* (New York: Random House, 2003).

5. Gary R. Bunt, *Virtually Islamic: Computer-Mediated Communication and Cyber Islamic Environments* (Cardiff: University of Wales Press, 2000); and Gary R. Bunt, *Islam in the Digital Age* (London: Pluto, 2003).

6. Bunt, *Virtually Islamic,* 10.

7. Ibid., 14.

8. http://www.ehj-navarre.org/index.html.

9. Tsfati and Weimann, "WWW.Terrorism.com," 323.

10. Ibid., 325.

11. Albert Bandura, "Mechanisms of Moral Disengagement," in *Origins of Terrorism: Psychologies, Ideologies, Theologies, States of Mind,* ed. W. Reich (Cambridge: Cambridge University Press, 1990), 161–191; Albert Bandura, "Moral Disengagement in the Perpetration of Inhumanities," *Personality and Social Psychology Review* (special issue on evil and violence) 3 (1999): 193–209; Albert Bandura, "Selective Moral Disengagement in the Exercise of Moral Agency," *Journal of Moral Education* 31, no. 2 (2002): 101–119; Albert Bandura, "The Role of Selective Moral Disengagement in Terrorism and Counterterrorism," in *Understanding Terrorism: Psychological Roots, Consequences and Interventions,* ed. F. M. Moghaddam and A. J. Marsella (Washington, D.C.: American Psychological Association, 2004), 121–150; Albert Bandura, Claudio Barbaranelli, Gian-Vittorio Caprara, and Concetta Pastorelli, "Mechanisms of Moral Disengagement in the Exercise of Moral Agency," *Journal of Personality and Social Psychology* 71 (1996): 364–374; Albert Bandura, Gian-Vittorio Caprara, and Laszlo Zsolnai, "Corporate Transgressions through Moral Disengagement," *Journal of Human Values* 6 (2000): 57–63.

12. Bandura, "Selective Moral Disengagement."

13. Ibid., 104.

14. Ibid., 105.

15. Bandura, "Moral Disengagement in the Perpetration of Inhumanities," 13.

16. From the ICT archive of terrorist organizations, http://www.ict.org.il/ inter_ter/orgdet.cfm?orgid=68.

17. Translated by SITE Institute, June 7, 2004, http://www.siteinstitute.org.

18. Translated by MEMRI and posted May 30, 2003, as a special dispatch on the MEMRI Web site, http://www.memri.org.

19. Ibid.

20. Ibid.

21. This incident was reported by Arnold Krushelnycky in "Chechnya: Rebels Use Internet in Propaganda War with Russians," Human Rights Information Network, 2000, http://www.hrea.org/lists/h.

22. Barton Gellman, "Cyber-Attacks by al-Qaeda Feared," *Washington Post,* June 27, 2002, A01.

23. On the history of al Qaeda, see Paul J. Smith, "Transnational Terrorism and the al Qaeda Model: Confronting New Realities," *Parameters* (Summer 2002): 33–46.

24. Ibid.

25. Paul Eedle, "Terrorism.com," *Guardian,* July 17, 2002, http://www.guardian .co.uk/print/0,3858,4462872-103680,00.html.

26. Mark Ward, "Websites Spread al-Qaeda Message," *BBC News Online,* December 12, 2002, http://news.bbc.co.uk/2/hi/technology/2566527.stm.

27. Cited in ibid.

28. From the (al Qaeda) Web site Azzam, cited in *Jihad Online: Islamic Terrorists and the Internet,* published by the Anti-Defamation League (ADL), 2000, http://www .adl.org/internet/jihad_online.pdf.

29. Ibid.

30. See "Islamist Websites and Their Hosts Part I: Islamist Terror Organizations" (online report, MEMRI, July 2004), http://www.memri.org/bin/articles.cgi?Area= jihad&ID=SR3104.

31. *Jihad Online.*

32. See " 'Why We Fight America': Al-Qa'ida Spokesman Explains September 11 and Declares Intentions to Kill 4 Million Americans with Weapons of Mass Destruction" (online report, MEMRI, June 2001), http://memri.org/bin/articles.cgi?Page=archives &Area=sd&ID=SP38802.

33. http://groups.yahoo.com/group/abubanan2/message/330.

34. See "Al-Qa'ida Claims Responsibility for Last Week's Blackout" (online report, MEMRI, August 2003), http://www.memri.org/bin/articles.cgi?Area=jihad&ID= SP55303.

35. Ibid.

36. Appeared first at http://www.cybcity.com/image900/index.htm and then changed sites.

37. For analysis of this magazine, see Reuvan Paz, "Sawt al-Jihad: New Indoctrination of Qa'idat al-Jihad" (Occasional Paper 1, no. 8, published by the Project for the Study of Islamist Movements [PRISM], 2003), http://www.e-prism.org/images/PRISM_no_8.doc.

38. Ibid.

39. Ibid.

40. This issue was translated and analyzed by SITE Institute in its report "Ninth Issue of *Sawt al-Jihad* Released," January 23, 2004, http://siteinstitute.org/bin/articles.cgi?ID=publications2504&Category=publications&Subcategory=0.

41. Ibid.

42. Ibid.

43. From "Women's War Daily—al Khansa Magazine and Azzam Publications Offers Handy Hints for Martyr Moms and Newlywed Jihadis," *Militant Islam Monitor,* August 24, 2004, http://www.militantislammonitor.org/article/id/258. See also "Cosmo for Jihadettes Debuts: Al Qaeda Starts Women's Magazine" (online report, Northeast Intelligence Network [NEIN], August 2004), http://www.homelandsecurityus.com/archives2d.asp.

44. This issue was translated and analyzed in "Al Qaeda Release Issue 17 of Voice of Jihad," (online report, NEIN, May 2004), http://www.homelandsecurityus.com/May2004/vj17.asp.

45. http://www.almuk.com/obm/.

46. http://www.almuk.com/obm/jihaad.html.

47. http://www.shareeah.org/.

48. Yotam Feldner, "Radical Islamist Profiles (1): London-Abu Hamza Al-Masi" (online report, MEMRI, October 16, 2001), http://www.memri.org/bin/articles.cgi?Page=subjects&Area=jihad&ID=IA7201.

49. Reported by the *Christian Science Monitor,* January 13, 1999.

50. Feldner, "Radical Islamist Profiles (1)."

51. This exchange appeared at http://www.shareeah.com/Eng/aj/aj2.html.

52. Most notable is http://www.farcep.org/.

53. Links to FARC's magazine can be found at http://www.resistancianacional.org.

54. Links to the international version are at http://six.swix.ch/farcep/Revista/Resistencia31/Web/index.html.

55. http://www.resistencianacional.org/.

56. nuevacolombia@resistencianacional.org.

57. http://six.swix.ch/farcep/Revista/Resistencia31/Web/index.html.

58. The charter can be found at http://www.nmsu.edu/~govdept/faculty/lapid/3.htm.

59. In English at "Hamas—the Islamic Resistance Movement," under "Communiqués," http://www.palestine-info.com/hamas/index.htm; in Arabic at "Sijil al-Majd—Amaliyat Hamas," under "The Record of Glory—Hamas Operations," http://www.palestine-info.net/arabic/hamas/glory/glory.htm.

60. From the Web site http://www.al-fateh.net/; text translated and posted at http://haganah.org.il.

61. http://www.islam-online.net/arabic/politics/2002/05/article25.shtml.

62. See "A May 2002 Interview with the Hamas Commander of the Al-Qassam Brigades, Salah Shehadeh" (online report, MEMRI, July 2002), http://www.memri.org/bin/articles.cgi?Area=jihad&ID=SP40302.

63. Reuvan Paz, "Rantisi vs. the United States: New Policy of a New Leader of Hamas?" (Occasional Paper 1, no. 5, published by PRISM, 2003), http://www.e-prism.org.

64. The Web site's IP is 216.244.106.208, hosted by CERVALIS, 1200 Bradford Street, Stamford, Conn. 06905, U.S.A.

65. Paz, "Rantisi vs. the United States."

66. Ibid.

67. Ibid.

68. Ibid.

69. See "Patterns of Global Terrorism: Background Information on Terrorist Groups," http://www.state.gov/s/ct/rls/pgtrpt/2000/2450.htm.

70. Jenine Abboushi Dallal, "Hizballa's Virtual Civil Society," *Television and New Media* 2, no. 4 (2001): 367–372.

71. Ibid., 367.

72. Ibid., 370.

73. http://www.hizbollah.org/english/frames/index_eg.htm.

74. *Jihad Online*, 26.

75. http://www.manartv.com/.

76. *Jihad Online*, 27.

77. http://www.nasrollah.org/arabic/hassan/khitabat/khitabat08.htm.

78. http://www.moqawama.tv/page2/main.htm.

79. The picture and text in English are included in the report "Educating Children for Hatred and Terrorism: Encouragement for Suicide Bombing Attacks and Hatred for Israel and the Jews Spread via the Internet on Hamas' Online Children's Magazine (Al-Fateh)," www.intelligence.org.il/eng/sib/11_04/edu.htm.

80. Text included in ibid.

81. Cited at http://www.worldnetdaily.com/news/article.asp?ARTICLE_ID=31323.

82. Ibid.

83. According to "IRA Splinter Groups," http://www.cfrterrorism.org/groups/realira.html.

84. Myra Philp and Dennis Rice, "Omagh Killers Target William," *Daily Express,* October 14, 2000, http://irelandsown.net/express.html.

85. Ibid.

86. Ibid.

87. http://www.guardian.co.uk/internetnews/story/0,7369,567864,00.html.

88. At http://archives.lists.indymedia.org/imc-seattle/2001-October/001703.html.

89. See Maura Conway's report on the Real IRA at http://www.fpa.org/.

90. James Middleton, "FBI Shuts Down 'IRA' Web Site," *VNUNET.Com,* October 12, 2001, http://www.vnunet.com/news/1126099.

91. Jimmy Burns, "Dissidents Defying the US Ban," June 4, 2001, at the Web site of the National Irish Freedom Committee, http://irishfreedom.net/rupert/overturnban.html.

92. Ibid.

93. Reported by RTE News, http://www.rte.ie/news/2000/1208/amazon.html.

94. The Alliance Party announcement is at http://www.allianceparty.org/news.asp?r=81.6376153304159&svr=4&id=229.

95. http://www.salafyahmojaheda.50megs.com (accessed July 5, 2004).

96. Jonathan Halevi, "Who Is Taking Credit for Attacks on the U.S. Army in Western Iraq? Al-Jama'a al-Salafiya al-Mujahida" (report published by the Jerusalem Center for Public Affairs, August 5, 2003), http://www.jcpa.org/brief/brief3-3.htm (accessed August 5, 2003).

97. Joel Leyden, "Al-Jama'a al-Salafiya al-Mujahida Takes Credit for Attacking US in Iraq," Israel News Agency, September 24, 2003, http://209.157.64.200/focus/f-news/988292/posts.

98. Halevi, "Who Is Taking Credit for Attacks?"

99. Michael Rubin, "Ansar al-Sunna: Iraq's New Terrorist Threat," May 2004, *Middle East Intelligence Bulletin,* http://www.meib.org/articles/0405_iraq1.htm.

100. Translated and posted by NEIN, http://www.homelandsecurityus.com/May2004/Laura0512.asp.

101. Ibid.

102. Robert S. Leiken and Steven Brooke, "Who Is Abu Zarqawi?," *Weekly Standard,* May 24, 2004, 25–27.

103. "Alleged Zarqawi Tape Threatens More Attacks on U.S. Forces, Shiites" (report published by the Muslim American Society, April 6, 2004), http://www.masnet.org/news.asp?id=1114.

104. Ibid.

105. Ibid.

106. MSNBC report, October 18, 2004, http://www.msnbc.msn.com/id/6268680/.

107. Rawya Rageh, "Online Magazine Pushes Message of al-Qaida in Iraq," *Chicago Sun-Times,* March, 4, 2005, http://www.suntimes.com/output/iraq/cst-nws-qaida04.html.

108. Daniel Benjamin and Gabriel Weimann, "What the Terrorists Have in Mind," *New York Times,* October 27, 2004, A31.

109. Ibid.

110. Letter cited in "Document: Text of a Letter Allegedly Written by Zarqawi to Bin Laden," *Terrorisme.Net,* September 18, 2004, http://www.terrorisme.net/p/article_125.html.

111. Benjamin and Weimann, "What the Terrorists Have in Mind."

112. Maura Conway, "Terrorist Web Sites: An Empirical Analysis" (paper presented at the annual meeting of the International Studies Association, Montreal, Canada, March 17, 2004).

113. Rachel Gibson and Stephen Ward, "A Proposed Methodology for Studying the Function and Effectiveness of Party and Candidate Web-Sites," *Social Science Computer Review* 18, no. 3 (2000): 301–319.

114. Ibid., 302.

115. Maura Conway, "Terrorist Web Sites: Their Contents, Functioning, and Effectiveness," in Philip Seib, ed., *Terrorism and the Internet* (New York: Palgrave, 2004).

116. Ibid., 36–37.

117. From the Internet site of the organization, quoted in *Yediot Aharonot*, December 16, 1998, 7.

118. SITE Institute, "Eleventh Issue of *Sawt Al-Jihad* Released."

119. SITE Institute online report, "Global Islamic Media Group Reports on Evolution of Media in Jihad," May, 10, 2005, http://siteinstitute.org/bin/articles .cgi?ID=publications44105&Category=publications&Subcategory=0.

120. Kumar Ramakrishna, "The Southeast Asian Approach to Counter-Terrorism: Learning from Indonesia and Malaysia" (paper presented at the annual meeting of the International Studies Association, Montreal, Canada, March 2004), 1.

121. Cited in Nick Britten, Rosie Waterhouse, and Sean O'Neill, "Al Muhajiroun under Scrutiny," *News.telegraph*, May 2, 2003, http://www.telegraph.co.uk/news/main .jhtml?xml=/news/2003/05/02/wbomb202.xml.

122. "Terror Groups Exploit Internet for Communications, Recruiting, Training," JINSA report, August 4, 2004, http://www.jinsa.org/articles/articles.html/function/ view/categoryid/1930/documentid/2621/history/3,2359,2166,1930,2621.

123. Gretchen Peters, "Al-Qaeda Publishes Magazine on the Net," *South China Morning Post*, February 13, 2004.

124. Arquilla and Ronfeldt, "Networks, Netwars, and the Fight for the Future"; Arquilla and Ronfeldt, "The Advent of Netwar"; and Arquilla, Ronfeldt, and Zanini, "Networks, Netwar and Information-Age Terrorism."

125. Hoffman, "Al Qaeda."

126. Shyam Tekwani, "The Web of Terror," *Media Asia* 29, no. 3 (2002): 146–149.

127. Ibid.

128. Cited in *Computer Crime Report*, http://www.crime-research.org/news/14.05 .2004/270.

4. Instrumental Uses of the Internet for Terrorism

1. Dan Verton, *Black Ice: The Invisible Threat of Cyber-Terrorism* (New York: McGraw-Hill Osborne Media, 2003).

2. Gellman, "Cyber-Attacks by al-Qaeda Feared."

3. From "Citing al Qaeda Manual, Rumsfeld Re-emphasizes Web Security," *InsideDefense.com*, January 15, 2003, http://www.insidedefense.com/.

4. Dan Verton, "Web Sites Seen as Terrorist Aids," *Computerworld*, February 11, 2002, http://www.computerworld.com/securitytopics/security/story/0,10801,68181,00 .html.

5. Thomas, "Al Qaeda and the Internet," 113.

6. Meir Suissa, "Hezbollah Penetrated Computers of Senior Israeli Journalists," *Maariv International,* May 17, 2004, http://maarivintl.com/index.cfm?fuseaction=article &articleID=7474.

7. See Internet Haganah, "State of Nevada Posts 'A Guide to Attacking Nuclear Waste Shipments,' " March 23, 2003, http://haganah.us/harchives/000385.html.

8. Ibid.

9. Simson L. Garfinkel, "Leaderless Resistance Today," *First Monday* 8, no. 3 (2003), http://firstmonday.org/issues/issue8_3/garfinkel/index.html.

10. Bruce Hoffman, "Plan of Attack," *Atlantic Monthly,* June 2004, http://www .theatlantic.com/issues/2004/07/hoffman.htm.

11. Ibid.

12. Arquilla, Ronfeldt, and Zanini, "Networks, Netwar and Information-Age Terrorism," 41.

13. "The Electronic Intrusion Threat to National Security and Emergency Preparedness (NS/EP) Internet Communications" (report by National Communications System, Arlington, Va., December 2000), 28–31, www.ncs.gov/library/reports/ electronic_intrusion_threat2000_final2.pdf.

14. Smith, "Transnational Terrorism and the al Qaeda Model," 33–46.

15. Steven Erlanger and Chris Hedges, "Terror Cells Slip through Europe's Grasp," *New York Times,* December 28, 2001, 1.

16. Zanini and Edwards, "Networking of Terror in the Information Age," 29.

17. Ibid., 35–36.

18. Ibid., 36.

19. Kevin J. Soo Hoo, Seymour E. Goodman, and Lawrence T. Greenberg, "Information Technology and the Terrorist Threat," *Survival* 39, no. 3 (1997): 135–155.

20. Bruce Hoffman, "Redefining Counterterrorism: The Terrorist Leader as CEO," *Rand Review* (Spring 2004): 1.

21. Marc Sageman, *Understanding Terror Networks* (Philadelphia: University of Pennsylvania Press, 2004).

22. Zanini and Edwards, "Networking of Terror in the Information Age," 43–44.

23. Michelle Malkin, "Trailing Attempted Espionage," *National Review Online,* February 13, 2004, http://www.nationalreview.com/comment/malkin200402130909.asp.

24. Niles Lathem, "Al-Qaeda Terror.com," *New York Post,* September 16, 2003, A12.

25. Cited in ibid.

26. Cited in Laura Rozen, "Forums Point the Way to Jihad," *Wired News,* 2003, http://www.wired.com/news/conflict/0,2100,59897,00.html.

27. Ibid.

28. This exchange is cited by Niles Lathem, "Al Qaeda Trolls Net," *New York Post,* September 15, 2003.

29. Etgar Lefkovitz, "Three Arabs Held in Jerusalem Cafe Poisoning Plot," *Jerusalem Post,* Sptember 10, 2002, http://www.jpost.com/.

30. Translated and published online, http://www.arabianews.org/english/article.cfm?qid=19&sid=6&printme=1 (accessed August 2004).

31. MEMRI, "Bahraini Author and Journalist: The Proponents of the Suicide Ideology Have Taken Advantage of Global Communications," *Special Dispatch,* May 17, 2005, http://memri.org/bin/articles.cgi?Page=archives&Area=sd&ID=SP90905.

32. The entire exchange was reported by Amit Cohen, "Hamas Dot Com," *Maariv Online,* July 2, 2003, http://www.maarivenglish.com/tour/Hamas%20Dot%20Com.htm.

33. Jeevan Vasagar, "Deadly Net Terror Websites Easy to Access," *Guardian,* July 1, 2000, http://www.guardian.co.uk/bombs/Story/0,2763,338617,00.html.

34. World Tribune.com, "How to Bomb Thy Neighbor: Hamas Offers Online 'Academy,'" October 3, 2002, http://216.26.163.62/2002/me_terrorism_10_02.html.

35. http://www.usdoj.gov/ag/trainingmanual.htm.

36. Ibid.

37. Reported by Lisa Myers, "Web Video Teaches Terrorists to Make Bomb Vest," *MSNBC News,* December 22, 2004, http://www.msnbc.msn.com/id/6746756/.

38. SITE Institute, "Manufacture of the Explosive Belt for Suicide Operations," December 22, 2004, http://siteinstitute.org/bin/articles.cgi?ID=publications13804&Category=publications&Subcategory=0.

39. Myers, "Web Video Teaches Terrorists to Make Bomb Vest."

40. Cited in SITE Institute, "Online Posting Lauds the Successful Use of Stinger Missiles by the Mujahideen," April 4, 2005, http://siteinstitute.org/bin/articles.cgi?ID=publications32505&Category=publications&Subcategory=0.

41. Toby Westerman, "Terror Training Online: Al Qaeda Franchises Out," *International News Analysis,* April 23, 2004, http://inatoday.com/terror%20training%20online%2042304.htm.

42. First issue posted at www.hostinganime.com/battar/b1word.zip. Translation and analysis in MEMRI, "Al Battar Training Camp," January 6, 2004, http://middleeastinfo.net/article3820.html.

43. Laura Mansfield, "Everything You Always Wanted to Know about Becoming a Terrorist, but Were Afraid to Ask," NEIN, March 24, 2004, http://www.homelandsecurityus.com/albattar.htm.

44. Translation of text is in SITE Institute, "Kidnapping the Focus of Al Battar Issue No. 10," May 24, 2004, http://siteinstitute.org/bin/articles.cgi?ID=publications 3804&Category=publications&Subcategory=0.

45. Ibid.

46. American Northeast Intelligence Network, online report, June 2, 2004, http://www.homelandsecurityus.com/.

47. Ibid.

48. Maria T. Welch, "Accumulating Digital Evidence Is Difficult," *Post Standard,* September 11, 2002, 11.

49. Thomas, "Al Qaeda and the Internet," 112–123.

50. "On the Internet, a Web of Dark Alleys," *Irunix News,* December 24, 2004, http://www.irunix.com/2004/12/on-internet-web-of-dark-alleys.html.

51. Yossi Melman, "Virtual Soldiers in a Holy War," *Haaretz,* September 17, 2002, http://www.haaretz.com.

52. Robyn Weisman, "Palestinian Woman Confesses to Internet Romance Murder," *NewsFactor Network,* February 26, 2001, http://www.newsfactor.com/perl/story/7757 .html.

53. MEMRI, "Voices of al-Qaida Leaders from Chechnya and Iraq," January 9, 2004, http://www.memri.de/uebersetzungen_analysen/themen/islamistische_ideologie/ isl_tschetsch_iraq_09_01_04.html.

54. Ibid.

55. Lia Brynjar and Thomas Hegghammer, "FFI Explains al Qaeda Document" (report published by the Norwegian Defense Research Establishment [FFI], March 19, 2004), http://www.mil.no/felles/ffi/start/article.jhtml?articleID=71589.

56. Ibid.

57. Susan Schmidt, "Spreading Saudi Fundamentalism in US," *Washington Post,* October 2, 2003, A1.

58. Thomas, "Al Qaeda and the Internet," 112–123.

59. Schmidt, "Spreading Saudi Fundamentalism in US," *Washington Post,* October 2, 2003, A1.

60. Ibid.

61. Daniel Pipes and Steve Emerson, "Rolling Back the Forces of Terror," *Wall Street Journal,* August 13, 2001.

62. http://www.americasvoices.org/.

63. Stephen Schwartz, "The Holy War Foundation," FrontPageMagazine.com, July 30, 2004, http://www.frontpagemagazine.com/Articles/ReadArticle.asp?ID=14435.

64. The site is not accessible anymore but its "mission" can be found at http://islam.about.com/library/weekly/aa120401a.htm.

65. http://www.islam-online.net/arabic/politics/2002/05/article25.shtml.

66. Translated in MEMRI, "A May 2002 Interview with the Hamas Commander of the al-Qassam Brigades," July 22, 2002, http://www.memri.org/bin/articles.cgi?Area=jihad&ID=SP40302.

67. Benjamin and Weimann, "What the Terrorists Have in Mind."

68. http://www.islamicjihad.com/urgent/appeal.html (May 2001), cited in *Jihad Online: Islamic Terrorists and the Internet.*

69. Jessica Stern, *Terror in the Name of God* (New York: HarperCollins, 2003), 112.

70. Maurice R. Greenberg, William F. Wechsler, and Lee S. Wolosky, "Terrorist Financing," report of an independent task force sponsored by the Council on Foreign Relations, 2002, http://www.cfr.org/publication.php?id=5080.

71. *Jihad Online.*

72. Kevin Johnson and Richard Willing, "Bosnian Evidence Makes FBI Case," *USA TODAY,* January 5, 2002, 12.

73. Ibid.

74. *Jihad Online,* 16.

75. On Hezbollah's activities in the United States, see Daniel Pipes, "The Hezbollah in America: An Alarming Network," *National Review,* August 28, 2000.

76. *Jihad Online.*

77. Paz, "Sawt al-Jihad."

78. Ibid.

79. The book is online at www.almaqdese.com/r?c=2.2.05&I=15; see also a long interview with al-Azdi, published in book form on the same Web site, www.almaqdese.com/r?c=2.3&I=23.

80. Reuven Paz, "Hizballah or Hizb al-Shaytan? Recent Jihadi-Salafi Attacks against the Shiite Group," (Occasional Paper 2, no. 1, PRISM, February 2004), www.e-prism.org.

81. http://www.d-sunnah.net/forum/index.php and http://www.d-sunnah.net.

82. Paz, "Hizballah or Hizb al-Shaytan?"

83. Ibid.

84. http://www.alerhap.com/vb/showthread.php?threadid=6136.

85. Translated by SITE Institute, http://siteinstitute.org/bin/articles.cgi?ID=publications2504&Category=publications&Subcategory=0.

86. Ibid.

87. Reuven Paz, "Hamas vs. al-Qaeda: The Condemnation of the Khobar Attack," (Special Dispatch 2, no. 3, PRISM, June 2, 2004), http://www.e-prism.org.

88. Ibid.

89. Cited in ibid.

90. Cited in "Happy Snaps of a Suicide Bomber," published in the South African *Star,* January 27, 2004, http://www.thestar.co.za/index.php?fSectionId=129&fArticleId=334925.

91. Cited in ibid.

92. Cited in Sudha Ramachandran, "Logging On to Terror.com," *Asia Times,* July 14, 2004, http://www.atimes.com/atimes/Front_Page/FG14Aa02.html.

93. Cited in ibid.

5. Cyberterrorism: How Real Is the Threat?

1. National Research Council, *Computers at Risk* (Washington, D.C.: National Academy Press, 1991).

2. Douglas Thomas, "Cyber Terrorism and Critical Infrastructure Protection" (statement to the Subcommittee on Government Efficiency, Financial Management and Intergovernmental Relations, 107th Cong., July 24, 2002).

3. James A. Lewis, "Assessing the Risks of Cyberterrorism, Cyber War, and Other Cyber Threats" (report submitted to the Center for Strategic and International Studies [CSIS], Washington, D.C., 2002), 1.

4. Joshua Green, "The Myth of Cyberterrorism," *Washington Monthly,* November 2, 2002, www.washingtonmonthly.com/features/2001/0211/green/html.

5. Cited in Ralf Bendrath, "The American Cyber-Angst and the Real World," in *Bombs and Bandwidth: The Emerging Relationship between IT and Security,* ed. Robert Latham (New York: New Press, 2003), 49–73.

6. Green, "Myth of Cyberterrorism."

7. Antone Gonsalves, "Security Expected to Take a Larger Bite of IT Budgets," *TechWeb News,* June 8, 2004, http://www.crime-research.org/news/08.06.2004/414.

8. Green, "Myth of Cyberterrorism."

9. Ibid.

10. Rick White and Stratton Sclavos, "Targeting Our Computers," *Washington Post,* August 15, 2003, A27.

11. Kevin Coleman, "Cyber Terrorism," *Directions Magazine,* October 10, 2003, http://www.directionsmag.com/article.php?article_id=432.

12. Maura Conway, "What Is Cyberterrorism? The Story So Far," *Journal of Information Warfare* 2, no. 2 (2003): 33–42; and Maura Conway, "Reality Bytes: Cyberterrorism and Terrorist 'Use' of the Internet," *First Monday* 7, no. 11, November 2002, http://firstmonday.org/issues/issue7_11/conway/index.html

13. Dorothy Denning, "Activism, Hacktivism, and Cyberterrorism: The Internet as a Tool for Influencing Foreign Policy," in *Networks and Netwars: The Future of Terror, Crime, and Militancy,* ed. J. Arquilla and D. F. Ronfeldt (Santa Monica, Calif.: RAND Corporation, 2001), 239–288, http://www.nautilus.org/info-policy/workshop/papers/denning.html; Dorothy Denning, "Testimony before the Special Oversight Panel on Terrorism," (statement to U.S. House of Representatives, Committee on Armed Services), http://www.cs.georgetown.edu/~denning/infosec/cyberterror.html (accessed May 23, 2000); Dorothy Denning, "Cyberterrorism," *Global Dialogue,* August 24, 2000, http://www.cs.georgetown.edu/~denning/infosec/cyberterror-GD.doc; Dorothy Denning, "Is Cyber Terror Next?" in *Understanding September 11,* ed. Craig Calhoun, Paul Price, and Ashley Timmer (New York: New Press, 2002).

14. Green, "Myth of Cyberterrorism."

15. Conway, "Reality Bytes."

16. Adam Savino, "Cyber-Terrorism," http://cybercrimes.net/Terrorism/ct.html.

17. Denning, "Activism, Hacktivism, and Cyberterrorism."

18. Conway, "Reality Bytes."

19. Denning, "Is Cyber Terror Next?"

20. Michael A. Vatis, "Cyber Attacks during the War on Terrorism: A Predictive Analysis" (special report, Institute for Security and Technology Studies, 2001), http://www.ists.dartmouth.edu/ISTS/counterterrorism/cyber_attacks.htm.

21. Ibid.

22. Thomas, "Cyber Terrorism and Critical Infrastructure Protection."

23. See http://2004.rsaconference.com/.

24. Cited in Elizabeth Montalbano, "Homeland Security Chair Likens 'Cyber Terrorists' to al Qaeda," *CRN News,* February 24, 2004, http://www.crn.com/sections/BreakingNews/dailyarchives.asp?ArticleID=48215.

25. Ibid.

26. Barry C. Collin, "The Future of Cyberterrorism," *Crime and Justice International* (March 1997): 15–18, http://afgen.com/terrorism1.html (accessed March 1997).

27. Mark M. Pollitt, "Cyberterrorism—Fact or Fancy?" Proceedings of the 20th National Information Systems Security Conference, 1997, 285–28, http://www.cs.georgetown.edu/~denning/infosec/pollitt.html.

28. Verton, *Black Ice.*

29. http://www.computerworld.com/securitytopics/security/story/.

30. Denning, "Is Cyber Terror Next?"

31. Robyn Greenspan, "Cyberterrorism Concerns IT Pros," *Computer Crime Research Center,* August 21, 2002, http://www.crime-research.org/library/Cyberterror2.htm.

32. Brian Krebs, "Feds Building Internet Monitoring Center," *Washington Post Online,* January 31, 2003, http://www.washingtonpost.com/ac2/wp-dyn/A3409-2003Jan30.

33. *Washington Post,* September 3, 2003, E05.

34. Anthony Lake, *Six Nightmares* (New York: Little, Brown and Company, 2000).

35. Cited in Caroline Benner, "The Phantom Cyber-Threat," *Salon.com,* April 4, 2001, http://archive.salon.com/tech/feature/2001/04/04/cyberterrorism/.

36. Green, "Myth of Cyberterrorism."

37. Thomas, "Cyber Terrorism and Critical Infrastructure Protection."

38. Ibid.

39. Lewis, "Assessing the Risks of Cyberterrorism."

40. Cited in Noah Shachtman, "Terrorists on the Net? Who Cares?" *Wired News,* December 20, 2002, www.wired.com/news/infostructure/0,1377,56935,00.html.

41. Green, "Myth of Cyberterrorism."

42. Denning, "Cyberterrorism" (testimony before the Special Oversight Panel on Terrorism, Committee on Armed Services, U.S. House of Representatives), http://www.cs.georgetown.edu/~denning/infosec/cyberterror.html (accessed May 23, 2000).

43. Green, "Myth of Cyberterrorism."

44. Denning, "Is Cyber Terror Next?"

45. Ibid.

46. Green, "Myth of Cyberterrorism."

47. Tim Spellman, "Expert: U.S. at Risk of Cyberterrorism," *Dartmouth Online,* http://www.thedartmouth.com/article.php?aid=2004041901010k/ (posted April 19, 2004).

48. Ibid.

49. Ted Bridis, "CIA Overseeing 3-Day War Game on Internet," Associated Press, May 25, 2005, http://apnews.myway.com/article/20050525/D8AAFUIO2.html.

50. "Virtually Unprotected," Editorial, *New York Times,* sec. A, June 2, 2005.

51. Denning, "Is Cyber Terror Next?"

52. Verton, *Black Ice,* 93.

53. Ausaf (Hamid Mir, editor), cited in Verton, *Black Ice,* 108.

54. Court transcript, *U.S. v. Osama bin Laden* (February 21, 2002), at http://lawcrawler.findlaw.com/scripts/lc.pl?entry=bin+laden&sites=news.

55. See the Anti-Terrorism Coalition, "The Anti-Terrorism Coalition's Database of Terrorist Websites and eGroups," http://www.geocities.com/atcterrorlistupdate12345/atcatcterrorlist.html.

56. Denning, "Is Cyber Terror Next?"

6. Fighting Back: Reponses to Terrorism on the Internet, and Their Cost

1. Arquilla and Ronfeldt, "The Advent of Netwar," 14.

2. "The USA Patriot Act," Electronic Privacy Information Center, May 24, 2005, http://www.epic.org/privacy/terrorism/usapatriot/.

3. Tonda MacCharles, "Sweeping Police Powers Planned," *Toronto Star,* October 14, 2001, 2.

4. Reported by CBC News, August 23, 2004, http://www.cbc.ca/story/canada/national/2004/08/23/wiretap_police040823.html.

5. Ibid.

6. Cited in CBS, "Predators of Digital Freedoms," *CBSNews.Com,* September 5, 2002, http://www.cbsnews.com/stories/2002/09/05/tech/main520928.shtml.

7. "The USA Patriot Act."

8. Orin S. Kerr, "Internet Surveillance Law after the USA Patriot Act: The Big Brother That Isn't," *Northwestern University Law Review* 97, no. 2 (2003): 607–673.

9. Ibid., 608.

10. Ibid., 673.

11. Cited by the Electronic Frontier Foundation, http://www.eff.org/Privacy/
Surveillance/Terrorism/son-of-patriot.php.

12. See Electronic Frontier Foundation, "Chilling Effects of Anti-Terrorism,"
November 13, 2001, http://www.eff.org/Privacy/Surveillance/Terrorism/antiterrorism
_chill.html.

13. ACLU, "ACLU Says New Ashcroft Anti-Terror Proposal Undermines Checks
and Balances" February 7, 2003, http://www.aclu.org/SafeandFree/SafeandFree.cfm?
ID=11803&c=206.

14. Ibid.

15. "Section of Patriot Act Ruled Invalid," *New York Times,* January 27, 2004,
http://www.nytimes.com/2004/01/27/politics/27PATR.html.

16. Brian Krebs, "Feds Building Internet Monitoring Center," *Washington Post
Online,* January 31, 2003, http://www.washingtonpost.com/ac2/wp-dyn/A3409-2003
Jan30.

17. John Markoff and John Schwartz, "Bush Administration to Propose System
for Monitoring Internet," *New York Times,* December 20, 2002.

18. John Schwartz, "Threats and Responses: Electronic Surveillance," *New York
Times,* December 20, 2002.

19. Ibid.

20. Pew Internet and American Life Project, "Americans' Views about What Government Agencies Should Post Online," 2003, http://www.pewinternet.org/reports/
reports.asp?Report=69&Section=ReportLevel2&Field=Level2ID&ID=531.

21. James Gomez, "Careful: Someone Is Watching You Surf," *Bandwidth Magazine,*
November–December 2003, http://www.commsday.com.au/magazine/asian_century/
nov_dec2003/nov_dec2003_03.htm.

22. Ibid.

23. Alan Boyd, "The Business of Stifling the Internet," *Asia Times,* January 31,
2004, http://www.thinkcentre.org/article.cfm?ArticleID=2316.

24. Gomez, "Careful: Someone Is Watching You Surf."

25. Ibid.

26. Garry Rodan, "The Internet and Political Control in Singapore," *Political Science Quarterly* 113, no. 1 (1998): 63–89. At http://epn.org/psq/rodan.html.

27. Ibid.

28. Gomez, "Careful: Someone Is Watching You Surf."

29. Reported by the *Globe and Mail* (Toronto), April 6, 2004, http://lists.jammed .com/ISN/2004/04/0016.html.

30. John Schwartz, "Tools for the Aftermath: In Investigation, Internet Offers Clues and Static," *New York Times,* September 26, 2001, H1.

31. John Markoff and John Schwartz, "Many Tools of Big Brother Are Now Up and Running," *New York Times,* December 23, 2002, C1.

32. Ibid.

33. Cited by *Washington Post,* March 13, 2004.

34. Ibid.

35. Tom Zeller, "On the Open Internet, a Web of Dark Alleys," *New York Times,* December 20, 2004.

36. Jack Karp, "Chewing on Carnivore," G4TechTV, http://www.g4techtv.com/ techtvvault/features/33634/Chewing_on_Carnivore.html (June 04, 2002).

37. See "Carnivore, Sniffers, and You," *Wireless,* September 17, 2000, http:// compnetworking.about.com/od/networksecurityprivacy/l/aa071900a.htm.

38. Pew Internet and American Life Project, "Opinions on Carnivore," 2002, http://www.pewinternet.org/reports/reports.asp?Report=32&Section=ReportLevel1& Field=Level1ID&ID=120.

39. "Stop Carinvore Now," http://stopcarnivore.org/threeproblems.htm (last accessed October 5, 2004).

40. Matthew P. Voors, "Encryption Regulation in the Wake of September 11, 2001: Must We Protect National Security at the Expense of the Economy?" *Federal Communications Law Journal* 55, no. 2 (2003): 331–352.

41. Bob Sullivan, "FBI Software Cracks Encryption Wall: 'Magic Lantern' Part of New 'Enhanced Carnivore Project,'" MSNBC, November 20, 2001, http://www .msnbc.com/news/660096.asp?0na=x21017M32&cp1=1.

42. Cited in ibid.

43. Ibid.

44. Voors, "Encryption Regulation in the Wake of September 11, 2001."

45. For a full report of this project, see Yuval Dror, "Cyberspace Warriors," *Haaretz,* April 22, 2004, http://www.haaretz.com/hasen/spages/415859.html.

46. Cited in ibid.

47. Richard B. Schmitt, "Demand Broadens the Field of Terror Experts," *Los Angeles Times,* April 14, 2004.

48. Cited in ibid.

49. Cited in ibid.

50. Evan Kohlmann, "A Web of Terror," *Journal of Counterterrorism* 6, no. 3 (Spring 2000), law.upenn.edu/~ekohlman/webterror.pdf.

51. The Anti-Terrorism Coalition (ATC) database was formerly at http://atcterrorlist.showsit.info/. The ATC is now up at http://www.atcoalition.net.

52. Pew Internet and American Life Project, "How the Terror Attacks Affected Americans' Views about Online Information and Their Internet Use," 2003, http://www.pewinternet.org/reports/reports.asp?Report=69&Section=ReportLevel1&Field=Level1ID&ID=305.

53. The list has since beeen updated. See http://www.ombwatch.org/article/articleview/213/1/1#agency.

54. Ibid.

55. From "Agencies Scrub Web Sites of Sensitive Chemical Data," *Washington Post,* October 4, 2001, http://www.washingtonpost.com/ac2/wp-dyn?pagename=article&node=&contentId=A2738-2001Oct3.

56. http://www.usdoj.gov/oip/foiapost/2001foiapost19.htm.

57. See Pew Internet and American Life Project, "Special Report: Americans' Views about What Government Agencies Should Post Online."

58. From Pew Internet and American Life Project, "A Year Later: The Internet and September 11," September 5, 2002, http://www.pewinternet.org/PPF/r/49/press_release.asp.

59. Ibid.

60. See Pew Internet and American Life Project, "Americans' Views about What Government Agencies Should Post Online."

61. John C. Baker et al., *Mapping the Risks: Assessing the Homeland Security Implications of Publicly Available Geospatial Information* (Washington, D.C.: RAND Corporation, 2004).

62. Ibid.

63. Cited in Lee Hockstader, "Pings and E-Arrows Fly in Mideast Cyber-War," *Washington Post,* October 27, 2000, A01.

64. Robyn Weisman, "Teen Hackers Crash Hizbollah ISP," *NewsFactor Network,* January 22, 2001, http://www.newsfactor.com/perl/story/6880.html#story-start.

65. Gabriel Weimann, cited in Gwen Ackerman, "A Virtual War," *Jerusalem Post,* December 18, 2000, http://www.jpost.com/Editions/2000/11/05/Features/Features.14883.html.

66. Robert Spencer, "Jihad Online," *PageMagazine.com,* December 16, 2003, http://www.frontpagemag.org/Articles/ReadArticle.asp?ID=11350.

67. From "US Shuts Down Somalia Internet," BBC News, November 23, 2001, http://news.bbc.co.uk/1/hi/world/africa/1672220.stm.

68. Reported by Agence France-Presse, October 10, 2003, http://www.why-wor.com/news/2003/10/10/usextend.html; and *Haaretz,* November 7, 2003, http://www.haaretz.com/hasen/spozes/358080.html.

69. From "US Extends Terrorism Blacklist to Cyberspace, Hits Radical Jewish Websites," Agence France-Presse, October 10, 2003, http://quickstart.clari.net/qs_se/webnews/wed/dg/Qus-attacks-internet.Ri8V_DOA.html.

7. Balancing Security and Civil Liberties

1. Vinton Cerf, "The Internet under Surveillance" (report published by Reporters Without Borders, 2003), http://www.rsf.org/article.php3?id_article=7280.

2. Ibid.

3. Stewart Baker, interview with the author, 2003.

4. From "Predators of Digital Freedoms," CBS News, September 5, 2002, http://www.cbsnews.com/stories/2002/09/05/tech/main520928.shtml.

5. "Using Terror as Pretext," *Wired News,* September 4, 2002, http://www.wired.com/news/politics/0,1283,54939,00.html.

6. Ibid.

7. Karen Kleiss, "Cyber-Dissidents under Attack," *Toronto Star,* November 16, 2003, A12.

8. Philip Pan, "China Releases 3 Internet Writers, but Convicts 1 Other," *Washington Post,* December 1, 2003, A14.

9. Kleiss, "Cyber-Dissidents under Attack."

10. Shanthi Kalathil and Taylor C. Boas, *Open Networks, Closed Regimes: The Impact of the Internet on Authoritarian Rule* (Washington, D.C.: Carnegie Endowment for International Peace, 2003).

11. Ibid.

12. Kleiss, "Cyber-Dissidents under Attack."

13. Ibid.

14. Stephen Schwartz, "The Islamic Terrorism Club," *FrontPageMagazine,* November 5, 2003, http://www.frontpagemag.org/Articles/ReadArticle.asp?ID=10634.

15. The Harvard study is available online at cyber.law.harvard.edu/filtering/saudiarabia.

16. Ibid., 287.

17. Denning, "Activism, Hacktivism, and Cyberterrorism."

18. Ibid., 246.

19. Ibid., 243–260.

20. Tania S. O'Neil, "Subnational Groups and the Internet: An Irritant to Globalization, Not a Threat," in *Information Technology and World Politics,* ed. Michael Mazarr (New York: Palgrave Macmillan, 2002), 42–54.

21. From "Zapatistas in Cyberspace," February 21, 2001, http://www.eco.utexas.edu/Homepages/Faculty/Cleaver/zapincyber.html#Analyses.

22. David Ronfeldt and John Arquilla, "Emergence and Influence of the Zapatista Social Netwar," in *Networks and Netwars,* ed. John Arquilla and David Ronfeldt (Santa Monica, Calif.: RAND Corporation, 2001), 171–199.

23. O'Neil, "Subnational Groups and the Internet," 49.

24. See Melody Ermachild Chavis, *Meena, Heroine of Afghanistan: The Martyr Who Founded RAWA, the Revolutionary Association of the Women of Afghanistan* (New York: St. Martin's, 2003).

25. Richard Solomon and Sheryl Brown, "Creating a Common Communications Culture" (paper presented at the Conference on Crisis Management and Information Technology, Helsinki, Finland, September 12, 2003), http://www.usip.org/virtualdiplomacy/.

26. Ibid.

27. Donna G. Bolz, "Information Technology and Peace Support Operations" (online research report, United States Institute of Peace, July 22, 2002), http://www.usip.org/virtualdiplomacy/publications/reports/13.html.

28. Solomon and Brown, "Creating a Common Communications Culture."

29. Jonathan Spalter and Kevin Moran, "Imagining Technology," *iMP: The Magazine on Information Impacts,* July 23, 2001, http://www.cisp.org/imp/.

30. Lindsey Wade, "Terrorism and the Internet: Resistance in the Information Age," *Knowledge, Technology, & Policy* 16 (2003): 104–127.

31. David Lyon, *Surveillance Society: Monitoring Everyday Life* (London: Open University Press, 2001).

32. "The Tools of Freedom and Security," PAR Worldwide Group, http://www.bioidentix.net/solutions/law.html.

33. Amitai Etzioni, "Seeking Middle Ground on Privacy vs. Security," *Commentary,* October 15, 2002.

34. Ibid.

35. See, for example, Cynthia Brown, ed., *Lost liberties: Ashcroft and the Assault on Personal Freedom* (New York: New Press, 2003); David Cole, *Enemy Aliens: Double Standards and Constitutional Freedoms in the War on Terrorism* (New York: New Press, 2003); Phillip B. Heymann, *Terrorism, Freedom, and Security: Winning without War* (Cambridge, Mass.: MIT Press, 2003); Richard C. Leone and Greg Anrig, eds., *The War on Our Freedoms: Civil Liberties in an Age of Terrorism* (New York: Public Affairs, 2004); Christian Parenti, *The Soft Cage: Surveillance in America from Slavery to the War on Terror* (New York: Basic Books, 2003); and Jeffrey Rosen, *The Naked Crowd: Reclaiming Security and Freedom in an Anxious Age* (New York: Random House, 2004).

36. "Tools of Freedom and Security."

37. Cited in Kim Zetter, "Snoopware: New Technologies, Laws Threaten Privacy," *PC World,* March 2002, http://www.pcworld.com/news/article/0,aid,78070,00.asp.

38. Ibid.

39. American Civil Liberties Union (ACLU), "Privacy and Technology" (n.d.), http://www.aclu.org/Privacy/PrivacyMain.cfm (accessed January 16, 2004); ACLU, "Urge Congress to Stop the FBI's Use of Privacy-Invading Software" (n.d.), http://www.aclu.org/Privacy/Privacy.cfm?ID=9958&c=130 (accesssed January 25, 2004); ACLU, "ACLU Recommends Modifications to Cyber-Crime Bill, Changes Would Protect Privacy Rights of Internet Users" (posted on April 24, 2002), http://www.aclu.org/Privacy/Privacy.cfm?ID=10160&c=131 (accessed April 25, 2002); ACLU, "ACLU Calls on Senate to Reject Misguided International Cybercrime Treaty; Pact Would Require U.S. Police to Enforce Foreign Laws" (posted on December 18, 2003), http://www.aclu.org/Privacy/Privacy.cfm?ID=14605&c=39 (accessed January 25, 2004); ACLU, "Feature on the International Cybercrime Treaty," (posted on December 18, 2003), http://www.aclu.org/Privacy/Privacy.cfm?ID=14489&c=252 (accessed January 25, 2004); ACLU, "ACLU Urges Congress to Reject Bush Call to Make Patriot Act Permanent" (posted on January 20, 2004), http://www.aclu.org/SafeandFree/SafeandFree.cfm?ID=14750&c=206 (accessed January 21, 2004); "Is the US Turning Into a Surveillance Society? Big Brother Is No Longer a Fiction," http://www.aclu.org/Privacy/Privacylist.cfm?c=39 (accessed January 2003); and Jay Stanley and Barry Steinhardt, "Bigger Monster, Weaker Chains: The Growth of an American Surveillance Society" (paper published for the Technology and Liberty Program, American Civil Liberties Union, Washington, D.C., 2003).

40. ACLU, "Is the US Turning Into a Surveillance Society? Big Brother Is No Longer a Fiction."

41. Stanley and Steinhardt, "Bigger Monster, Weaker Chains," 15.

42. Ibid., 16.

43. Ibid., 17.

44. Center for Democracy and Technology (CDT), "CDT Statement Preserving Democratic Freedoms in Times of Peril," http://www.cdt.org/security/010914cdtstatement.shtml (statement posted online on September 14, 2001).

45. Ibid.

46. Ibid.; CDT, "Support Legislation to Fix the Patriot Act" (n.d.), http://www.cdt.org/action/safe/; CDT, "Special Report: Justice Dept. Drafts Sweeping Expansion of Anti-Terrorism Act," February 7, 2004, http://www.publicintegrity.org/dtaweb/report.asp?ReportID=502&L1=10&L2=10&L3=0&L4=0&L5=0.

47. CDT, "Support Legislation to Fix the Patriot Act."

48. From the Lawyers' Committee for Human Rights Report "Imbalance of Powers" (March 1, 2003), http://www.humanrightsfirst.org/us_law/loss/imbalance/powers_recmms.pdf. The selected recommendations are at http://www.humanrights first.org/us_law/after_911/PDF/PRIVACY%20-%20recommendations.pdf.

49. See http://www.eff.org/.

50. Electronic Frontier Foundation (EFF), "EFF Analysis of the Provisions of the USA PATRIOT Act that Relate to Online Activities," October 31, 2001, http://www.eff.org/Privacy/Surveillance/Terrorism/20011031_eff_usa_patriot_analysis.php; and EFF, "Electronic Frontier Foundation Files Comments on FBI Plan," April 13, 2004, http://www.eff.org/news/breaking/archives/2004_04.php#001412.

51. See http://www.epic.org/.

52. Electronic Privacy Information Center (EPIC), "Letter to Congress on Proposed Anti-Terrorism Legislation," 2001, http://www.epic.org/privacy/terrorism/cong_ltr_10_02_01.html.

53. Wade, "Terrorism and the Internet."

54. John Schwartz, "Seeking Privacy Online, Even as Security Tightens," *New York Times,* November 11, 2001, 10.

55. Kip W. Viscusi and Richard J. Zeckhauser, "Sacrificing Civil Liberties to Reduce Terrorism Risks" (Working Paper 03-1, AEI-Brookings Joint Center for Regulatory Studies, 2003), http://www.aei-brookings.org/admin/authorpdfs/page.php?id=240.

56. Ibid.

57. Louis Kaplow and Steven Shavell, *Fairness and Welfare* (Cambridge, Mass.: Harvard University Press, 2002).

58. Viscusi and Zeckhauser, "Sacrificing Civil Liberties."

59. Jonathan Zittrain, "Beware the Cyber Cops," *Forbes* 170, July 8, 2002, 62.

60. Ibid.

61. Ibid.

62. From "The Internet and the USA PATRIOT Act: Potential Implications for Electronic Privacy, Security, Commerce, and Government" (CRS Report for Congress, March 4, 2004), http://www.epic.org/privacy/terrorism/usapatriot/RL31289.pdf.

63. The Northeast Intelligence Network (NEIN) is an all-volunteer group of analysts that monitors terrorism, terrorist actions, terrorist Web sites, and counter-terrorism. See http://www.homelandsecurityus.com/.

64. Laura Mansfield, "U.S. Advertisers Unwittingly Support Terrorism?" (online report, NEIN, April 12, 2002), http://www.homelandsecurityus.com/.

65. Ibid.

66. Ibid.

67. Ibid.

68. The first report in this series was Marie-Helene Boccara, "Islamist Websites and Their Hosts Part I: Islamist Terror Organizations" (Special Report no. 31, MEMRI, July 16, 2004), http://memri.org/bin/articles.cgi?Page=subjects&Area=jihad&ID=SR3 104. The second report in the series was Marie-Helene Boccara and Alex Greenberg, "Islamist Websites and Their Hosts Part II: Clerics" (Special Report no. 35, MEMRI, November 11, 2004), http://www.memri.org/bin/opener_latest.cgi?ID=SR3504#_edn1.

69. Sean Beesley, "America Hosts 76 Percent of Islamic Terrorist Websites," *Canada Free Press,* July 19, 2004, http://www.canadafreepress.com/2004/main072004.htm.

70. Mark Hosenball, Michael Hirsh, Colin Soloway, and Emily Flynn, "Al Qaeda's New Life," *Newsweek,* January 6, 2003, 47.

71. http://haganah.us/haganah/.

72. http://docs.yahoo.com/info/terms/.

73. http://datapipe.net/acceptableuse.aspx.

74. http://docs.yahoo.com/info/terms/.

75. http://docs.yahoo.com/info/terms/.

76. http://legal.web.aol.com/aol/aolpol/comguide.html.

77. http://datapipe.net/acceptableuse.aspx.

78. http://www.drmac.org/aup.php.

79. Frederick S. Siebert, Theodore Peterson, and Wilbur Schramm, *Four Theories of the Press* (Urbana, Ill.: University of Illinois Press, 1963).

80. Taken from "Freedom of the Press," http://faculty.ncwc.edu/mstevens/410/410lect09.htm.

81. John Stuart Mill, *On Liberty* (London: Longman, Roberts and Green, 1869).

82. Jack M. McLeod and Jay G. Blumler, "The Macrosocial Level of Communication Science," in *Handbook of Communication Science,* ed. Charles R. Berger and Steven H. Chaffee (Beverly Hills, Calif.: Sage, 1989), 271–322.

83. Siebert, Peterson, and Schramm, *Four Theories of the Press.*

84. http://www.apme.com/ethics/.

85. Robert L. Stevenson, "Freedom of the Press around the World," in *Global Journalism: Topical Issues and Media Systems,* 4th edition, ed. Arnold S. de Beer and John C. Merrill (Boston: Allyn and Bacon, 2003), 20.

86. Ibid., 12.

87. Ibid., 21.

88. Ibid., 22.

89. Cited in Adrian Humphreys, " 'Mouthpiece of al-Qaeda' Hacks Alaskan Tourism Web Site," *National Post,* March 25, 2003, http://www.globalsecurity.org/org/news/2003/030325-alqaeda-hack01.htm.

90. Hosenball, Hirsh, Soloway, and Flynn, "Al Qaeda's New Life," 47.

91. Ibid., 47.

92. Stevenson, "Freedom of the Press around the World," 21.

93. Ibid., 22.

94. Ibid., 22–23.

95. Joelle Diderich, "G8 to Work Together against Cyber Crime," Reuters, May 14, 2002, http://www.zdnet.com/zdnn/stories/news/0,458,2569402,00.html; Ekaterina Drozdova, "Civil Liberties and Security in Cyberspace," in *Transnational Dimension of Cyber Crime and Terrorism,* ed. Abraham D. Sofaer and Seymour E. Goodman (Washington, D.C.: Hoover Institution Press, 2001); and Anne Swardson, "International Officials Admit Internet Security Holes," May 16, 2000, *Washington Post Online,* washingtonpost.com/wp-dyn/articles/A12013-000May16.html.

96. Abraham D. Sofaer, Seymour E. Goodman, Mariano-Florentino Cuéllar, Ekaterina A. Drozdova, David D. Elliott, Gregory D. Grove, Stephen J. Lukasik, Tonya L. Putnam, and George D. Wilson, "A Proposal for an International Convention on Cyber Crime and Terrorism" (report posted on August 15, 2000), http://www.iwar.org.uk/law/resources/cybercrime/stanford/cisac-draft.htm.

97. Described by Drozdova, "Civil Liberties and Security in Cyberspace."

98. Ibid., 16.

99. Ibid., 16.

100. "MI5 Security Advice Goes Online," BBC News, April 30, 2004, http://news
.bbc.co.uk/1/hi/uk/3672221.stm.

101. Ibid.

102. Cory Smith, interview by Alison Talbott, United States Institute of Peace
research assistant, April 7, 2004.

103. Timothy Lynch, "Breaking the Vicious Cycle: Preserving Our Liberties While
Fighting Terrorism" (Cato Policy Analysis no. 443, June 26, 2002), http://www.cato.org/
pubs/pas/pa-443es.html.

Appendix: Terrorist Organizations on the Internet

1. The following lists are based on "Foreign Terrorist Organizations," published
by the U.S. State Department, http://www.state.gov/s/ct/rls/fs/2003/17067.htm.

2. Ibid.

Index

C

About the Author

Gabriel Weimann is professor of communication at Haifa University and a former Senior Fellow at the United States Institute of Peace. A prolific analyst of terrorism and the mass media, he has written five books, including *Communicating Unreality, The Influentials: People Who Influence People, The Theater of Terror, Hate on Trial,* and *The Singaporean Enigma.* He has also written more than one hundred book chapters and articles, including papers in the *Journal of Communication, Public Opinion Quarterly, Communication Research, Journal of Broadcasting and Electronic Media,* and *American Sociological Review.* He received numerous grants and awards from international foundations, including the Fulbright Foundation, the Canadian-Israel Foundation, the Alexander von Humboldt-Stiftung, the German National Research Foundation, the Sasakawa Foundation, and United States Institute of Peace. He has also held visiting professorships at universities throughout the world, including the University of Pennsylvania, Stanford University, Hofstra University, Lehigh University, Universitaet Mainz (Germany), the National University of Singapore, and Carleton University in Ottawa, Canada.

United States Institute of Peace

The United States Institute of Peace is an independent, nonpartisan federal institution created by Congress to promote the prevention, management, and peaceful resolution of international conflicts. Established in 1984, the Institute meets its congressional mandate through an array of programs, including research grants, fellowships, professional training, education programs from high school through graduate school, conferences and workshops, library services, and publications. The Institute's Board of Directors is appointed by the President of the United States and confirmed by the Senate.

Chairman of the Board: J. Robinson West
Vice Chairman: María Otero
President: Richard H. Solomon
Executive Vice President: Harriet Hentges
Vice President: Charles E. Nelson

Board of Directors

J. Robinson West (Chairman), Chairman, PFC Energy, Washington, D.C.

María Otero (Vice Chairman), President, ACCION International, Boston, Mass.

Betty F. Bumpers, Founder and former President, Peace Links, Washington, D.C.

Holly J. Burkhalter, Director of U.S. Policy, Physicians for Human Rights, Washington, D.C.

Chester A. Crocker, James R. Schlesinger Professor of Strategic Studies, School of Foreign Service, Georgetown University

Laurie S. Fulton, Williams and Connolly, Washington, D.C.

Charles Horner, Senior Fellow, Hudson Institute, Washington, D.C.

Seymour Martin Lipset, Hazel Professor of Public Policy, George Mason University

Mora L. McLean, Esq., President, Africa-America Institute, New York, N.Y.

Barbara W. Snelling, former State Senator and former Lieutenant Governor, Shelburne, Vt.

Members ex officio

Michael M. Dunn, Lieutenant General, U.S. Air Force; President, National Defense University

Barry F. Lowenkron, Assistant Secretary of State for Democracy, Human Rights, and Labor

Peter W. Rodman, Assistant Secretary of Defense for International Security Affairs

Richard H. Solomon, President, United States Institute of Peace (nonvoting)

Terror on the Internet

This book is set in Adobe Garamond; the display type is Eurostile. The Creative Shop designed the book's cover. EEI Communications made up the pages. The text was edited by Kurt Volkan and Michael Carr and proofread by Karen Stough. The index was prepared by Sonsie Conroy.